2/80

light stains noted—
8-11-18

ERICH MARIA REMARQUE

ERICH MARIA REMARQUE

by

CHRISTINE R. BARKER

and

R. W. LAST

LONDON : OSWALD WOLFF
NEW YORK : BARNES & NOBLE BOOKS
(a Division of Harper & Row Publishers, Inc.)

© 1979 Oswald Wolff (Publishers) Ltd.
London W1M 6DR

Published by
Oswald Wolff (Publishers) Ltd., London
and
Harper & Row, Publishers, Inc., New York
Barnes & Noble Import Division

British Library Cataloguing in Publication Data

Barker, Christine R.
  Erich Maria Remarque.
  1. Remarque, Erich Maria — Criticism and
  interpretation.
  I. Last, Rex William
  833'.9'12   PT2635.E68Z/   79—10837
  ISBN UK 0-85496-060-0
      US 0-06-490308-4

Produced in Great Britain by
J. M. Dent & Sons (Letchworth)

CONTENTS

ACKNOWLEDGEMENTS

The authors wish to express their gratitude to the following individuals and institutions: to H-G Rabe, who put together the Remarque Collection housed in the Niedersächsisches Staatsarchiv in Osnabrück, for discussing with us his first-hand knowledge of Remarque's life and personality; to the Niedersächsisches Staatsarchiv for access to the Remarque Collection; to K Witsch and Professor Walter Sorell for information relating to the different versions of *Zeit zu leben und Zeit zu sterben*; to *Quinquereme*, University of Bath, for permission to use some of the material from the article by RW Last, "The 'Castration' of Erich Maria Remarque" (Vol. II, no. 1, 1979); and to the German Academic Exchange Service for grants enabling us to research in Osnabrück. All foreign language quotations have been rendered into English and all translations are our own.

INTRODUCTION

Imagine a pallid youth, his soul chilled by disappointment in love, listlessly watching a performance of Goethe's *Faust*. During the Walpurgis Night scene, he is moved (whether by indifferent acting, we are not informed) to cast his gaze about the audience. A woman's face rivets his attention: her eyes are the very eyes he has so often seen in his dreams of an ideal love. The performance over, he espies her anew on the steps of the theatre — "it was as if roses were scattered beneath her feet" — and in a wondrous voice she utters these words to him: "Come home".

He follows her. After suitable musical preliminaries on the pianoforte, he possesses her in a fleeting moment of erotic ecstasy. Then they part — for ever, "because I love you," he says, "... and to possess love means to yield it up. All things are transient..." This brief rhapsody in prose, culled from the pages of the right-wing journal *Die Schönheit* (Beauty) in 1918, leaves the youth languishing in the afterglow of a unique fragment of time, playing Chopin on the piano and recalling his lady with the wondrous eyes.[1]

Or imagine a cartoon strip from *Echo-Continental*, the house magazine of the international German-based Continental tyre and rubber goods manufacturing company. It recounts, with accompanying verses, Captain Priemke's Fourth Adventure, the cautionary tale of his endeavours to win himself a wife. He and his intended, Friederike Ziemke (whose patronymic conveniently supplies a much-needed rhyme-word), go swimming together, she wearing a rubber bathing cap. Alas, the cap is swept from her head by a passing wave, removing in addition the lady's wig and revealing her to be entirely bald. Priemke hastily steps back from the brink, expressing his gratitude at such a narrow escape from matrimony in lines, which, loosely rendered into English, go like this:

So he swore right there and then:
"I'll never seek to wed again.
Just fancy: if the reprobate
Had a *Conti-Cap* upon her pate,
The wig'd ne'er been swept away,
And I'd be duped and wed today!"[2]

1

It is no easy matter to reconcile the perpetrator of these two pieces — which respectively represent the ridiculously sublime and the sublimely ridiculous — and many more in similar vein, with Erich Maria Remarque, international celebrity and *bon viveur*, friend of the Hollywood stars, one of the most glittering of whom he married, and author of the greatest best-selling novel of all time. But indeed it was Remarque — or, as some would have him, "Remark" (or even "Kramer") — who penned such deathless prose and verse in the course of his early career as a writer. These youthful indiscretions, as we shall see, leave a vapour trail of sucrose sentimentality and superficial triteness which on occasion make an embarrassing appearance in his major novels, but, by and large, the gulf between his mature work and his juvenilia is such that it is hard indeed to credit that they all flowed from the pen of one and the same man.

This study sets out to define for the first time the principal themes and preoccupations of Remarque's work and to define its significance in twentieth-century German literature. Most readers will be familiar with *Im Westen nichts Neues*,[3] the very title of which has found its way into current German — and English — usage, but his other novels are much less widely known, except perhaps for those which have been adapted for the screen. A proper evaluation of Remarque's mature work is long overdue, not least because *Im Westen nichts Neues*, for all the unprecedented success and controversy which attended it, is far from being his best novel.

But this does not mean that we come either to bury Remarque in technical exegesis or to praise him by making exaggerated claims for the significance of his work by covering up its weaknesses, which can at times be substantial. Nor shall we jump on the fashionable bandwaggon of that barbarous neologism *Rezeptions-ästhetik* — literally, the aesthetics of the reception (of literature) — although the analysis of *Im Westen nichts Neues* almost inevitably takes as its point of departure the furore which surrounded the novel's first appearance and the running battle which has been dogging it ever since. Remarque's novels do merit serious critical analysis in their own right, and much of what follows is old-fashioned literary criticism. When Remarque embarked on his career proper as a novelist in 1928, his style soon stabilized, so it is not particularly meaningful to seek to discuss his "development", for the simple reason that he developed little, either stylistically or theoretically, once he had found himself as a writer and had defined his thematic objectives. For this reason his novels are considered here slightly out of sequence as far as their order of composition is concerned; they are grouped according to their subject-matter, setting, and the chronological position they occupy.

The transformation from limp disciple of the worst aspects of *Jugendstil* and rather indifferent journalist and copywriter into accomplished novelist is surprising enough; but what is perhaps even more astonishing is the deafening critical silence which has reigned over his not inconsiderable achievements; apart, that is, from the flood of articles, pamphlets and monographs which served as ammunition in the paper war of attrition which was fought at the end of the 'twenties, more over the issues raised by *Im Westen nichts Neues* and the personality of its author than over the book itself. *Im Westen nichts Neues* apart, Remarque has to date been the object of a mere scattering of articles, the occasional thesis weighing him in the Marxist-Leninist balance (and finding him wanting), and one rather sketchy and indifferent monograph, which the reviewer in *Die Zeit* justly pillories as a Readers Digest-like compilation of other men's efforts which is "crawling with errors", and whose author "evidently appears to be inadequately acquainted with Remarque's literary work", a dubious distinction which he is not alone in holding.[4]

If the critical fraternity has been somewhat reticent about Remarque, his native town of Osnabrück has at least named a section of the road which follows the line of the town walls after him: the "Erich-Maria-Remarque-Ring" is part of the ring road which changes names eight times in its circuit of the inner town. Whether Remarque himself would have approved of rubbing shoulders with the "Goethe-Ring" and the "Konrad-Adenauer-Ring" is quite a different matter.

Before turning to his novels it is necessary to sketch in the background with an account of Remarque's life which in many ways is, if not stranger, then at the very least more unpredictable and adventurous than his fiction. Few writers have put so much of themselves and their personal experiences — especially those of his earlier years — so directly into their work. Much of what Remarque wrote is semi-autobiographical, and it would not be far from the truth to dub the majority of his novels *romans à clef*.

This is not the place for a definitive biography: what follows simply seeks to provide sufficient basis for an understanding of the extraordinarily intimate relationship between man and work; only incidentally could it be regarded as prolegomena to such a study — which, when the time comes, it will be no easy task to compose, since Remarque himself resisted all attempts to chronicle his life.[5]

3

Like his novels, Remarque's life is surrounded by all manner of misrepresentations, plain libels and woeful inaccuracies. Doubts have even been expressed as to his true identity.

CHAPTER ONE

LIFE

"Did Erich Maria Remarque really exist?" This question was posed, ironically enough, by another writer working under an even more assumed name, Mynona ("Anonym" backwards), *alias* Dr Salomo Friedlaender, in the title of his full-length diatribe against Remarque and *Im Westen nichts Neues.*[1] Exist he most certainly did and not under the name of Kramer ("Remark" backwards) as other rumours have suggested.

The son of Peter Franz and Anna Maria Remark, the author of *Im Westen nichts Neues* was born on 22 June 1898 in the Knollstrasse, Osnabrück, and christened Erich Paul. The French version "Remarque", which he adopted in 1923, having previously exchanged his second Christian name for that of his mother, does in fact derive from his French ancestry, for his great-grandfather was called Johannes Adam Remarque.[2]

Erich's family was poor: his father was a book-binder by trade and worked for the firm of Prelle in Osnabrück. During Erich's childhood, the financial situation of the family obliged them to move house several times. In those days, strangely enough, new accommodation with its damp plasterwork could be the cheapest, and between Erich's birth and 1917 the Remark family lived in eleven different places in Osnabrück. In addition to Erich, there were also two daughters, Elfriede and Erna.

Several of the flats in which they lived were in the same street, the Jahnstrasse, and it was here that Erich spent most of his youth up to 1914. The streets and scenes of his childhood were to make an abiding impression on him. The Jahnstrasse backs on to one end of Am Pappelgraben, where Erich frequently played and which he describes in terms of a happy youthful memory both in *Im Westen nichts Neues* and *Der Weg zurück.*

A flat on the second storey of a house in the Hakenstrasse, which belonged to the firm of Prelle (the name still remains on the house side), became a home for the errant Remark family from 1917 to 1935, and for Erich himself until 1922, in which year he left Osnabrück. It was here that he completed his first novel, *Die Traumbude,* and his earliest poems. Much of the action on which

Der Weg zurück is based took place during this period in Remarque's life, and the view from his attic window of a chestnut tree in an inn garden and of the tower of the Katharinenkirche beyond is described in some detail not only in *Im Westen nichts Neues* and *Der Weg zurück* but also in many of his subsequent novels.

Erich's parents were both Catholic, and so it is hardly surprising that he should have received a Catholic education. As a result of the family's frequent change of abode, he attended two different primary schools in Osnabrück, from 1904-1908 the Domschule and from 1908-1912 the Johannisschule. At that time, almost the only career which stood open to the intelligent son of poor parents was school-teaching, since the training for a primary school teacher did not present the parents with any financial burden. Consequently, Erich underwent the first stage of his teacher-training in the Catholic *Präparande* between 1912-1915. This was situated behind the Marienkirche in the old part of the town, and it was run by Rektor Korthaus, known by the nickname of "Schlächter" (Butcher), with whom, according to a fellow pupil, Joseph Witt,[3] Erich had many an argument. (One of his teachers there, Konschorek, was to become the Kantorek of *Im Westen nichts Neues,* although the resemblance is confined to the name alone.) Erich himself went by the nickname of "Schmieren" (Smudge) at school, and it is by this name that he often signed the letters he wrote from the hospital in Duisberg where he remained for some time in 1917-1918 recovering from war wounds. From 1915 until 21 November 1916, Erich attended the *Lehrerseminar,* an establishment for training elementary teachers.

Remarque's hobbies as a child and young man are also worthy of mention, since they too find their way into his novels. He collected butterflies, stones and stamps, and was interested in painting and music. He was particularly gifted as a musician, and played both piano and organ extremely well. In 1916 he gave piano lessons in order to supplement his pocket money. At that time, clothes too were already becoming an obsession with him: he considered it essential to be well-dressed in order to make the right kind of social impression.[4]

His association with the aesthetic circle of the "Traumbude" (Dream-Den), after which his first novel was named, began in 1915-1916, when he became acquainted with its leader Fritz Hörstemeier (1882-1918) whilst he was living in the Luisestrasse. At this time Hörstemeier had attic rooms in the Liebigstrasse, which they dubbed the "Traumbude." In addition to Hörstemeier and Remarque, the circle comprised Paula Spenker, Erika Haase (the leading female member of the group), Rudolf Kottmann, and the artist Friedrich Vordemberge. They were all idealists in the *Jugendstil* (Art Nouveau) vein, seeking to transform drab reality into an idealized world of beauty. Remarque's first novel, *Die Traumbude,* is dedicated to Fritz Hörstemeier, whom he faithfully portrays as Onkel Fritz. Remarque was later to describe *Die Traumbude,* with more than a little justification, as "a really terrible book", and maintained that two years after its publication he would have bought up all the copies remaining, if he had had the money. Ullstein, the publishers of *Im Westen nichts Neues,* subsequently performed this service for him. "If I had not written something better later," he said, "this book would have justified suicide."[5]

In another later interview, Remarque admitted that the publication of *Die Traumbude* under the name of Erich Remark was the chief reason for his assuming a new name:

> Under the name of Remark, I published an early work, a novel, whose title I will not name, even under torture. For this reason Remark became Remarque.[6]

Remarque might equally have disowned his first published piece of prose, printed in 1916 in the Osnabrück journal *Heimatfreund.* Entitled "Aus der Heimat: Von den Freuden und Mühen der Jugendwehr" (From the Homeland: Concerning the Pleasures and Problems of the Youth Cadets), Remarque's prize-winning essay is a controlled piece of writing, well paced, ably capturing the tension and excitement of a patrol exercise he is leading, although he does tend — not for the last time — to drift into sentimentality, and, not surprisingly, shows no real understanding of war. Some of the descriptive writing would perhaps be more at home in *Die Traumbude* and expresses sentiments which, when seen with the clarity of hindsight, have more than a tinge of irony about them:

> A feeling of strength overwhelms one, such a sunny, splendid feeling of strength, that the ancient Titanic defiance of the Germans is born anew, a defiance which, trusting only in itself, obliterates one world and builds a new one.[7]

We now turn to the most controversial period of Remarque's life — his army career. Contrary to the assertions of many critics, Remarque did in fact serve as a soldier in the First World War, although it is true that he never actually got as far as the front line. Along with others in his school class, he was called up on 26 November 1916. Three young men from the same class had volunteered two years earlier, and one of them had had an arm amputated as a result of a war wound. Remarque was first housed in the Caprivi barracks on the Westerberg (the Klosterberg of *Im Westen nichts Neues*) under Corporal Schwarze. After his basic training, Remarque joined the Reserve Battalion IR. 78 and underwent further training, but, as his mother was seriously ill, he obtained frequent compassionate leave to return to Osnabrück.

On 12 June 1917 he was moved towards the Western front and assigned to the Second Company of the Field Recruiting Depot of the Guards Reserve Division, which was located in Ham-Lenglet, behind the Arras front. He was subsequently allocated to a trench unit which was based somewhere between Thourout and the forest of Houthult. According to Rabe, several of Remarque's contemporaries from Osnabrück were in the same troop, including Georg Middendorf (Kropp in *Im Westen nichts Neues*), Wilhelm Katschinsky (Kat), Seppel Oelfke (Haie Westhus), Detering, and Theo Troske.[8] Troske was badly wounded by grenade splinters in July 1917 and Remarque carried him back behind the line of fire; but Troske later died in hospital of head wounds which at first passed unnoticed, and was buried in Osnabrück on 24 August. Rabe suggests that this incident formed the basis of the fate which befell Kat in Remarque's novel.[9] According to the account of his closest friend during the war years, Georg Middendorf, Remarque was a reasonably competent soldier, always calm and self-possessed and valued by his comrades, whom he frequently entertained by playing the piano or by performing hypnotic tricks.[10]

During the battle of Flanders, which began on 31 July 1917, Rabe states that Remarque carried another comrade behind the line of fire, before being wounded himself by several grenade splinters in a surprise attack by the British.[11] Remarque was taken first to a field-hospital and then to the St Vincenz hospital in Duisberg. According to letters he wrote to Middendorf (whose nickname was "Dopp") his time in hospital passed fairly pleasantly (in stark contrast to the broadly unsympathetic view of military hospitals given in *Im Westen nichts Neues*):

> How are you? All right? I am very well. I am walking about, can go out whenever I wish, am getting good food. What more could one desire? . . . For the time being I have obtained a post as orderly room clerk. I have no intention of giving that up before I have to.[12]

Remarque also found time to develop a friendship with a hospital official's daughter, to give piano lessons to the doctor's children, and to compose music, including some settings of poems by Ludwig Bäte. A particular point of interest in another letter, written in pseudo-Upper Silesian, a style occasionally affected by

Remarque in his correspondence with Middendorf, is the following:

> Write and tell me about life as it is now. This is of great interest to me as I am writing a novel.[13]

The novel referred to must have been *Die Traumbude,* which was begun in Duisberg and finally published in 1920 by the *Die Schönheit* press in Dresden, although it is difficult indeed to conceive of such a book being written in the midst of the horrors of war.

It was at this time that Remarque's mother died.[14] Her death, which Remarque announced in a letter to Middendorf on 26 September 1917, came as a great blow to him; it was shortly to be followed by another, the death on 6 March 1918 of the thirty-six-year-old Fritz Hörstemeier. Remarque played the organ at Hörstemeier's cremation in Bremen later that month, an occasion which is described in *Die Traumbude.*[15] It was in this same year that Remarque began publishing poems and short prose pieces in the journal *Die Schönheit.* These early efforts are couched in the same exaggeratedly aesthetic mode as *Die Traumbude* and were probably composed in Duisberg. On 30 October 1918, Remarque returned to Osnabrück for further training, but the end of the war supervened before he was able to return to active service.

The controversy which was to surround Remarque's army career after the publication of *Im Westen nichts Neues* was given added fuel by his own somewhat unorthodox conduct after the end of the war. First, an announcement appeared in the *Osnabrücker Tageblatt* in November 1918 to the effect that a certain Erich Remark had been awarded the Iron Cross First Class. The announcement was accompanied by a photograph of master and dog, with the former dressed in officer's uniform and wearing the Iron Cross First and Second Class, the "Verwundetenabzeichen" (equivalent of the Gold Stripe for the Wounded) and another medal. When Georg Middendorf later remonstrated with Remarque for wearing medals to which he had no right, he showed Middendorf a document from the *Arbeiter- und Soldatenrat* (Council for Workers and Soldiers),[16] testifying to his right to wear them. How he came by this document and the medals remains a mystery (like so much of his life at this time), as do the motives behind Remarque's declaration, which his friend Rabe attributes to his undeniable tendency towards showing off.[17] In 1919 Remarque was required by the Osnabrück authorities to answer charges relating to this deception and obliged to sign a "confession".

Together with Middendorf and others of his fellow soldiers, Remarque returned to school in 1919, where the "mature students" received no sympathy from the older members of staff, none of whom had served as soldiers. Trouble inevitably arose when the teachers attempted to impose petty school discipline on their now adult pupils, whom they persisted in treating as the teenagers they had been before they went off to war. During the ensuing enquiry, Remarque acted as spokesman for the Catholic Seminar (and his subsequent friend Hanns-Gerd Rabe for its Protestant counterpart). Remarque depicts this period of his life in *Der Weg zurück*.

During these years, Remarque's home was an attic room in the Hakenstrasse, which was equipped with a desk, a piano (which he sold in 1919 to meet the printing costs of *Die Traumbude*), and his books, including works by Thomas and Heinrich Mann, Werfel, Hofmannsthal, Poe, Stendhal and Hölderlin. Remarque's reading matter during the early post-war years also included Schopenhauer, Nietzsche, Rilke, Balzac, Flaubert, Proust, Rolland, and Jack London. He dabbled in painting, attended concerts and went to the theatre. As the episode of the Iron Crosses and officer's uniform indicates, Remarque was fond of display and placed great emphasis on clothes. He was always elegantly dressed, with a proclivity towards large flamboyant ties and panama hats. He appears to have entertained certain aspirations towards becoming a professional pianist, but later claimed that a war wound just above his right wrist prevented him from making this his career.[18] Instead he successfully completed his training as a teacher in June 1919, attaining average grades in every subject except art and religious knowledge, in which he fared better, and took up his first appointment in Lohne during August of that year.

The Osnabrück authorities have records dating from 1919 accusing Remarque of being involved in Sparticist activities, a charge he consistently denied. He asked them for proof, but this was not forthcoming, although his behaviour while at the Seminar after his return from the war was criticized,[19] and the official letter of recommendation which he presented for his first teaching appointment stated that he was more "freethinking" than the average schoolteacher. Despite this, and despite Remarque's self-confessed interest in the infamous Nietzsche, Dr G Wöste, the son of Remarque's headmaster, subsequently stated that Remarque was a competent teacher who conducted himself most correctly and as part of his duties accompanied the children to church.[20] Dr Wöste also reports that Remarque often visited the family and entertained them by playing the latest operetta hits on the piano. He had lodgings with the Schomaker family, not far from the school, and was visited by his girlfriend Fräulein Diederichs. Wöste and "Mutter Schomaker" both feature in *Der Weg zurück*.

Remarque left the peaceful Lohne region in March 1920 on the return of the teacher whom he had been replacing, and his next post was at Klein-Berssen, Hümmling, again as a supply teacher, replacing a man by the name of Nieberg, who was on sick-leave. Although he once more found himself in a quiet country school, Remarque's new post was to offer little of the tranquillity which he had experienced in Lohne. He was accommodated over the single school-room with Nieberg and his family. The school was, in both a literal and a figurative sense, in the shadow of the church: it was a strict Catholic area, and the local priest Brand continually interfered with Remarque's duties.

The altercation between Remarque and Brand eventually developed to such a pitch that the matter was taken up by the authorities in Osnabrück. Remarque was regarded with suspicion from the outset, since he went out walking carrying a riding whip and invariably accompanied by his Alsatian (which he claimed had saved his life in the trenches),[21] and, to the horror of the priest, failed to attend church on Sundays. However, Remarque was by no means entirely to blame: Brand had already had disputes with Nieberg, whose illness Remarque attributed directly to the priest's constant meddling with school matters, maintaining that he had "quite literally brought the family to a state of despair".[22]

Rabe's copies of the correspondence between the two men reveal a lively and often acrid exchange, although it must be confessed that one is compelled to judge the matter almost entirely from Remarque's point of view: the priest's handwriting, as Remarque himself frequently points out in the most forthright of terms, is almost totally illegible. He often returned Brand's letters unread for this very reason, as the following extract from one of Remarque's replies indicates:

In answer to your enquiry whether I can now read your handwriting, I must say in your favour that you have greatly improved. If you continue to practise industriously you may yet attain a pretty high standard.[23]

When criticized by the authorities for his sarcastic and discourteous observations, Remarque pointed out that his correspondence with Brand had been entirely personal in nature, and should, therefore, not be judged by the same standards as an official document, despite the fact that Brand submitted all the letters to the local authority in Osnabrück. Remarque in fact welcomed Brand's publicizing of the affair, and threatened in his turn to take the matter up in the Social Democratic press:

> I have other material as well which could be most unpleasant for you! I have been patient. But if a cleric makes false statements to the authorities and even seeks to vilify me, then it is time to put an end to it! Now to battle! I am not afraid! . . . I am in the right and consequently will conduct the battle openly. You cannot frighten me; I have already conquered other opponents.[24]

As well as interfering with Remarque's duties, Brand was also guilty of witholding his salary, which, even when it was eventually paid to him, fell short of the stipulated amount.

Following the investigation of the correspondence between Remarque and Brand by the local authority in Osnabrück, Remarque was yet again summoned by this august body to submit a written explanation of his behaviour. This he duly did in a lengthy document of 12 September 1920, which he opens with this dogmatic assertion: "The statements made by Father Brand are *untrue*".[25] The pronouncements that Remarque refutes so categorically relate to his salary, but he also alludes to Brand's accusations of misconduct in matters concerning religion: these accusations he equally refutes, again calling Brand's credibility into question. In the issue of salary at least Remarque was vindicated, but he left his post on 31 July 1920 after only two months, and stated that he wished to be employed nearer to Osnabrück so that he could pursue his studies. His request was granted, and the following month he took up an appointment in Nahne, just outside Osnabrück, where he remained until November of that year, once again replacing a teacher on sick-leave. Although he encountered no problems in this post, Remarque formed the resolution to leave teaching for good. In submitting his resignation to the Osnabrück authorities, he gave no reason for this decision, but in a later interview he said that, while he had enjoyed teaching and got on well with his pupils, he felt the career to be too restrictive.[26]

For Remarque, as for countless others in post-war Germany, the early 'twenties were hard times. During this period he earned his living by a variety of means, as he indicates in the same interview:

> Then I did all kinds of things: for a time I wandered around with a suit-case and sold pieces of material . . . Later I was a representative for a memorial mason and much else besides, and I was also an organist in a lunatic asylum of all things.

This phase of Remarque's life, which is reflected in *Der schwarze Obelisk,* was doubtless one of the most disadvantaged from a financial point of view, but it was evidently not without its interesting aspects. His job as organist on Sundays earned him a free lunch (with wine) and also led to friendship with Father

Biedendieck, who had been Remarque's confessor before the war, and who proved to be a priest rather more to Remarque's liking than Brand. Biedendieck, who figures under the name of Bodendiek in *Der schwarze Obelisk* and under his own name in *Zeit zu leben und Zeit zu sterben,* is described by Rabe in these terms:

> He was not a spiritual priest, but rather a materialist, a lover of food and drink ... He was tall, a giant of a man, not always popular among his parishioners because he was not slow to speak his mind and let his views be known. He was quite blunt in showing his flock the error of their ways.[27]

From 1921 onwards, Remarque visited Rabe fairly frequently, enjoying the hospitality of his newly-married friend, where the food was less spartan than at home. He and Rabe shared similar interests, they were both theatre critics (Remarque for the short-lived *Osnabrücker Landeszeitung*) and both had aspirations as writers. (Rabe appears in *Der Weg zurück* and *Zeit zu leben* under the name of Lieutenant Georg Rahe.) Remarque was also writing sketches and short stories at the time, but the money he earned was quickly swallowed up by the galloping inflation. When his sentimental love-poem "Abendlied" (Evening Song) was published in 1920 in the *Osnabrücker Tageblatt,* it was surprisingly well received.[28] A noted poet of the time, Henckell, said of it: "It is one of the profoundest love-songs I have ever read",[29] and he praised the emotional intensity with which Remarque had charged the simple vocabulary of his poem.

Remarque began working for the Vogt brothers, who were monumental masons in the Süsterstrasse, in 1922 and later said of his time there:

> We designed and sold atrocities depicting lions with toothache or bronze eagles bereft of wings, whenever possible with golden crowns.[30]

While at Vogt's, Remarque made contact with the "Continental Caoutchouc- und Gutta-Percha-Compagnie" in Hanover, and began writing advertising copy and editorial material for its house magazine *Echo-Continental.* In October 1922 he moved to Hanover to take up full-time employment with the firm. In reply to an offer of a teaching post from the local authority in Osnabrück, Remarque writes, with a degree of pride: "I am publicity manager and chief editor for the Continental Company of Hanover".[31] This letter he signs Erich *Maria* Remark. For the years 1922-1923, Remarque is listed in the Osnabrück directory as "Erich Remark, writer", a title which he had earlier employed in his correspondence.

For the *Echo-Continental* Remarque wrote short and often humorous prose pieces advertising tyres, cycles and cars, together with a number of short verses accompanying strip cartoons celebrating the adventures of the Conti-Buben (Conti-Lads) and Captain Priemke.[32] Remarque's love of cars and motor-racing found ample outlet with Continental and also plays a major rôle in three of his novels, the early *Station am Horizont* (serialized in *Sport im Bild* 1927-28), *Drei Kameraden,* and *Der Himmel kennt keine Günstlinge.* Other key themes in Remarque's novels also make their first appearance in these pieces. In one article, for example, he advocates participation in sport as part of the fight against tuberculosis, which was particularly widespread during the early twentieth century.[33] Another preoccupation which emerges in his journalistic writing of this period is Remarque's interest in alchohol. This finds its way into a number of articles under such titles as "Uber das Mixen kostbarer Schnäpse".[34] The extravagant clichés which Remarque employs in his descriptions of cocktails and other alchoholic beverages are seized upon gleefully by Mynona in *Hat Erich Maria Remarque wirklich gelebt?* [35]

In 1925 Remarque moved to Berlin, where he worked as an editor for the journal *Sport im Bild,* writing articles similar in theme and style to those he penned for the *Echo-Continental* and equal in literary merit. Remarque was quick to point out in an interview shortly after the publication and success of *Im Westen nichts Neues* that his work for *Echo-Continental* and *Sport im Bild* was done solely in order to earn a living:

> I wrote lots of articles about rubber tyres, cars, collapsible canoes, engines and goodness knows what, simply because I had to make a living from it.[36]

He was rapidly acquiring a taste for society life, and could frequently be seen, monocled and chiquely attired, adorning the bars at the major sport events. He also accompanied the racing driver Rudolf Caracciolo on motor-racing trips.[37]

Those who knew Remarque during the late 'twenties have described him as a very personable young man, strikingly good-looking, blond and athletic (in fact, typically Aryan!).[38] He was evidently considered to be quite a man of the world, and when he mentioned to acquaintances that he had written a novel, no one took very much notice, little dreaming that they were speaking to the man who was destined to write the most celebrated war novel of all time. On 14 October 1925 Remarque married the twenty-four-year-old actress and dancer Jutta Ilse Ingeborg Ellen Zambona in Charlottenburg.

During 1927-1928 Remarque's *Station am Horizont* (which several critics have erroneously referred to as *Segel am* (or *im*) *Horizont*[39]) appeared in serial form in *Sport im Bild.* Antkowiak states that this is a fluent piece of story-telling, but it contains the "creed of a snob", since it is concerned with the glossy exterior of society life — and presumably rather more in the vein that Remarque's motor-racing acquaintances might have expected of him than *Im Westen nichts Neues*:

> The heroes move in a mundane tinsel-world, where waiters in evening dress serve select meals, and where flirtation and motor-racing are the substitute for real life ... Platitudes are served up as profound thoughts.[40]

Station am Horizont, many of whose themes are taken up again later, notably in *Der Himmel kennt keine Günstlinge,* was never published in book form. Although Ullstein allegedly acquired the rights to it, they treated it in the same manner as *Die Traumbude* and allowed it to remain in well-deserved oblivion. Remarque himself has dismissed the book as a disastrous experiment:

> Earlier I worked quite differently. I had experimented ... in order to find a style, but everything remained dull and colourless and I was never satisfied. Probably because I was on entirely the wrong track.[41]

Like *Die Traumbude,* then, *Station am Horizont* was an essential but unsuccessful exploratory phase for Remarque, and in many ways a strange preparation for the best-selling war novel which was to follow soon after.

Im Westen nichts Neues was written during the latter part of 1927. The manuscript remained in Remarque's desk for six months before being submitted to Fischer and then to Ullstein.[42] Having accepted the novel, Ullstein first serialized it in the *Vossische Zeitung* between 10 November and 9 December 1928. It appeared in book form in January 1929. Remarque's overnight success drastically and irrevocably altered the course of his entire life, and the hitherto unknown journalist became a world-famous author: loved or hated but never regarded with indifference, he found himself relentlessly pursued by public and media alike. While not exactly shunning publicity, Remarque always sought to maintain a degree of privacy and very rarely gave interviews. Asked once why he never intervened in the heated debates about *Im Westen nichts Neues* he replied:

> Because I didn't and don't consider it necessary ... Once a work is finished, the author has nothing further to say about it, even if there is a risk of being misunderstood. If this is the case, then his work has not succeeded, and talking about it serves no purpose. But I am of the opinion that I was only misunderstood where people went out of their way to misunderstand me.[43]

During the controversy surrounding *Im Westen nichts Neues,* Remarque and his wife lived in Berlin, and their house at 5 Wittelsbacher Strasse today bears the inevitable memorial plaque. The questions and theories regarding Remarque's personal identity received little enlightenment from the fact that he was registered in Berlin as Erich, Freiherr von Buchwaldt.

Unable to work in Berlin on a sequel to *Im Westen nichts Neues* because of the publicity stimulated by his first novel (as he chose to call *Im Westen nichts Neues,* conveniently sweeping his earlier efforts under the carpet), Remarque advertised in a newspaper in Osnabrück for a quiet flat in which he could work for a while undisturbed. A certain Frau Maria Hoberg answered his advertisement, and during November and December of 1929 he spent some four weeks in her spacious house, occupying rooms overlooking private gardens which extended along the Süsterstrasse, opposite Vogt's stonemasonry where he had once worked.

Remarque had often admired the gardens from his office at Vogt's and was well pleased with his new working environment. During the summer of 1930, Remarque, together with his Irish setter, Billy, spent a further couple of months in the Hoberg house, where he completed *Der Weg zurück.* In a letter to Frau Hoberg during her absence from the house, he gives the following reasons for his tardiness in writing to her:

> Seriously: during these crowded weeks I have lost the ability to hear and see, and I could think of nothing but work. Besides, for ten days I was in pretty poor shape physically, as if I really was about to have a nervous breakdown ... My wife was here for a day, but only for one day; my work makes so many demands on me.[44]

Karla Hoberg, Frau Hoberg's daughter, has confirmed that Remarque worked most industriously in a well-lit room overlooking the garden, with music from his own collection of gramophone records playing in the background. He never typed his novels, preferring to use well-sharpened pencils and neatly erasing any mistakes: "I always write in longhand, otherwise I'd feel like my own stenographer. I also concentrate better if I write by hand".[45]

Despite his industry, Remarque did not make the progress he wished on his novel, which did not flow from his pen — or rather, his pencil — with anything like the fluency of *Im Westen nichts Neues.* This was probably due to his anxiety to produce a worthy successor to his "first" novel; he also felt under a certain amount of pressure to produce a new novel fairly rapidly. According to Karla Hoberg, Remarque was also discontented because of the prolonged absences from his wife, and felt that his marriage was being sacrificed on the altar of his success as a writer:

He was often depressed. He was not content with his book, he felt he was being rushed . . . In addition, he was oppressed at being apart from his wife. He felt that she was slowly slipping away from him through the turmoil that attended his success. He once spoke of it, saying that he now had so much money and success, but the one thing he was really concerned about, his wife, was slipping away from him more and more.[46]

There was more than a measure of truth in these views, since Remarque's marriage ended in divorce shortly after his stay in Osnabrück.

Remarque always retained a great affection for the Hoberg house, as is shown in a letter he wrote in the last year of his life to HG Hoberg. Remarque is writing to thank Hoberg for a picture of the Süsterstrasse taken in the 'twenties:

The picture happened to arrive here during a lengthy illness, and I have had it standing by my bed all these weeks; it has aroused so many memories of those days when I was in the Vogt house up to the time when I wrote my second book in your beautiful house . . . When I last went through the town, shortly after the war, I could hardly find anything again. Everything had been destroyed.[47]

Remarque's stay in Osnabrück during 1930 was, in fact, destined to be his last, and even then the people of Osnabrück saw very little of him. He was, then as always, unwilling to permit his fame to intrude upon his personal life and, apart from occasional gatherings with Rabe and other friends from his school and army days, was rarely seen in his home town. Rabe reports that Remarque remained a most likeable person, unspoilt by his wealth and fame (although there is no doubt that they meant a great deal to him) and relates as an instance of Remarque's generosity that, having been invited to visit Remarque in Berlin, Rabe received a first class rail ticket, was accommodated in one of the best hotels, and was even given a purseful of money to supplement his meagre teacher's salary.[48]

In 1930, Remarque suddenly found himself hounded by the National Socialists. It was they who really turned *Im Westen nichts Neues* into a political issue (Remarque always insisted that he was "unpolitical") by attacking its anti-heroic stance in relation to the First World War. They never forgave him for challenging the Nazi myth of individual heroism in the armed conflict which they regarded as the fire in which the iron spirit of National Socialism had been forged. In the words of Erika and Klaus Mann:

Remarque, already bewildered by the immense and unforeseen success of this, his first book, suddenly found himself in the middle of a political scandal he had not the least intention of provoking.[49]

The witch-hunt against Remarque, epitomized by the disturbances caused by members of the Hitler youth during the screening of the American film version of *Im Westen nichts Neues* in 1930, was to drive Remarque not only from Berlin but also from his native land:

> In the year 1931 I had to leave Germany, because my life was threatened. I was neither a Jew nor orientated towards the left politically. I was the same then as I am today: a militant pacifist.[50]

Along with his contemporary Erich Kästner, Remarque was a "don't know" rather than a convinced anti-Nazi at the beginning of the 'thirties, and is reputed to have stated later to Thomas Mann: "It's more by luck than good judgement that I am on the side I now stand on. But I know that it happens to be the right one".[51]

The campaign against Remarque was spearheaded by Goebbels, who is later said to have repented and sent a deputy to invite Remarque back to Berlin, suggesting at the same time that without the National Socialists his anti-war book would never have topped the million sales.[52] Remarque counters this assertion by stating that it was the very success of the book which brought about the political attacks:

> It is unpolitical. And at first the impression it made was entirely non-political. Only through its success was it drawn into the political debating arena. I think it was more the number of copies sold than the book itself which was the object of attack.[53]

It is certainly the case that most of the attacks made on Remarque were personal and political rather than literary in nature, and one of the chief reproaches levelled against him by many German critics — and not only from those in the National Socialist party — appears to have been that he knew and catered for public taste. The offer from Goebbels was, of course, declined by Remarque and — again according to the account of E and K Mann — he is alleged to have said: "What? 65 million people would like to get away and I'm to go back of my own free will? Not on your life".[54]

Among the many stories surrounding Remarque's departure from Berlin is one which he himself was fond of repeating. It concerns a restaurant in Berlin which he was in the habit of frequenting — in the company of Carl Zuckmayer among others — and which had accumulated a large stock of Remarque's favourite wine, Pfälzer. Remarque was apparently told that, after he had left Germany, Göring went into the restaurant and asked for the same wine, adding: "You don't need to save it up for Remarque any more, he won't be coming back". But the waiter replied

apologetically that Remarque had drunk every last bottle.[55]
Zuckmayer too includes a variation of this story in the play *Des Teufels General* (The Devil's General), where General Harras is told that a particular wine he orders has been reserved for Remarque:

> Dr. Schmidt-Lausitz *has come closer:* For Erich Maria Remarque? The emigrant?
> Harras *more and more amused:* Just imagine! And the lad is sitting in America and has to drink whisky.[56]

Remarque emigrated to Porto Ronco in Switzerland at the beginning of the 'thirties, to a villa falsely claimed to have once belonged to the nineteenth century artist Böcklin, who painted the famous "Island of the Dead".[57] A newspaper article reports that Remarque's German bank account was seized in April 1932:

> On Friday of last week money desposited in the Darmstadt and National bank by the writer Erich Maria Remarque was confiscated by officials of the customs office.[58]

This was done ostensibly because he had been living abroad for an extended period and had tax arrears. The article also records that the police (quite correctly) suspected that Remarque had transferred most of the money he had earned from his books abroad, since the account contained only a relatively small sum. As well as most of his money, Remarque also managed to rescue his collection of Impressionist paintings — including works by Cézanne, Van Gogh, Renoir and Degas — and the Lancia Cabriolet presented to him by Ullstein.

Remarque became very attached to his beautiful Ascona home, which he renamed "Casa Remarque", and over the years filled it with many valuable antiques, notably early Chinese and Egyptian bronze figures, Venetian mirrors, and Persian carpets. Until 1939, Remarque divided his time between Porto Ronco and France, and after the Second World War spent a good deal of time there. It was in Porto Ronco that he completed *Drei Kameraden,* which he had begun in Berlin. The novel was finally published in Amsterdam in 1937:

> When Hitler forced me out of Germany, my third novel *Drei Kameraden* was almost finished. It was such a shock for me to have to leave Germany that I took four years to complete the book.[59]

Meanwhile his two earlier novels, *Im Westen nichts Neues* and *Der Weg zurück,* had been placed on the index of prohibited literature by the Nazi régime and had been burned in the notorious book-burning ceremony in Berlin in 1933. (Ironically, Remarque's novels were also banned by Russia and the Eastern Bloc in 1949.)

Rumour has it that in 1933 Remarque braved the dangers to himself in order to rescue his ex-wife from Berlin,[60] but the following account by Remarque of this period in his life makes no reference to the incident:

> I was at the time (1929) married to a very beautiful woman. But after the flight to Switzerland I divorced her. So that she did not lose her residence permit for Switzerland, I then married her again. I couldn't allow her to be sent back to Germany just because we weren't in love any more.[61]

Reports vary as to when the divorce actually took place: the *New York Times* obituary gives 1932, [62] and a report in the *Frankfurter Neue Presse* states that Remarque divorced his wife in 1931 and married her again in 1932.[63] The generally reliable Hans Wagener, on the other hand, maintains that Remarque was divorced in 1930 and did not re-marry until 1938, after which time he and his wife mostly lived apart.[64] The circumstances surrounding Remarque's divorce and re-marriage remain veiled in an obscurity which Felicitas von Reznicek's recollections of Remarque do little to illuminate. She was acquainted with both Remarque and his wife, since she did some work for *Sport im Bild* while Remarque was an editor there. She appears to have last seen the couple together in Davos in Switzerland during the winter of 1929, where Remarque's wife was undergoing some kind of health cure (she suffered from tuberculosis), and declares enigmatically that in the question of the divorce she "was not in agreement with the way he put his divorce through", although she "was in no doubt as to its necessity", and took the side of his wife.[65] Felicitas von Reznicek gives no further details other than to add that Remarque later told her that he admired her for supporting his wife at a time when others sided with the world-famous author.

A letter to *Der Spiegel* in 1971[66] maintains that Erna Zambona, the sister of Remarque's wife, was in fact married to Professor Heinrich Göring, a relative of the notorious Hermann. According to this letter, Professor Göring helped many people who had opposed the Hitler régime, and it seems doubly mysterious that Remarque's estranged wife should have felt "threatened by the National Socialists in Berlin",[67] although the writer of the letter does add that Remarque never availed himself of his connection with Professor Göring.

Remarque was deprived of his German citizenship in 1938 and went to America — via France — in the following year. The most dramatic account of his flight is given in a book entitled *Die grossen Namen* (The big Names), in which its author, Constantine, Prince of Bavaria, relates that, having decided to return from France to Switzerland because of the increasing threat of war, Remarque was warned that the Gestapo were waiting for him on the Italian border. He therefore jumped into his Lancia and headed for Paris, blowing first one cylinder, then another, and just making it to the Hotel Lancaster in Paris before the car finally ground to a halt. By chance he obtained a returned ticket for the Queen Mary, on which he sailed to New York, hearing the declaration of war on board ship.[68]

Wagener, on the other hand, claims that Remarque's first trip to New York was to be attributed not least to his close friendship with Marlene Dietrich (whom he had met in Berlin) rather than to any real wish to emigrate to America, for soon after disembarking in New York he went to Marlene Dietrich's home in Hollywood.[69] Still reluctant to believe in the possibility of war, says Wagener, Remarque returned to France, accompanied by Marlene Dietrich, and returned to America in September of 1939, again on the Queen Mary. It was allegedly on the advice of Joseph Kennedy (father of the former US President) that Remarque decided to leave Europe for America.[70] Kennedy was at that time American ambassador in London, and Remarque met him in Antibes while holidaying on the Côte d'Azur with Miss Dietrich, and according to Franz Baumer, Remarque many years later remembered with gratitude the assistance he received from Joseph Kennedy in establishing himself in America. Baumer also quotes from an interview Remarque gave on his arrival in New York in which, after denying that there was any real reason for a war, he added prophetically: "This will not be a war against frontiers, but a war against women and children". [71]

Remarque's wife, who had initially remained in Europe, made her own fairly dramatic entry into the United States shortly after her husband. She arrived in New York at the end of October 1939, but was detained because of passport difficulties. She eventually obtained permission to take the usual emigré route via Mexico, and, according to Wagener, crossed the Mexican border on 4 January 1940, the very day that her temporary US permit expired, and waited for Remarque in Mexico City. She then went back into the United States with her husband, but again lived apart from him and finally divorced him in 1951.[72] Remarque himself experienced none of the usual difficulties of the war refugees which he describes so graphically in his novels. When his Swiss papers expired he was given a temporary pass by Panama; Mexico then offered him somewhere to live and a refugee pass. In the meantime, Roosevelt ensured that he was put on the quota list of immigrants to the United States and renewed his Swiss papers. It was in 1941 that he first decided to apply for American citizenship. This entailed returning to Mexico and registering with the American consulate and, after the statutory five years, Remarque became an American citizen in 1947. Although he had acquired a great liking for America, Remarque was evidently distressed at the loss of his German citizenship, as the following bitter comment demonstrates:

> As far as I know, none of the mass murderers of the Third Reich have been deprived of their citizenship. The emigrants, therefore, are far worse off than they are.[73]

Apparently it was not possible for Remarque to be automatically reinstated — a regulation he felt most embittered about — and an application for German citizenship would have cost him his American rights. More important than this, however, to reapply for German citizenship would have been to acknowledge that he had been deprived of it in the first place, and this Remarque categorically refused to do, even though Fritz von Opel managed to obtain permission for him to make a verbal request only: "I did not apply to be deprived of my citizenship, and therefore shall not apply to be reinstated".[74]

Remarque and his family suffered in other ways at the hands of the Nazis. In 1943 Remarque's youngest sister Elfriede was beheaded, having been accused of subversive propaganda. In a letter to Georg Kruezmann, which was printed in an Osnabrück newspaper in 1968, [75] Remarque's father asserted his daughter's innocence, and it was generally assumed that Elfriede's death was, in part at least, a result of Nazi antipathy towards her brother. Certainly reference was made to Remarque during Elfriede's "trial" by Freisler, but in an interview Remarque has the following to say:

> The fact that she was my sister probably had something to do with the verdict. But the main reason was that she belonged to the resistance circle around the Scholls.[76]

In a letter to Rabe, Remarque also says: "My youngest sister . . . was executed by the people's court because, in 1942, she didn't believe in a German victory".[77] Twenty-five years after her death, in 1968, a street on the western outskirts of Osnabrück was named after Elfriede Scholz (née Remark), and the letter which Remarque wrote in January 1969 to thank the town shows how deeply he was moved by this gesture.[78] In June 1971 Remarque himself was posthumously accorded a similar honour:

the Karlsring in Osnabrück was renamed the Erich-Maria-Remarque-Ring.

From 1939 to 1942 Remarque spent most of his time in Hollywood, where he rented a bungalow. He was evidently quite at home in the centre of the film world, as David Niven records:

> When Erich Maria Remarque was not wrapped around Marlene Dietrich or other local beauties, he acted as a sort of liason officer between the German-speaking foreigners, the Garden of Allah Set and Musso and Frank's Restaurant on Hollywood Boulevard.[79]

Remarque's friendship with Marlene Dietrich lasted until 1946 or thereabouts, and she is credited with having named Remarque as the most attractive man in the world. Remarque, in an interview, modestly blames this statement for the "rumours" that he and Marlene Dietrich had a love-affair of several years duration:

> They probably arrived at that conclusion because once in a questionnaire Marlene put me at the top of her list of the ten most attractive men in the world.[80]

Although Remarque here attempts to cast doubt upon the closeness of his relationship with Marlene Dietrich, he certainly knew her very well indeed, and Victoria Wolff, who was similarly "exiled" in Ascona, claims that Remarque once told her that Marlene Dietrich kept some letters from him in a bank safe and expressed fears that she would publish them after his death, thereby causing embarrassment to his wife, Paulette Goddard, as well as allowing the public to intrude even further into his private life.[81] His fears, however, appear to have been unfounded.

Another of his more celebrated female companions was the elusive Greta Garbo — "I accompanied her frequently, and enjoyed doing so"[82] — and among his male friends he numbered Charlie Chaplin, Cole Porter and the American writers F Scott Fitzgerald and Ernest Hemingway. The latter he particularly admired, once remarking to film director Douglas Sirk: "You know, I'm only a small man in comparison to Hemingway".[83] It was in the late 'forties that he made the acquaintance of the actress Paulette Goddard, whom he said was one of the most intelligent women he had ever met, and they married in 1958.

Although involved for some time in the social whirl of Hollywood, where his expertise in mixing the more recherché alchoholic beverages as well as his personal charms ensured his success at parties, the glittering unreality of Hollywood soon drove Remarque to New York, where he felt far more at home. He first settled there in 1942, and the enthusiasm with which he extols its virtues in a letter to Rabe in 1966 proves that the "Big Apple" had lost none of its appeal for Remarque twenty-seven years after he first set foot there:

> New York! That really is a city without the melancholy and oppressive charm of the past! An explosion of life! The future.[84]

The buoyant life of New York afforded a welcome contrast to the tranquillity of Porto Ronco, where Remarque spent the summer months after the end of the Second World War. Most of all, he loved the freedom of America and the easy-going friendliness of the people. It is certainly true to say that Remarque was more readily accepted by critics and public alike in America than in his native Germany:

> In America ... they react in this way: "The man is successful, so there must be something in him". In Germany they say: "He's successful, so he can't be worthwhile".[85]

There is more than a little truth in these words, and despite being accorded a certain measure of official recognition from Germany during the latter part of his life in the form of medallions and the *Grosses Verdienstkreuz* (which he was awarded in 1963), Remarque never seemed to feel that he had been totally accepted by his fellow countrymen and made only brief return trips to Germany after the Second World War. Instead, he spent his time alternating between New York and Porto Ronco until a serious illness in the mid 'sixties obliged him to choose Rome instead of America for his winter quarters. In an article written shortly after Remarque died in 1971, Hans Habe points out that, while Remarque's books were hardly ever reviewed in the German press during his lifetime, a number of favourable reviews of his work suddenly appeared in the days following his death. He comments with a tinge of irony:

> The people like their writers good and dead ... How dead does a German author have to be in order to be able to live?[86]

The Germans, it seemed, could never forgive Remarque for enjoying so much success with his brand of writing.

The Americans, on the other hand, were restrained by no such inhibitions. His popularity in the USA knew no bounds, and the number of films made from his books was such that he gained the title "King of Hollywood". Remarque's follow-up to *Drei Kameraden* was published in America in 1941 under the title *Flotsam*, but it was not until twelve years later that it was

published in Germany as *Liebe deinen Nächsten*. His second
worldwide bestseller, *Arc de Triomphe*, was also written and first
published in America. He composed the novel in California just
after America's entry into the Second World War, when German
and Japanese refugees were confined to their houses by curfew
after eight in the evening:

> At that time I developed a longing for Paris, where I could move about
> freely even though I didn't have a passport. In the course of the long
> Californian evenings I had enough time to call to mind all the places I
> knew so well.[87]

Remarque seemed fated all his life to enjoy fame for non-literary
reasons. With *Arc de Triomphe* it was his choice of Calvados for
his hero's favourite drink which seized the imagination of his
public — and of the liquor merchants. He chose Calvados not
because he himself was particularly fond of the drink but simply
because it was cheaper than whisky and had a somewhat more
exotic ring to its name. Sales of the apple schnapps soared as
Remarque's novel climbed the bestseller charts:

> I believe the sales increased tremendously after the publication of the
> book. In New York I discovered copies of my book decorating barrels full
> of Calvados in the liquor stores. That is how people like myself succeed in
> being taken seriously by the spirits merchants.[88]

The grateful distributors kept sending Remarque bottles of the
drink, and, not liking to tell them he was really not so fond of
Calvados, he appears to have amassed quite a large stock. When
Rabe went to Porto Ronco with other members of a delegation
from Osnabrück to present Remarque with the Möser medallion,
he was presented with a five litre bottle![89]

Three of Remarque's novels had been made into films before his
arrival in America, with Scott Fitzgerald contributing — in his
more sober moments — to the screenplay of *Three Comrades*.
While the films *All Quiet on the Western Front* and *The Road
Back* adhered fairly closely to Remarque's texts, *Three Comrades*
did not: anything which might have upset the sensibilities of the
American public was omitted. Hence, with references to the First
World War and the revolts which followed obliterated and
anything remotely "political" excised, together with drastic
alterations in the basic love story, little of Remarque's original
plot remained. The entire film was excessively sentimental, and,
hardly surprisingly, received adverse reviews. *So Ends Our Night*,
the film of *Liebe deinen Nächsten* (or rather, *Flotsam*), which was
made in 1941, did not fare much better, but this time for the
contrary reason that the screenplay followed the book too

slavishly, and the resultant film lacked dramatic tension and laid itself open to the charge of tediousness.

Undeterred by the relative lack of success of these enterprises, United Artists turned to an unpublished short story by Remarque for their film *The Other Love* (1947). Originally entitled *Beyond,* Remarque's story was written in the early 'forties and, according to Wagener, was conceived from the outset as the basis for a potential screenplay.[90]   United Artists had also bought up a number of short stories which Remarque had written a decade before: these, however, were never filmed and have apparently disappeared without trace.[91]   Remarque had been anxious for Marlene Dietrich to take the star rôle in *The Other Love* but the studio overruled him: Dietrich was rejected in favour of Barbara Stanwyck, who co-starred with David Niven and Richard Conte. The line of the action bears a striking resemblance to that of *Der Himmel kennt keine Günstlinge* (published in 1961), and it seems reasonable to speculate that it may have constituted a half-way stage between *Station am Horizont* and the later novel. Parallels with Thomas Mann's *Der Zauberberg,* still apparent in *Der Himmel kennt keine Günstlinge,* were soon unearthed by the critics, whose general response was surprisingly favourable, particularly in England.

Arc de Triomphe, so successful as a book, was a financial disaster as a film, despite the signing of the popular Ingrid Bergman, Charles Boyer and Charles Laughton for the leading rôles. Remarque is again said to have had Marlene Dietrich in mind for the leading female rôle, and she herself is thought to have entertained a similar notion and to have been very disappointed that she was not offered it by the film studio. In a later interview Remarque maintained that Ingrid Bergman was too "heavy" and "earthy" for the part of Joan.[92] The *Los Angeles Times,* in a review of the film in 1948, was also of the opinion that Ingrid Bergman as leading lady was miscast and would have preferred Marlene Dietrich in the part.[93]   Again, the "political" aspects of the story were pruned back and the plight of the emigré was completely subordinated to the love relationship between Ravic and Joan. This was not all: Dr Ravic's illegal surgical operations only narrowly escaped the studio's own cutting-room floor. Even the famous Calvados was not spared the screenwriter's axe.

At the beginning of the 'fifties Remarque returned briefly to Germany to collect material for *Zeit zu leben,* which was published in 1954, two years after his concentration camp novel *Der Funke Leben.* Douglas Sirk's 1957 film of *Zeit zu leben,* whose American title, *A Time to Love and a Time to die,* taken from the English language version of the novel, was in keeping with the Hollywood dream machine in emphasizing the love story, constituted a significant landmark in Remarque's career in more than one way. First, it marked his début as an actor: at Sirk's request, Remarque portrayed the schoolmaster Pohlmann, a performance which was acclaimed by the critics (more so than those of his professional co-stars, in fact); secondly, Remarque (with Sirk) had written the original screenplay for the film — in English. This was not only the first time that Remarque had written the screenplay for one of his own films (he had previously claimed that he was too close to the text to be able to achieve a successful adaptation), it was also his début as a writer in English for, although his grasp of the language was excellent, he always returned to German for his novels. It is Orin Jannings, however, who is credited with the scenario, for Sirk employed the American dialogue writer for the final version, Remarque — according to Sirk — having refused either payment or credit for the work he had done.[94]

Remarque had earlier written for the cinema in German. In 1955 he had produced the screenplay for the Austrian film *Der letzte Akt* (The last Act), based on the book *Ten Days to Die* by Michael A Musmanno. This film, very successful in the English language version under the title *The Last Ten Days,* depicts the closing scenes in the life of Hitler in his Berlin underground bunker.

The last of Remarque's own novels to be filmed was *Die Nacht von Lissabon,* which was made into a television film in Germany in 1970. The highlight of the film, in the reviewers' eyes at least, appears to have been a pre-war telephone box which was transported from Bremen and installed outside the cathedral in Osnabrück. The German press was again critical of the excess of clichés and platitudes in the language and Remarque once more found himself accused of being "superficial".[95]

In 1956, he embarked on yet another new career and one which had always attracted him; namely, that of playwright. He was fascinated by the theatre and described himself as an out-and-out theatrical man.[96] His own narrative technique has indeed always been closely allied to that of the dramatist, as he himself has repeatedly underlined. When asked what he regarded as the key to his success as a writer, Remarque replied:

Perhaps because I'm a playwright manqué ... All my books are written like plays. One scene follows upon another. [97]

Remarque, for whom the act of writing was more of a chore than a pleasure, always maintained that what came easiest to him was the dialogue, and the reader of his novels cannot but agree that his chief strength lies in his rapier-edged exchanges, which have been likened to those of Oscar Wilde.[98] Remarque attributes his skill in this regard to his "musical ear":

> I write by ear. I hear everything that I write. I choose words for their sound. Because I am musical, because I was once quite a good organist, because I really wanted to be a musician, my novels all sound good when they're read out loud. I find easy what other authors find most difficult: writing dialogue.[99]

Instead of assuming a mantle of authorial omniscience, Remarque allows his characters to speak for themselves and the action to unfold naturally. This approach to creative writing is, of course, admirably suited to the dramatic form and contributed greatly to the success of his stage play *Die letzte Station,* the tense love story of a refugee from a concentration camp set against the background of the last days of the war in Berlin. The play — which has not yet been published in book form — had its première in Berlin and was subsequently produced on Broadway. It was a success with both German and American audiences, but did not meet with universal acclaim from the reviewers. Throughout his life, Remarque found it practically impossible to please both his public and the professional critics.

Remarque went to Berlin for the première of *Die letzte Station* in 1956 , and had also made another flying visit to Germany shortly before to attend the funeral of his father, Peter Remark. His relationship with his father was by no means as close as that with his mother had been, and there had, in fact, been little contact between the two since 1932. Peter Remark had remarried after the death of Remarque's mother, and his second wife had died not long after Elfriede's execution in 1943.[100] The account of his father's death which Remarque offers in a newspaper interview has the same apocryphal and anecdotal ring as many of the stories associated with himself:

> My father also died of a heart complaint. At eighty-three. He caught cold in church because he was without a coat. He hadn't put one on in order to impress his lady friend. When he got home he was freezing. My sister asked if he would like some cognac. He said he would. Then he died. Is there any finer death than to die awaiting a cognac?[101]

Although his father's funeral took place no great distance from Osnabrück, Remarque held back from visiting his home-town, the setting for so many of his novels. *Der schwarze Obelisk*, a semi-autobiographical novel published in 1956 but set in 1923, draws on his own experiences as an employee at Vogt's stonemasonry in

Osnabrück, and bears witness to the fact that Remarque was still very much attached to his native town, but the prospect of actually returning there evidently gave rise to very mixed feelings. Writing to Rabe in 1957, Remarque rejects the view that he has a "love-hate relationship" with Osnabrück, and writes eloquently of his love for the place:

> The town is very dear to me as it is to you — we were, after all, born there and grew up there. To you over there I am considered a "cosmopolitan" — here my friends call me "the man from Osnabrück". One should never disown anything and, as you see, almost all my books have a touch of Osnabrück background.[102]

However, none of the projected visits to his home town referred to time and again in Remarque's letters to Rabe and others in Osnabrück came to fruition. Phrases expressing the hope of visiting the town in the not too distant future became a regular feature of Remarque's letters from the late 'fifties until the time of his death, but each proposed journey was postponed for one reason or another.

As old age approached, memories of his youth became dearer to Remarque, particularly when illness, resulting from a series of heart attacks in the late 'sixties, brought thoughts of death crowding into his mind:

> Please send my greetings to all my school-friends again, and tell them that I very often think of the happy old days of our youth — that's probably always the case when one gets older. Youth then often seems strangely close, as if it were only a few years past instead of more than half a lifetime away.[103]

As the pull of Osnabrück became stronger, however, so did Remarque's fears that the emotional upheaval caused by such a journey would be too much for his precarious state of health:

> Nothing will come of my trip to Osnabrück this year, it is too far and too exhausting, also emotionally, strange as that might sound.[104]

One major factor which deterred Remarque from revisiting Osnabrück was his awareness of the many changes which had taken place there since the days of his youth. The Osnabrück he loved was not the bustling rebuilt town with its pedestrian precincts and strident prosperity but the old streets of the pre-war days, precious few of which survived the combined efforts of Allied bombing and municipal planning. The letter to Hoberg refers to the fact that when Remarque last saw Osnabrück, shortly after the Second World War, he scarcely recognized it, so great had been the devastation.[105] Further bitterness was doubtless caused by the refusal of a petty bureaucracy to restore his German citizenship without a formal request on Remarque's part.

Thus it was in America, Switzerland and Italy that Remarque spent the closing years of his life, travelling less frequently to New York as his health deteriorated. In addition to the series of heart attacks which began in the mid 'sixties, Remarque on two occasions narrowly escaped a dramatic death in a manner which by now seems inevitable: "With me everything is a story, even the things that concern me directly".[106] In the winter of 1965-1966 an avalanche swept down upon the garden and garage of Remarque's Ascona home, but the house itself was spared from destruction, and in the same year the ship in which he and his wife had booked a passage was hit by a freak wave. The Remarques had decided against travelling on the Michelangelo since Paulette wanted to break the journey in Paris in order to stock up her wardrobe with fashionable French clothes, and the two of them were more than a little shocked when they learned that bodies of victims of the tragedy were found in the very cabin which they had booked on the ship.[107]

Throughout the ill health which dogged him in the latter part of his life, Remarque was working on the manuscript of another novel, the posthumously published *Schatten im Paradies*, which represents a sequel to *Die Nacht von Lissabon*, in the sense that it deals with the arrival and subsequent experiences of a German emigré in America after a successful flight from the mainland of Europe. Until Remarque's death, the subject-matter of this last novel was a close-kept secret; Remarque even refused to discuss with his wife any project he was currently engaged on:

> I am superstitious and fear that I'll harm my work if I do . . . I have never discussed my manuscripts with anyone.[108]

Once a book had been completed, however, Remarque was reluctant to go through it again, even at the proof-reading stage. Remarque, who never possessed a study, worked erratically, continually altering his manuscripts, which were always left ready to hand in case a sudden thought came to him for an addition or alteration to the text. He envied Thomas Mann his ability to discipline himself and work to a regular pattern:

> I always had the worst conscience in the world. If only I had written as regularly as other writers I should have had a much happier life. Only now am I beginning to get some pleasure from my work. Ever since the doctor has tried to prevent me from writing, the whole business has acquired something dangerous and attractive.[109]

Despite six years of work, *Schatten im Paradies* was never completed to Remarque's satisfaction, and it is doubtful whether he would have allowed the book to be published in its existing form, had he lived.

Remarque was seventy-two when he passed away in a hospital in Locarno on 25 September 1970. He was given a Catholic funeral. Tributes from the world's press were many, varied, and often inaccurate, not least in his native Germany, where Remarque — virtually ignored for years by the critics — suddenly became the centre of renewed interest. Many of the rumours about him persisted and found their way into the obituaries. The *Rheinischer Merkur,* for example, states: "Remarque, who died in Locarno, was really called Kramer",[110] and Remarque's erstwhile friend Hans Habe comments upon the fact that even so renowned a journal as *Der Spiegel* should have managed to write an obituary of Remarque without mentioning the fact that he had written "the greatest war-book of the century", concentrating instead on Remarque the "dandy".[111] This widespread conviction among the journalist fraternity that the public is more interested in the Hollywood superstars that swam, however briefly, into Remarque's ken than in his actual novels had dogged Remarque ever since the publication of *Im Westen nichts Neues.* Typically, Remarque had a curt and pertinent counter to such an attitude towards his achievement:

Life has nothing to do with literature, but literature has everything to do with life.[112]

CHAPTER TWO

ALL QUIET ON THE WESTERN FRONT

In 1936, the National Socialist newspaper *Völkischer Beobachter* made this proud announcement to its readers:

> After all the lies told by people like Remarque, we now bring to you the experience of a soldier who took part in the war, of which you will say at once: that is what it was really like.[1]

There then follows an extract from an account of life at the front which, on closer examination, turns out to be nothing other than part of Remarque's *Im Westen nichts Neues* (presumably sent in anonymously by a third party), and this really was heaping insult on injury, since Joseph Goebbels's *Angriff* had already been similarly duped into printing a "genuine tale from the front line" at the height of his anti-Remarque campaign, which had also turned out to have been culled from the pages of *Im Westen nichts Neues*.[2] These were among the more bizarre consequences of the publication of what rapidly became one of the most successful books ever written — that is, if success is to be measured in terms of the number of copies sold, a proposition which many might be inclined to challenge.

When *Im Westen nichts Neues* was serialized in the *Vossische Zeitung* in November and December 1928, the paper's circulation tripled as eager readers snatched the latest issue from the news vendors with an avidity matched only by those in quest of the latest news of Pickwick or the fate of Little Nell in nineteenth-century England. The book edition, preceded by a concentrated advertising campaign in the press and on street hoardings, sold a million copies in a single year; its author was nominated for the Nobel literature prize; and the work set in train the most amazing storm of controversy, in the course of which it was hailed by one faction as the greatest anti-war novel of all time, denounced by the National Socialists as denigratory to the German *Volk*, and ultimately burned in the Opernplatz in Berlin during the infamous Nazi book-burning ceremony on 10 May 1933 (in such distinguished company as the works of Thomas and Heinrich Mann, Kästner, Brecht, Joyce, Hemingway and Gorki), to the accompaniment of these solemn words:

> As a protest against the literary betrayal of the soldiers of the Great War, and on behalf of the education of our people in the spirit of truth, I consign to the flames the writings of Erich Maria Remarque.[3]

Remarque found himself pilloried by his opponents, and accused of all manner of misrepresentation and misconduct; books and articles galore were written about him and his bestseller, many of them factually inaccurate, not to say libellous; a parody appeared, transposing the setting from the Western front to the Greek camp outside the walls of Troy; and the writer and critic Dr Salomo Friedlaender, under his pseudonym of Mynona, published a full-length attack on Remarque and his masterpiece in mediocrity, as he was pleased to call it.

Not surprisingly, the circumstances surrounding the composition of *Im Westen nichts Neues* and its submission to publishing houses are surrounded with confusion and contradictions. One thing, however, is clear, and that is that Remarque did not compose the novel as a deliberate money-making exercise, as Rowley for one seems to indicate: "The particular blend of suffering, sensuality and sentiment suggests that Remarque had gauged public taste".[4] In an interview with Axel Eggebrecht in 1929, Remarque presents his own reasons for writing the novel. He had, he states, been suffering from serious bouts of depression, the underlying cause of which remained a mystery to him until he made a sustained effort to ascertain why his mood was so consistently bleak:

> It was through these deliberate acts of self-analysis that I found my way back to my war experiences. I could observe a similar phenomenon in many of my friends and acquaintances. The shadow of war hung over us, especially when we tried to shut our minds to it. The very day this thought struck me, I put pen to paper, without much in the way of prior thought.[5]

Working quickly during the evenings after doing a day's work at the offices of *Sport im Bild,* Remarque completed the novel in a mere six weeks — keeping himself awake with strong cigars and large quantities of coffee, if we are to believe a rather inflated account by Riess, who also cuts the time of composition in half.[6]

The finished work was submitted to S Fischer Verlag, the celebrated publishers of that other great German success of this century, Thomas Mann's *Buddenbrooks,* who were an obvious choice for any novelist eager to establish a solid reputation for himself. The manuscript was read by Bermann Fischer, who is recorded as having said that, to the best of his recollection, he read the novel at a single sitting, the night before a month's holiday touring, placed it before Samuel Fischer on the following morning and urged him to read it at once and draw up a contract with the author without delay, before any other publishers got sight of it.[7]

Bermann Fischer was convinced that he had brought off a really outstanding coup, but Samuel Fischer would go no further than to tell Remarque that he would take the book if no other publisher was prepared to accept it. When he heard about this, Bermann Fischer anxiously sought to retrieve the manuscript from Remarque, but by this time it was too late.

Remarque records that Samuel Fischer had informed him that, in his opinion, the book would not sell, since no one wanted to hear about the war any more.[8] But the real reason was that Samuel Fischer had very fixed ideas about what his firm should or should not put into print, and he was convinced that *Im Westen nichts Neues* did not accord with his notion of a work suitable for publication under the Fischer imprint, and he held to this view, apparently without a trace of regret, even when the novel turned out to be a huge and instantaneous success.

In the Eggebrecht interview, Remarque does not refer to the Fischer episode, but this seems more attributable to the fact that he was a reluctant interviewee than to any more sinister motive on his part; instead, he simply states that the manuscript lay untouched in his writing desk for close on six months until, at the insistence of friends, he put it in the hands of Ullstein's Propyläen Verlag.

As to the exact circumstances of its acceptance by Ullstein, there was a brief, if acrimonious, exchange of views in the correspondence columns of the *Frankfurter Allgemeine Zeitung* in 1962.[9] Professor Paul Frischauer claimed that it was he who came to know Remarque when the latter was working for *Sport im Bild,* and as a result of their meeting mentioned *Im Westen nichts Neues* to Dr Franz Ullstein at a social gathering. Ullstein then ensured that the work was seen by his reader Max Krell, who instantly recognized its qualities. So much for Professor Frischauer's account; Ullstein himself went on record as stating that it was a certain Herr Ross who first read it and strongly recommended its acceptance. In his memoirs, Krell does at least confirm that the novel came on to his desk shortly after Whitsun 1928.

Whatever the details, the Propyläen Verlag decided to give the work the full treatment: it was to come out first in instalments in the *Vossiche Zeitung* and then — in a slightly revised form — in a blaze of publicity in a first edition of 50,000 copies. The rest is history.

The reaction to the novel in Germany was violent in the extreme, and opinions soon polarized; but it is instructive to turn first to the response on the other side of the Channel, where a more stable political climate and the fact that Britain was not smarting under a humiliating defeat and the crippling terms of the Versailles treaty enabled the novel to be considered more dispassionately, first and foremost as a piece of literature rather than as a political manifesto.

The traditionally anonymous reviewer in the *Times Literary Supplement* accorded *Im Westen nichts Neues* a muted reception when it appeared in English translation by AW Wheen under the title *All Quiet on the Western Front*, published by Putnam for the princely sum of seven shillings and sixpence. The reviewer expresses surprise at the outstanding popularity of the work, which sold, as he records, 275,000 copies in just over six weeks:

> Very good as it undoubtedly is, this figure is astonishing; and one finds oneself wondering whether an extra nought has not slipped in.[10]

The *Times Literary Supplement* article sets the pattern for other English reviews, both in the slight note of incredulity at such success attending a novel of this nature and also in the careful reading which the reviewer undertakes of the work on its own merits which, even at this early stage, resulted in the emergence of interesting if somewhat inaccurate observations, such as the suggestion that the tale is "obviously autobiographical", or that "the real hero of the story is the narrator's particular friend, Katczinsky".

Im Westen nichts Neues in its English guise must have come as a welcome change from the tidal wave of what might be dubbed the "soft porn" of war literature flooding the British market. On the column adjacent to the *Times Literary Supplement* review, an advertiser announces — with unwitting irony and uncomfortable propinquity — the publication of *War Birds:*

> Still the best-selling war book. Life, death, praying, cursing, women and the snarl of shrapnel! All the wild ecstasy and stark tragedy in this unexpurgated diary of a flying man!

The advertisement closes with a glowing extract from the review of *War Birds* by Gerald Gould of the *Daily Express,* who must have been busily preparing to eat his words: "It is the finest book on the war that has ever appeared, and a finer will never be written!"

The *Times Literary Supplement* reviewer also takes up one issue raised in the lurid apotheosis of *War Birds*, namely, that the novel contains references to certain areas of life not normally discussed in polite company and, significantly, he adds that such references are "of a type that (the reader) will not find in English novels". This prudish British insularity was particularly strong in the 1920's; indeed, it had continued unabated from the early years of the century, and is epitomized by the chauvinistic assertion in Erskine Childers's anti-German spy novel, *The Riddle of the Sands*: "It was something in his looks and manner, you know how different we are from foreigners".[11]

The review in *The New Statesman* reflects a similar cast of mind, and points out in mitigation that, of course, the Germans had the worst of it in the Great War,

> for on that side everything was a little more so — militarism was a little more militaristic; parade ground imbecilities were a little more imbecile; the squalor of the trenches (in the last year or two) was more squalid.[12]

And it concludes on a not untypical note of faint praise, commending the strengths of the work on the one hand, yet on the other stating that this level of achievement was not beyond the reach of any competent writer who happened to have served in the trenches:

> For the rest, anyone who was sufficiently in the thick of it for a long period, on one side or the other, might have written this grim, monotonous record, if he had the gift, which the author has, of remembering clearly, and setting down his memories truly, in naked and violent words.

Grudging though the recognition may have been in many quarters, the reception of *Im Westen nichts Neues* in Britain did at least focus attention on the novel as literature, but, when we turn to the reaction within Remarque's home country, it is clear that we find ourselves faced with an entirely different situation.

In Germany, the emphasis was not so much on the book as on the impact which it had on individuals and political factions alike. All the varied reactions have one thing in common, as can be illustrated by the case of the angry Doctor of Medicine Karl Kroner, writing in the *Neue Preussische Kreuz-Zeitung*, who protests mendaciously that nowhere in *Im Westen nichts Neues* is the medical profession depicted with humanity or sympathy. Even the ancillary staff, he complains, come off badly. No one would believe from Remarque's novel that there were actually doctors up in the front line itself, facing the same dangers as the troops in action. Remarque, claims Dr Kroner, gives the totally erroneous impression that the wounded soldier was obliged to pick his own way back to the field stations. And, worse still, all the old tales of horror about the Germans, now happily long forgotten, and which sprang up in the war psychosis, will now be resurrected. People abroad will draw the following conclusions: if German doctors deal with their own fellow countrymen in this manner, what acts of inhumanity will they not perpetrate against helpless prisoners delivered up into their hands or against the populations of occupied territory?[13]

Dr Kroner reads *Im Westen nichts Neues* as documentary fiction, as if it staked some kind of claim to being representative both of German attitudes and German actions at the front and behind the lines during the Great War.

The novel is also regarded as aspiring to present the "truth" on a literal, autobiographical level. The *Times Literary Supplement* and *New Statesmen* reviewers were far from being alone in their insistence that the reader is being presented with an account of events that actually took place, and more than one critic has gone so far as to chastise Remarque for not giving precise details of time or place, so that they might be checked for accuracy.[14] A certain Peter Kropp, who had been a patient in the same military hospital at Duisberg as Remarque, and who knew him, as Erich Remark, of course, was outraged at his former comrade's descriptions of the hospital in *Im Westen nichts Neues*.[15] Remarque, he protests, presents a very partial view which is not without its serious inaccuracies. Of course there was a great deal of suffering in the hospital, but there was much silent heroism too. The hospital, asserts Kropp, was run in an exemplary fashion, the patients were tended by a nursing order of Catholic nuns, and Remarque is entirely erroneous in his assertion that the patients were disturbed by the noisy praying of the sisters in the corridors. (*Im Westen*, p.226) Kropp goes on to describe the exact location of the chapel in the hospital, thus "proving" that their prayers could not have been heard by the wounded soldiers, as Remarque claims in his novel. From this point, Kropp proceeds to try and indentify individual patients with characters in the novel, and lights in particular on the forty-year-old Lewandowski, who has been in the hospital for ten months, and who in the novel is excitedly anticipating a first visit from his wife. Lewandowski tells the others — "for in the army we have no secrets of that kind" (*Im Westen*, p.238) — that he is desperate to make love to his wife when she comes to see him, and the others stand guard as the blushing couple embrace in the hospital bed. This is too much for Kropp, who protests that this kind of thing simply could not have happened: "I should certainly have known about it," he complains.

In more general terms, Kropp castigates Remarque for accentuating the negative:

I find no front-line spirit in Remark's book. There were other front-line soldiers who were different from the way Remark depicts them. There were such soldiers to whom the protection of homeland, protection of house and homestead, protection of the family was their highest objective, and to whom this will to protect their homeland gave the strength to endure any extremities.[15]

This assumption that, in *Im Westen nichts Neues*, Remarque was seeking to encapsulate a piece of personal and national history in literary form was immediately taken up by both sides in the critical debate.

In his celebrated review for *Die literarische Welt*, the dramatist Ernst Toller claims that Remarque "has spoken on behalf of all of us".[16] Not only does the book describe in unforgettably graphic terms the horrific experiences and privations to which the front-line soldier was exposed, but so exemplary is it, Toller argues, that it should be read by everyone as an anti-war document, and especially in the schools. *Im Westen nichts Neues* says more about the nation and its involvement in the Great War than any statistics or weighty historical tomes ever could.

A publicity pamphlet produced by the Ullstein Propyläen Verlag entitled *Der Kampf um Remarque* (The Battle over Remarque),[17] which consists of a compilation of criticism, both positive and negative, of *Im Westen nichts Neues*, cites a letter from a war-blinded schoolteacher who welcomes the novel with open arms as the one book with which to instruct the minds of the young on the subject of the Great War. This work, he writes, fortuitously employing a turn of phrase which, as we shall see later, is crucial to a proper understanding of the novel, represents "my own release (= Erlösung) from the front".

Almost alone among the reviews of *Im Westen nichts Neues*, the Berlin *Die Welt am Montag*, quoted in the Propyläen Verlag pamphlet, at least begins to spell out the nature of the real problem posed by the novel:

What makes it so unique? . . . the fact that Remarque does not spoon-feed his reader page by page with ready-made attitudes, but leaves him to draw his own conclusions from the book.

But, by and large, *Im Westen nichts Neues* came to be regarded by the vast majority of people as the anti-war book *par excellence* (or the worst kind of pacifist propaganda, depending on which camp one belonged to), a successor to Bertha von Suttner's *Die Waffen nieder!* (Lay down your Arms, 1892), which had been instrumental in giving an early impetus to the International Arbitration and Peace Association because of its stark portrayal of the horrors of war, not least in its famous depiction of the heroine, Martha von

Tilling, picking her way among the dead and dying on the battle-field of Königgrätz in search of her missing husband. Suttner it was who persuaded her life-long admirer, the industrialist Alfred Nobel, to institute his peace prize, one of whose recipients she became in 1905.[18] But, although this peace movement outlived the First World War in various forms, it had already passed its second peak in Germany before the appearance of *Im Westen nichts Neues*, and the right-wing backlash was already in full swing; and, as Shuster has pointed out, "the excesses of the earlier pacifism only served to swell the forces which were now ushering in a rebirth of militarism".[19]

This militarism assumed two forms in the context of the onslaught launched against *Im Westen nichts Neues* and its author. In its milder manifestation, it outraged all those who were instinctively appalled at the desecration, as they saw it, both of the sacrifices made by the front-line soldiers and of the idea of the German nation. The most closely-argued contemporary critical attack on the novel by Heisler states that, for all its undoubted merits, the work represents a threat, since it tends to sap the energies of the German nation at a time when it has to assert itself in the face of a hostile world if it is to survive.[20]

Not unexpectedly, the main opposition to *Im Westen nichts Neues* came from the National Socialists, who regarded the book — which, as they were not slow to point out, was produced by a Jewish publisher — as part of a well-financed international conspiracy on the part of Bolshevists and Jews against the German *Volk*. At that time, the theorists of National Socialism were claiming insistently that the Great War represented nothing less than the fire in which the spirit of the emergent German Reich had been forged, and that, as a consequence, *Im Westen nichts Neues* constituted a betrayal of all that is great and noble in Germany and the German nation.

Remarque is accused of partiality in his depiction of the front-line soldier, since he presents only "how a few emotionally unbalanced people conducted themselves before they ever went into battle".[21] What the National Socialists found most offensive in Remarque's portrayal of the men in the trenches was his demythologizing of front-line warfare, of the concept of the "hero" which is so crucial to the National Socialist foundation myth. Life, it is argued, is a relentless Darwinian struggle, in which the individual, if he is to survive, has to assert himself in the face of others; and similarly, the strongest nation is the one that has the will to survive more successfully than any of its rivals. The individual cannot exist as a separate selfish entity — to coin a phrase, no man is an island — since he is part of a greater whole, the race or nation, and the selfless surrender of his own life on the part of the hero in order that the whole might survive, is the greatest and noblest act that a human being can perform.

Remarque's negative attitude to war in general was equally anathema to the National Socialists in that it embodied two of their *bêtes noires*: namely, pacifism and internationalism. The proponents of internationalism may proclaim from the rooftops that the life of the individual is the highest good, but the ineluctable laws of nature, which antedate the appearance of man on this planet and to which he is subordinate, dictate that this simply is not so. In a grotesque prefiguration of the biogeneticists' concept of "non-selfish" behaviour, the National Socialists argue that it is the survival of the race, the nation, that matters, not that of the individual. Hence internationalism, which is more or less equated with Marxism, is, like pacifism, a dangerous aberration: "Pacifism is the same heresy on the ethical plane as is Marxism in the social sphere".[22] If the life of the individual is sacred, as the pacifists claim, then how much more sacred must be the life of the nation:

> The projected utopia of the pacifists has one thing in common with that of the Marxists — and that is, that it will never be realized. As long as men are men, as long as death remains a fact of life, its twin servants, sickness and war, will remain with us too.[23]

Disease is equated with war, and the argument goes that getting rid of doctors will not result in the disappearance of disease, but will inevitably bring about its spread and ultimate domination. Therefore the soldier is not fomenting war and militarism; on the contrary, he is actually fighting *against* war, just like the doctor combatting disease.

This insidiously plausible line of argumentation was brought to bear with particular force on the figures in *Im Westen nichts Neues* who violated the notion of the Great War as a positive rather than a destructive force — regrettable though it was, of course, and rendered necessary only by the aggression of others:

> The war was a test; in the thunder of the cannon all masks fell away, and men stood there naked, in their true qualities. He who had eyes to see and ears to hear learned at the front to distinguish the wheat from the chaff.[24]

And, in contrast to Remarque's negative concept of comradeship, the community of soldiers at the front in reality paved the way for the new national community of the coming Reich, under the leadership of the Führer, of course.

Despite their vocal protests, the National Socialists were unable to prevent the publication and sale of *Im Westen nichts Neues*, but Joseph Goebbels, at the time Gauleiter of the Berlin section of the National Socialist party, found himself presented with a golden opportunity to bring off a major propaganda coup when the celebrated American film based on the book, *All Quiet on the Western Front*, was screened in the German capital. The film, directed by Lewis Milestone and produced by Universal Pictures, was one of the early talkies and has since come to be recognized as one of the great classics of the cinema. The National Socialists seemed to be losing the initiative in the parliamentary battle in the *Reichstag*, but Goebbels leaped at this unique chance of bringing the fight out on to the streets. He organized a gang of Hitler Youth to storm the auditorium where the film was to be premiered, and they rampaged through the building, hurling stink bombs, scattering white mice and shouting "Germany awake!" Goebbels's tactic of stirring up controversy over an issue at the centre of public attention certainly paid off; not only did he attract considerable publicity, he even succeeded in getting the film banned in Germany. And, as we saw earlier, the book itself was also burned — and banned — when the dream of a Third Reich became a political reality in 1933.

Remarque was also the object of attack from a quite different quarter, this time on largely unpolitical grounds. The slight but acid parody *Vor Troja nichts Neues* (All Quiet before the Walls of Troy), supposedly by one Emil Marius Requark, has an overweening first-person narrator whose sole ambition it is to amass great wealth after the war is over: "I will become a rich man, all Greece will read my book".[25] And, in fact, the whole Trojan war seems to be taking place simply so that he can write a book about it. Nor is the narrator inclined to underestimate his own abilities: "One has such incredibly clever thoughts and one gets to feel the importance of one's person".[26] He inflates his ego to its fullest extent and proclaims: "Thus it is that I am writing a war diary. It will contain a great deal about me and just a very little about the war".[27] The rest of the world is in a state of utter confusion; the soldiers alone have retained their clear-sightedness and integrity.

The great poet Homer is also present, compiling the official version of the war and evidently enjoying himself. The narrator, hearing him mutter hexameters out loud, assumes that he is inebriated, and bids him forget about noble heroes and all that kind of thing and write instead about the sordid realities of war, the mud and the lice (to which latter the narrator has, it seems, become quite attached). The soldiers, as a sentence picked out in large type stresses, "belong to a generation which will never

41

recover from the impact of war. Our lives are ruined beyond recall".[28] The parody in *Vor Troja nichts Neues* is directed partly against Remarque's pacifist tendencies, but even more against his personal vanity in arrogating to himself the rôle of the omniscient recording angel of the Great War, the sole repository of the whole truth about the armed conflict on the Western front.

This latter view is also espoused by Mynona's *Hat Erich Maria Remarque wirklich gelebt?*[29] an exceedingly witty and entirely libellous assault on Remarque, which follows the pattern of Mynona's equally venomous onslaught on Freud, in the publisher's announcement for which he is elevated to the dubious status of the "Chaplin of German philosophy". Employing the time-honoured principle that the least strenuous means of demolishing the work is to discredit the man, Mynona summons up every pun, turn of wit, and allusion to his victim's life, employment and previous writing — especially his advertising career (there is much play on Conti-dummies for babies and the like) and, of course, *Die Traumbude* — in his character assassination attempt, and tops the whole thing off with a "Documentary Appendix for Sceptics" quoting Remarque's birth certificate and other information "proving" that he falsely assumed the French tail on his name. The book closes with a list of "Erich Maria Remark's Collected Werques" (sic). He finds Remarque guilty of outstanding mediocrity, and expresses his utter astonishment that such a thoroughly ordinary piece of pen-pushing should have attracted such a hugely disproportionate amount of public attention and stand at the epicentre of such an earth-shattering storm of controversy.

Osnabrück — "the mouse that gave birth to this mountain"[30] — has a great deal to answer for, claims Mynona, since in *Im Westen nichts Neues* that town's celebrated son does little more than hold up a dull mirror to a drab age. Mynona reminds his readers of the orator in Classical times who started with fright when he received universal applause, fearful that he might have said something ridiculous, for "only the uttermost folly gains instant thunderous approbation, the truth in contrast is greeted by an audience of deaf mutes".[31]

Mynona describes his attack as a satirical apotheosis; but, in reality, it is no more than an enormous ego-trip, a romp of *Schadenfreude* on the part of a writer who really ought to have known better. His attack becomes more understandable — but even less forgivable — when it is realized that, under his real appellation of Dr Salomo Friedlaender, Mynona was a less than successful poet and writer, a minor member of the circle of contributors to the Expressionist periodical *Der Sturm* with pretensions as a philosopher in the wake of Nietzsche. He had, he was convinced, "solved" the post-Kantian dilemma of subjectivity and the destruction of absolute values by means of a strong creative individual operating a positive, but still subjective ethic. Unfortunately, no one was inclined to listen to him.[32]   And nothing could have been more repugnant to the aspirations of Dr Friedlaender than the attitudes of the characters in *Im Westen nichts Neues.* The instinctive revulsion on the part of Mynona, of our anonymous parodist, and indeed of others, to the popularity of this work prefigures most of what little critical attention the novel has been accorded in the West in recent years.

Im Westen nichts Neues hardly receives more than a passing — and not always accurate — mention in histories of contemporary literature published in the West: Soergel and Hohoff only accord it a handful of lines in a nine-page section on the First World War in literature, stating that "in the case of Remarque, too, comradeship and sacrifice were values which outlived the war" (the first part of the assertion may be true, the second certainly is not);[33] a five-hundred page compendium on German literature in the Weimar Republic is even more parsimonious, squeezing out just three mentions of *Im Westen nichts Neues* by title in a whole section devoted exclusively to the novel of the Great War;[34] Lange, skating across the surface of modern literature between 1870 and 1940, simply refers to the novel as "one of the first, but not one of the most substantial of the war books",[35] an *ex cathedra* pronouncement not untypical of this brand of general survey; a more considered reaction from Rühle none the less insists that the work is political and pacifist, which "explains the hypnotic mass impact of the novel and its effectiveness as a pacifist manifesto";[36] and Kerker goes to the other extreme in a somewhat idiosyncratic interpretation of the work, in which he claims that, far from being an anti-war novel, it actually helped to bring about the Second World War, but he is clearly confusing analysis of the novel as such with the impact which it happened to have in certain quarters.[37]

Of the handful of scholars who have undertaken detailed consideration of *Im Westen nichts Neues* in the West, Liedloff has some kind words to say about it, but his attention is diverted by the fact that he is writing a descriptive comparatist essay, relating it to Hemingway's *A Farewell to Arms;*[38] Swados defends the artistic value of the novel, praising its directness in depicting the horrors of war;[39] in another comparatist study, this time with reference to F Manning's *Her Privates We,* Klein underlines the literary merit of *Im Westen nichts Neues* and stresses its highly organized structure, although he does not go into a great deal of detail on this vital issue;[40] and Rowley, in a sensitive essay, echoes Klein's views about the novel's structure, and stresses that the style — which he dubs "journalistic"[41] — is deliberately chosen by Remarque, and not a sign of weakness on his part.

One suspects that the scant attention now paid to Remarque in the West is attributable, in part at least, to the huge success of the work — for how, the argument goes in the groves of academe, can something so overwhelmingly popular be great literature in an age when the true artist seems inevitably to be alienated from the public at large? Such considerations seem to loom particularly large for the German academic critic: witness, for example, the very mixed reception accorded to a dramatist like Fritz Hochwälder, who insists on writing "well-made plays" when everyone knows they are *passé* in an era of theatrical experimentation, or another dramatist, Rolf Hochhuth, who actually has the nerve to write about individual responsibility when the fashionable critic has long since pronounced it dead and buried — both, needless to say, very successful writers who have attracted a large public following. And, apart from the issue as to whether the novel can be regarded as "serious literature" or not, *Im Westen nichts Neues* has become almost totally submerged under the weight of the political and ideological battles that have been waged around it.

In the East, on the other hand, there have been no aesthetic reservations, for the social — not to say socialist — content of a work far outweighs any such decadent Western consideration, and *Im Westen nichts Neues* has attracted a fair amount of interest in academic circles there, largely as an illustration of a liberal Western piece which, on the social plane, puts a finger on the evils of the world but regrettably goes no further.

With not untypical circular argumentation, Marxist critics assert that the novel *is* political despite itself — its inability to advocate positive action being itself regarded as the assumption of a political stand. The principal complaint of the Marxist critic is that *Im Westen nichts Neues* fails in its social obligations: having recognized the disease, it avoids taking the next logical step, that of pronouncing a means (Marxist-Leninist, perhaps?) towards a cure. Remarque, and others like him, "indeed recognized the growing Fascist threat but did not have the will to make the revolutionary response to it".[42]

So the wheel turns full circle, and once more *Im Westen nichts*

Neues is regarded as a representative work, but this time it is criticized for failing to draw any positive conclusions from the evils it detects and depicts in the militarism of Germany in World War One, which at least makes a change from being attacked for not being militaristic enough.

The novel is also found wanting on the grounds that, in its portrayal of the war scene, it is too limited in perspective: in presenting, for example, the martinet figure of the corporal Himmelstoss, Remarque is accused of concentrating shortsightedly on the symptoms, not the root cause, and for this reason if for no other the novel is incapable of advancing any kind of positive solution. Left-wing totalitarianism comes close to its arch-enemy, Fascism, when one Marxist critic, Wegner, complains that Remarque is only depicting the "little man" of the time who needs, but lacks entirely, some sense of spiritual direction, a purposeful rôle for himself in society.[43] One can almost hear a demand for the *Führerprinzip* behind these words.

Hardly any of the host of reviewers, critics and political theorists who have put pen to paper on the subject of *Im Westen nichts Neues* — or, more frequently, on issues raised by the novel — have made any real contribution to a proper understanding of the actual work itself; in fact, most of them have succeeded in going beyond the point at which the novel ceases to be relevant to their discussion. The first English critics tended to misconstrue it because of its "foreign-ness"; the Germans because it was used as ammunition in the battle between the liberals and pacifists on the one hand and the militarists and National Socialists on the other; and, after the Second World War, Western critics were either preoccupied with whether or not it was fit to be considered as "art" at all, or were again busily looking at the circumstances surrounding the work, either as comparatists or practitioners of the currently fashionable art of the aesthetics of the reception of literature; and, behind the Iron Curtain, the Marxist critics have been holding it up against the yardstick of social and political commitment and finding it wanting.

But, for all that, *Im Westen nichts Neues* — like many another work — has managed to survive its critics; yet the main issue still remains largely unanswered: What makes it such a compelling and successful work? And the only way to answer that question is actually to take a look at the novel itself.

Im Westen nichts Neues concerns the war experiences of a

45

school class of young men who volunteer for active service under patriotic pressure from Kantorek, their schoolmaster, and another group of men whom they have closely befriended in the army. Of the class, originally twenty in all, only a handful remain, and the attention is focussed on four of them — Kropp, Müller, Leer and Bäumer — and this quartet is balanced by four others: Tjaden, a mechanic, Westhus, a turf-cutter, Detering, a farmer, and Katczinsky (referred to by the nickname of "Kat"), at forty the oldest of the group.

This numerical equilibrium which Remarque establishes between the more intelligent but inexperienced young soldiers on the one hand and the academically less able ex-workers on the other, who compensate for their lack of intellectual attainment by a wider experience of life, points to a strong sense of organization on the part of the author which, as we shall see in due course, is fundamental to the entire work and has been studiously ignored by most critics.

It is told, principally in the historic present (which will be retained in quotations although it rings awkwardly in English), by a first-person narrator, Paul Bäumer, whose surname has been assiduously dismembered by Liedloff into "Baum" (= tree) and "Träumer" (dreamer), which by a tangential leap of the imagination is caused to represent two supposedly key constituents of Bäumer's nature: his "yearning for beauty" encapsulated in the "organic growth" of the tree; and his reflective and inward-turned personality.[44] However, there is not a shred of evidence, internal or external, which might indicate that this is anything other than a perfectly ordinary German name, chosen precisely because of its ordinariness. The "Paul", on the other hand, is a direct reference to Remarque's original second Christian name and suggests that the novel is obliquely autobiographical. (Until Mynona dredged up the "truth" about Remarque's "real" name, of course, that autobiographical element remained hidden from the reader.) The problem is, to what extent and in what manner does it reflect the life and convictions of the author? This question could equally be posed in relation to the vast majority of Remarque's output. Critics — especially those hostile towards *Im Westen nichts Neues* — have all too eagerly tended to fall into the trap of arguing themselves into a logically absurd position: on the one hand, Remarque is castigated for not adhering faithfully to the "facts" of his own personal life, and yet on the other he is reprimanded by the same people for presenting a personal, partial and biased picture of the war on the Western front.

To some extent, at least, Remarque is to blame for this state of affairs; he describes the experiences and emotions of his central figure with such vividness and with such an aura of authenticity that one is all too readily tempted to assume that the events described actually took place precisely as he depicts them, or, if they did not, that some kind of fraud is being perpetrated; it is, to borrow an observation from an entirely different context, "a reproof to that large body of readers, who, when a novelist has really carried conviction to them, assert off-hand: 'O, that must be autobiography!' "[45] The sentiments are Remarque's, the words those of Arnold Bennett.

The most superficial examination of, say, place-names, in *Im Westen nichts Neues,* makes it abundantly clear that Remarque has selectively plundered his own past experiences and environment in the composition of his novel. When Bäumer (why do critics patronizingly tend to refer to him as "Paul" all the time?) is entering his home town by train on leave from the front, for example, he passes over the Bremer Strasse before entering the main station. And there is no denying that the railway line to Remarque's home town of Osnabrück does precisely that (but the more pernickety critic might have observed that this is the route from the *east,* and therefore less likely to have been travelled upon by a soldier returning from the Western front). When Bäumer leaves the station, he sees the river rushing out from the sluices under the mill bridge; he looks up at the old watch tower, now used as a wash house; he crosses the bridge, finds his way home, climbs the stairs to his parents' flat, and later sits at his bedroom window looking out at the chestnut tree in the garden of the inn across the way — and every detail is "almost photographically accurate".[46]

Although Remarque keeps close to reality in his depiction of the setting of his home town, leaving the front line deliberately imprecise because of its uniformity of appearance and the irrelevance of geographical designations, there is much less to be found in the way of parallels between the characters and their actions and any real life equivalents, save on the most superficial level: Bäumer's class "volunteers" under the chiding tongue of Kantorek, whereas all but three of Remarque's class waited until they were conscripted in 1916 (including our author himself). Other parallels are more or less on the level of, for example, the name of the corporal Himmelstoss being based on that of a family living in the Jahnstrasse in Osnabrück.[47]

So it is quite evident that we are considering here a writer who, by preference, draws fairly directly but none the less selectively on his own experiences and background, although he is by no means seeking to present us with fictionalized autobiography. The reader unfamiliar with the topography of Osnabrück is not one whit the poorer. Were it not for all the nonsense penned about Remarque and his supposed "distortions" of reality, it would hardly be necessary to state the obvious; namely, that Remarque uses his home town or city and experiences close to his own as a convenient basis for his imaginative work.

Instead of fussing about the supposed authenticity or otherwise of Remarque's work, it might be less quixotic to consider the internal parallels between novel and reality. In order to do so, we must return to the words of the blind schoolteacher in the Propyläen publicity pamphlet, for whom the novel represented a release or "Erlösung" from the experiences of the war, a cathartic purging of the emotional residue of the front line. It enabled him to sort out within himself the tangled memories and emotions of the Great War, and to come to terms with them. And it is precisely in this light that Remarque himself regarded *Im Westen nichts Neues*. In the interview with Eggebrecht, Remarque too talks of a sense of release that came with the writing of his novel, and he uses exactly the same word, "Erlösung".[48] He had experienced an inexplicable sense of depression, and the act of writing had enabled him to recognize the symptoms and their cause and to work towards some kind of accommodation with the past.

But more than that: Remarque succeeded in transcending his own personal situation; he touched on a nerve of his time, reflecting the experiences of a whole generation of young men on whom the war had left an indelible mark. Remarque uses his own personal experiences in a similar fashion as the starting point for nearly all his subsequent novels. This exorcism of his own doubts and conflicts enabled him to make a huge step forward away from the preciosities of *Die Traumbude* and of the little prose and verse pieces penned for *Die Schönheit*.

Although the novel is divided into twelve chapters of varying length, they do not necessarily point to more than one facet of the basic structure of *Im Westen nichts Neues*. In this novel he is introducing a structural technique — which he was to refine in his subsequent works — which involves a series of small episodes as building bricks, not necessarily related to one another causally (that is to say, the "plot" is not particularly important), but cumulative in effect. Bäumer's account is very much like a diary, consisting in the main of either description of a sequence of events or internal monologue, without linking passages of any kind. It is, one might say, without seeking to over-stretch the comparison, a

kind of "Stationenroman" on the lines of the Brechtian epic
theatre with its "Stationendramen", that is, a novel held together,
not by the traditional glue of a developing action culminating in a
climax and denouement, but rather by broader thematic links,
such as character or ideas. And, as far as Remarque's novels in
general are concerned, there is a strange inverse relationship
between their literary quality and the tightness of their plot.

Im Westen nichts Neues falls into three parts plus a contemplative interlude. The first part (Chapters I-VI) explores the
experiences of the private soldier at the front and behind the lines,
together with reflections back on home, the last days in school
and life in the training barracks. It opens with a depleted company
newly returned from the front, only eighty men out of a hundred
and fifty, and concludes in similar vein with the return of another
company, this time reduced to a mere thirty-two men. The central
section (Chapter VII, the longest in the book) deals partly with
women (of whom a little more later), aspirations towards a world
of love beyond the war, and partly with Bäumer's disastrous
experience of leave, when he fails to regain contact with his past.
There then follows a contemplative interlude (Chapter VIII),
principally devoted to Bäumer's thoughts as he stands guard over
a group of Russian prisoners of war; in this section, he actually
ponders on the wider political and moral issues raised by the armed
conflict (not a few critics must have had faulty copies of *Im
Westen nichts Neues* with these particular pages expunged!). In the
final section (Chapters IX-XII), the action becomes more
concentrated: vignettes of fellow soldiers, each ending in their
death, are sandwiched between periods of reflection and
contemplation, and the narrative technique — unusually for
Remarque — switches over from blocks of description and action
with a high content of dialogue to a summarized, compressed
account of the concluding phase of the war, as time seems to
become suspended and the comrades' emotions utterly numbed.
And, at the end, Bäumer dies, just as peace is approaching.

Reading critics of *Im Westen nichts Neues,* one might all too
readily gain the impression that the novel is a succession of night-
marish situations and unrelieved gloom, but this is far from being
the case. Remarque skilfully paces the development of the action,
interposing scenes of real happiness and contentment, some of
which contain episodes that are extemely funny. On one such
occasion, Bäumer clumsily attempts to "liberate" a brace of
geese from a farmyard; he is cornered by the farm bulldog and
pinned to the ground by that animal; and, finally, he manages to
extricate his revolver:

When I get my revolver in my hand, it starts to shake. I press my hand on to the ground and tell myself: raise the revolver, fire before the dog can get at me and make myself scarce. Slowly I take my breath and calm down. Then, holding my breath, I jerk the revolver into the air, it goes off, the dog leaps yowling to one side, I reach the stable door and go head over heels over one of the geese which had fled from me. *(Im Westen,* p.89)

So he makes a grab for it, hurls it over the wall to Kat, who puts the bird out of its misery; and Bäumer joins them, having just escaped the fangs of the frustrated bulldog. (Almost as funny, but unintentionally so, is the National Socialist critic Nickl's accusation against Remarque that this is another instance of double standards: on the one hand, men protest violently against the sufferings of horses in warfare, but on the other they are quite prepared to kill and eat geese. Nickl must have been a vegetarian as well as a National Socialist.)[49]

Another amusing episode which is equally concerned with food, but this time, so to speak, from a different point of view, relates to the inevitable outcome of gastronomic excess. Kat manages to acquire two sucking pigs, and these are roasted with all the trimmings:

We fall asleep chewing. But things get bad in the night. We have eaten too much fat. Fresh roast sucking pig has a devastating effect on the bowels. There is an incessant to-ing and fro-ing in the dugout. Men are squatting about outside in twos and threes with their trousers down, cursing. Getting on for four in the morning we achieve a record: all eleven men . . . on their haunches outside together. (*Im Westen,* p.213-14)

Even the tyrannical corporal Himmelstoss gives occasion for some amusement, as when the soldiers obey his orders with excessive slowness, thus whipping him into a hoarse frenzy (*Im Westen,* p.28); but there is a grimmer side to the humour, too, both in the scene where Himmelstoss is swathed in a sheet and beaten by the vengeful group of comrades, (*Im Westen,* p.48f) and when their ex-teacher Kantorek is also humiliated by a former pupil of his in the barracks when the rôles are reversed and Kantorek is actually a subordinate to his erstwhile student. (*Im Westen,* p.160)

Such episodes, however, are not scattered randomly about the novel; in this, as in all else, Remarque pays considerable attention to the detailed organization of his material. Opening on a positive note, the novel alternates light and dark episodes, the intensity of both increasing as the narrative progresses. In Chapter I, the comrades sit *al fresco* on latrine buckets in a circle playing cards in a scene of tranquil contentment; and this sequence is closely followed by a visit to the dying Kemmerich. Chapter V brings the *contretemps* with the goose, which is then consumed with considerable relish in an atmosphere of peace and fulfilment; and this comes just before the comrades move up to the front line past coffins piled high in readiness for the victims of the coming offensive. And, finally, in Chapter X there is a sequence in an evacuated village — "an idyll of guzzling and sleeping" (*Im Westen*, p.210) — which they are supposed to be guarding, and where they have been left more or less to their own devices; and this is immediately followed by Bäumer and Kropp sustaining wounds in action. Each of the positive scenes, it will have been noted, is concerned with basic functions of the human body; and we shall be returning to this preoccupation with the essentials of life later.

Similarly, Remarque establishes a series of contrasts between scenes at the front and behind the lines, in an alternating sequence in which more and more stress comes to be placed on the front as the struggle becomes grimmer and the small group of comrades finds its numbers gradually whittled down. This aspect of the novel's structure is reflected in the chapter endings, each of which — with the exception of the Russian prisoners interlude in Chapter VIII — is concerned with a departure or a return of some kind, and the novel ends with the final departure from this life by Bäumer.

The process being depicted is one of a decreasing freedom of action and a growing sense of claustrophobia; there is, it becomes increasingly evident, no way out save through death. This relentless crushing of life and the closing in of death is underlined by the motif of Kemmerich's English flying boots. At the beginning of the novel, he lies dying, one leg amputated, and Müller is obsessed with the desire to inherit them. When Kemmerich realizes that he is close to death, he hands them over to Müller. When the latter dies in Chapter XI and Bäumer comes into their possession, we know that he too is marked for death. Of the original group of eight comrades, only one remains, Tjaden, and he in turn inherits the boots; but "Tjaden has luck as always" (*Im Westen*, p. 120) and he alone also will survive, despite the ill-fated boots, and indeed he reappears in the sequel *Der Weg zurück*.

The whole of *Im Westen nichts Neues* is in fact based on a series of antitheses which reflect various levels of alienation in the minds of the small and dwindling band of comrades. The first of these to come to light is that between "them" and "us":

Whilst they were still writing and speechifying, we saw field hospitals and dying men; — whilst they were proclaiming service of the state as the highest good, we knew already that fear of death is the stronger. This did not turn us into rebels, deserters, or cowards — all these words came so readily to their lips — we loved our homeland just as much as they did, and we advanced bravely with every attack; — but . . . we had suddenly had our eyes opened. And we saw that of their world nothing remained.(*Im Westen*, p.17)

51

There are two immediate consequences that flow from this gulf: the first is that the private soldiers form a closed and self-contained group, that is, they acquire and foster a sense of "comradeship" which dominates every aspect of their existence, but not in the meaning of the word coined by the National Socialists: this is not a case of the "Frontgemeinschaft" (brother-hood of the front)[50] which is such a key concept in their interpretation of the rôle of the First World War, far from it. It is, rather, a negative state, a protective shrinking within a cocoon of intense intimacy with fellow soldiers as an essential means towards self-preservation and the maintenance of sanity in a world gone mad. After being lost for endless hours in No Man's Land, Bäumer hears the voices of his comrades who are out searching for him:

> An uncommon warmth flows through me all of a sudden. Those voices, those few, softly-spoken words, those footsteps in the trench to my rear suddenly wrench me out of the terrible isolation of the mortal fear to which I had all but succumbed. Those voices mean more to me than my life . . . they are the most powerful and protective thing that there can ever be: they are the voices of my comrades.(*Im Westen*, pp.191-92)

The second consequence of the gulf between "them" and "us" is that the comrades have lost all sense of belonging to that hierarchy of rôles that sustained them as they grew up: father, mother, schoolmaster and the rest have forfeited their validity; and a new hierarchy has come to be established within the confines of the closed group of comrades. In *Im Westen nichts Neues,* it is Kat, twice the age of the others, who acts out the rôle of the father: he is the source of authority, the leader, the indestructible one whose death by a stray piece of shrapnel as Bäumer is carrying him to a field station to have his wounds dressed so poignantly parallels the wasting away of Bäumer's disease-stricken mother at home. Parent substitute and "real" parent are now both irretrievably lost. (Of Bäumer's father we hear virtually nothing, save that he is a book-binder; and the French soldier Gérard Duval, whom Bäumer stabs in a crater in No Man's Land, and who dies slowly and in great pain before his eyes, also followed that trade.)

Significantly, Kat's qualities are vastly different from those of the group's parents and other figures of authority: he is admired for his ability both to survive in a cruel environment and to care for the needs of his comrades. This finds its sharpest expression in relation to his skill at conjuring food and other necessities of life apparently out of empty air. And so it is hardly surprising to find Bäumer writing about Kat in these terms when he wakens in the night during a rest-break after a wire-laying party, frightened by a sudden sound:

> It is so strange, am I a child?... and then I recognize Katczinsky's silhouette. He is sitting there quietly, the old soldier ... I sit upright: I feel strangely alone. It is good that Kat is there. (*Im Westen*, pp.58-59)

And again, as the captured goose is being roasted in the gathering gloom, Bäumer falls into a reverie and is roused by Kat:

> Is my face wet, and where am I? Kat stands before me, his giant shadow bent over me like home. (*Im Westen*, p.91)

But, for Kat, as for the rest of them, "home" is the barracks (*Im Westen*, p.63); and the nostalgic reminiscences of the group are directed, not back at their schooldays and childhood, but towards their experiences in the training barracks, when, for example, the order was given for piano-players to take two paces forward, and the unfortunates who did so were briskly marched off to the cookhouse for spud-bashing; or when Himmselstoss made them practise time and again what he evidently regarded as the difficult art of "changing trains in Löhne", which meant that they were obliged to crawl beneath their beds — which served to simulate the underpass at the station — and emerge smartly on the other side. (*Im Westen*, p.43)

Thus a second area of alienation is on the temporal plane. The little group of comrades is effectively cut off from the past: "Since we have been here, our earlier life has been excluded from us, without our having done anything to bring that about". (*Im Westen*, p.23) The years prior to the outbreak of war, and the values and knowledge which the comrades had acquired then have no meaning for them now. "Between today and the past there is a gulf ... it is a different world." (*Im Westen*, p.155) The past is an alien realm to which they could return only as strangers. It is as if the past has died; and, in order to underline this, Remarque twice employs the image of the photograph: when Kemmerich is expiring of his wounds in the hospital bed, he is described as looking blurred and indeterminate in outline, "like a photographic plate which has been double exposed", (*Im Westen*, p.19) just a hazy shadow of the man he once was. And this image recurs when Bäumer is on guard duty in the darkness reflecting back on the scenes and experiences of his younger days and recognizes that, for him, they are irretrievably lost:

> It would be just like pondering over a photograph of a dead comrade; it is his features, it is his face, and the days we spent together would acquire a deceptive life in our memory, but it is not the thing itself. (*Im Westen*, p.115)

In the front line, what they learned in school is utterly useless to them. At one point, the comrades joke about the knowledge they acquired in school, throwing the old questions at one another: "How many inhabitants has Melbourne?" "What were the goals of the Göttinger Hain?" (A circle of sentimental eighteenth-century poets.) "How many children has Charles the Bold?"

> We can't remember very much about all that rubbish. Nor has it been of any use to us. No one taught us in school how to light a cigarette under attack in the rain, how to make a fire with wet wood — or that the best place to thrust a bayonette is in the stomach, because it doesn't get stuck fast there like it does in the ribs. (*Im Westen*, p.82)

On entering the army, they were thoroughly brainwashed into forgetting their previous scale of values, although these simply lay dormant at first; it was not until their exposure to front-line fighting over an extended period of time that they became obliterated altogether. In another example of Remarque's skilful use of theme and variation, the recruits were taught "that a polished button is more important than four volumes of Schopenhauer". (*Im Westen*, p. 25) This is then neatly stood on its head in the sequence where Bäumer is observing to his amusement his former schoolmaster Kantorek being drilled in the barracks square by his former pupil, Mittelstaedt, who cries out: "Landsturmmann Kantorek, is that what you call cleaning buttons? You never seem to learn. Unsatisfactory, Kantorek, unsatisfactory". (*Im Westen*, p. 161) He turns the schoolmaster's words against him, destroying all the man's values in a sour act of revenge for the fact that Kantorek, in encouraging his pupils to enlist, had caused precisely the same fate to befall them. This rupture with the past is one of the dominant themes of Remarque's work, the discontinuity of life, this jolting from one plane of existence to another for which man is completely unprepared.

Not only are they cut off from the past; a gulf also extends between them and the future. The inability of those who survive the war to readjust to peacetime conditions is suggested by the way in which Bäumer, walking along the streets of his home town while on leave, starts with fright at the screeching sound of the tramcars, mistaking the noise for that of a grenade whistling through the air. (*Im Westen*, p. 153. The identical motif is repeated in *Der Weg zurück*, p.82.) The knowledge they have acquired in the trenches is as useless to them in time of peace as their school lessons in time of war.

Only those of the older generation, like Kat, will be able to slip back more or less unscarred into civilian life, since they came to war as mature adults, with a firm foundation in life, and they have something to build on when they return; Kat, for example, has his wife and, significantly, a young son to provide hope for the future.

But, as Bäumer writes of his own generation: "The war has ruined us for everything". (*Im Westen,* p.84) They have been caught up in the war when the hold of school and parents was slackening, but before they had had the opportunity to enter upon adult life: none are married, none have a job, none know which direction they want their future to take.

The young comrades feel equally alienated from the political and social issues of the day; it is not "their" war, and they can see no sense in the notion, say, of a nation actually wanting to attack another nation, a personification of abstractions which, to them, is nonsensical. And when the Kaiser himself appears to review the troops, their reaction is one of bemused disappointment; surely he cannot be the much-vaunted embodiment of the highest ideals of the German nation, they ask themselves; and this leads them on to challenge the whole question of the war, its origins and objectives. In the end, Albert Kropp speaks for them all when he bursts out: "It's better not to talk about all this nonsense at all". (*Im Westen,* p.187)

Worse still, they feel cut off from reality itself and from their own humanity by the horrific routine of death and suffering in the trenches. They come to lose all sense of time,

> and all that keeps us going is the fact that there are even weaker . . . yet more helpless men who look up at us with wide-open eyes as gods who are able for a while to evade death. (*Im Westen,* p. 125)

All they possess is life and freedom from injury. They have even lost all sense of their youthful vitality:

> Iron youth. Youth! None of us is more than twenty years old. But young? Youth? That's way back in the past. We are old men. (*Im Westen,* p.22)

And in the trenches they are coming to discover that even life itself does not belong to them. At the very beginning of the novel, when Kemmerich is dying, it is stressed that the life has already drained out of him, that "the face already bears the alien lines" of death, that "there is no life pulsing under the skin any more", that he has the mark of death upon him. (*Im Westen,* pp. 18-19) When Kemmerich has expired, Bäumer's reaction is one of terrible exultation, for he is alive, he has life within him, and he is filled with the most powerful desire to cling on to that elusive force whatever the cost:

> Streams of energy flow through the earth, surging up into me through the soles of my feet . . . My limbs move freely, I feel my joints strong . . . The night lives, I live. I feel a hunger, more powerful than for mere food. (*Im Westen,* p. 35)

The ground is frequently referred to in *Im Westen nichts Neues* as the source of a life-giving power, and the strength and significance of the "life force" — which has been conveniently overlooked by the critics — lies at the heart of all Remarque's mature work, and, as we shall see, it is a concept which he develops in the novels which follow upon *Im Westen nichts Neues*. One of them, *Der Funke Leben* (meaning: the spark of life) has the life force as its central theme, and the title of this novel, which explores the power of life in the midst of death and torture in the concentration camps, is prefigured in the scene where the goose is being roasted, and Bäumer describes Kat and himself as "two tiny sparks of life" in the darkness. (*Im Westen*, p. 90)

So when Bäumer and his comrades state that "we want to live at any price", (*Im Westen*, p. 130) the sentiments expressed have nothing to do with cowardice or selfishness. Running away from the fighting is never once contemplated as a possibility (the only exception being the farmer Detering, whose mind snaps when he catches sight of some cherry blossom which swamps him with recollections of his home). Life seems all the more precious when death is so close, but this does not cause them to falter when the call comes to attack the enemy. They fight like dangerous animals, but their adversary is not the French or the British — it is death itself, the negation of the life force:

> We are not hurling grenades against people, we are oblivious of all that at this moment, for there is Death in full cry against us. (*Im Westen*, p. 108)

This existence on the border of death causes them to concern themselves only with the basic essentials; and this is why the episodes of happiness we discussed earlier all concerned the basic physical needs of the comrades: food, defecation, sleep.

The one thing that keeps Remarque's characters determined to maintain their hold on life, even in the face of the most terrible injuries, or frightful tortures in *Der Funke Leben*, is hope; and when Bäumer confesses in the closing pages of *Im Westen nichts Neues* that "we are without hope", (*Im Westen*, p. 251) we know that his end is near. If, Bäumer acknowledges, the war had been over in 1916, it would have been possible for them to return to normality, but now they have been exposed to the front line for too long, they know nothing else any more, and in the words of one study of war fiction, "the front line has become the soldier's home, and it is best to die at home".[51]

Despite all the critical assertions to the contrary, however, the comrades do not actively embrace their lives as savages, for perhaps the most tragic level of alienation which the novel explores is their separation from their true nature as human beings. When

Bäumer comes out of the hospital ward where Kemmerich has just died of his wounds, he is filled, not with grief, but with an overwhelming longing, a hunger greater than that for mere sustenance could ever be, a burning desire to reach out and capture life itself.

Their adjustment to life at the front is more apparent than real; they adopt a deliberately superficial mode of existence, cutting themselves off from all emotion and passion in order to be able to survive at all. This causes them to yearn all the more intensely to be able once more to live as complete human beings. The goal of their aspirations is, however, far beyond their grasp: "It is unattainable, and we know it. It is as vain as the expectation of becoming a general". (*Im Westen,* p. 115)

When Bäumer returns home on leave, he recognizes that even those once attainable and modest aspirations which used to fill him — pursuing his studies, reading his books — have been driven out of him by the experience of war. The last words that Bäumer writes before he is killed reflect this loss of hope of ever returning to normality, although the life force within him will continue to "seek its way" (*Im Westen,* p. 263) for as long as he or others of his contemporaries are spared; and the use of the word "way" ("Weg" in German) forges the link with the title of the sequel *Der Weg zurück,* in which Bäumer's generation tries to find a way back to normality, even though the impossibility of the task is clear from the outset. The life force within them will struggle on, just as it now does in Bäumer, whether they will or no.

But the hardest lesson of all that the group of comrades is forced to learn in the war is that the ordered and meaningful pattern of life which they had once found in parents, home and school is a lost illusion; the causality which they had been taught was one cornerstone of their lives does not exist in the front line. There all life hangs on a sequence of blind chances, and chance is the only faith left to the soldier:

> The front is a cage in which you have to wait nervously for whatever is going to happen . . . When a shot comes towards me I may duck down, but that is all; where it strikes I can neither know exactly nor influence . . . Every soldier only remains alive by a thousand chances. And every soldier believes and trusts in chance. (*Im Westen,* p.96)

The good do not necessarily prosper, nor do the bad meet their just deserts; in fact, the exact opposite seems to obtain. Joseph Behm, for example, a fat, contented lad, does not want to go to war, but lets himself be persuaded, for fear that he would have been branded a coward. Behm is one of the first to fall; wounded in the eyes, he rushes aimlessly about blind and crazed with pain, and is shot down before any of his comrades can reach him and bring him back to safety. Even the apparently indestructible Kat, who has a wife and son to return to, is killed by a tiny stray splinter of shrapnel.

The only apparent exception to this total disruption of causality is the fate of Himmelstoss, the corporal whose reign of terror over the comrades when they are undergoing their basic training culminates in his vicious treatment of Tjaden and another soldier. The two are bed-wetters, and he assigns them to a two-tier bunk, where each is to take turns at sleeping in the lower bunk. Vengeance for this and his other actions is meted out to him on the night before the trainees depart for the front line: Himmelstoss is caught as he returns from his favourite bar, covered in a sheet, tied up, and soundly beaten. When he subsequently appears behind the lines, Tjaden and Kropp insult him, but only receive token punishment when Tjaden explains in the orderly room about the bed-wetting episode. So in this case, it seems, justice is done and seen to be done twice over; the wicked Himmelstoss does not profit from his evil ways, and later in the novel he is shown to be a reformed character; when one of the kitchen orderlies goes on leave, he puts Tjaden in charge of supplies and ensures that the rest of the group are assigned to three days on kitchen fatigue so that they get "the two things which the soldier needs to be happy: food and rest". (*Im Westen*, p. 130)

The semblance of causality in this sequence of events relating to Himmelstoss only serves to heighten the overall absence of causality from the principal strand of the action. And, if the Himmelstoss subplot is considered in the light of Remarque's later novels, it soon becomes evident that it really has little to do with causality as such; it is rather related to the motif of revenge which becomes so prominent in the novels of emigration, where the act of revenge is a protest against the absence of causality in a blindly cruel world.

Since the soldier lives by chance, all the skill and moral probity in the world are powerless to protect him against a falling shell or a stray bullet; and this situation is reflected in the structure of *Im Westen nichts Neues,* which has no real plot in the proper sense of the term at all, but operates instead on the basis of theme and variation, a sequence of antithetical patterns, and also of a highly developed substructure of recurrent images. We have already encountered the motif of the English flying boots and the photographic plate, but the most poignant of such motifs relates back to the days before the war; the two most important of these are butterflies and poplar trees. Like Remarque himself, Bäumer used to collect butterflies as a child, and when he returns home on leave he looks again at his collection, and reflects on the past which is now irretrievably lost:

> My mother is there, my sister is there, my case of butterflies there and the mahogany piano there — but I am not yet quite there ... There's a veil, a gap between us. (*Im Westen*, p.149)

Needless to say, the optimism expressed in the words "not yet quite there" is far from justified.

Earlier in the novel, this same gulf between the world beyond the trenches and the front line is underlined by a grotesque juxtaposition of two incidents, again in the context of the butterfly: two brimstone butterflies (in German, "Zitronenfalter", i.e. "lemon butterflies") flutter all morning over the trench in which the comrades are on duty, and rest for a while on the teeth of a skull. A few lines further on comes a description of a huddle of corpses after a grenade attack; two of them have literally been blown to pieces, and one

> rests his head in death on his chest in the trench, his face is lemon yellow, in his bearded mouth a cigarette is still glowing. It glows until it hisses out on his lips. (*Im Westen*, p.121)

The colour of the butterflies is transferred to the face of the dead soldier, and their alighting on the skull's teeth is paralleled by the glowing cigarette on the lifeless lips.

The butterfly motif is taken up to very great effect in the film *All Quiet on the Western Front;* in its celebrated closing sequence, Bäumer's hand is seen reaching out to touch a butterfly, only to fall back limply in death as he is fatally wounded. In a parallel sequence in the novel, in which Detering is overwhelmed with a longing to return to the past, it is the delicate colour of cherry blossom which causes him to lose his reason. His comrades find him holding a twig of cherrry blossom, and ask him why he has picked it. He replies that this is the time of year when his cherry orchard back home is transformed into a sea of white blossom; and so powerful is the pull of this recollection of past happiness that Detering simply disappears, presumably seeking to find his way back home. The comrades hear no more of him, but his fate is almost certainly that of the deserter: "For what do court martial judges a hundred kilometres behind the lines understand about that kind of thing?" (*Im Westen*, p.248)

For Bäumer, the trenches represent the antithesis of the fragile, gentle and ever-present beauty of Nature, the "lost world of beauty", as Liedloff puts it.[52] As far as Nature is concerned, Remarque never quite shakes off the sentimentality of his

Jugendstil days. The butterfly and the cherry blossom symbolize the irrevocable disappearance of the comrades' past lives. Towards the end of the novel — it is the summer of 1918, and it is clear that the Germans have lost the war — Bäumer writes: "The days stand like angels in gold and blue, beyond our grasp, over the circle of destruction". (*Im Westen*, p.254) Nature is totally detached from the conflict being acted out beneath.

Only once in the novel is there a reference to any military object as being pictorially attractive, and the circumstances are quite special: the comrades are waiting behind the lines for transport; it is a misty night, and there is a strange atmosphere of suspension from reality. A column of men goes past, but they are not like men, only a pattern of shapes against the gloom. And then more men pass, this time on horseback, but equally unreal: "The riders with their steel helmets look like knights of a past age; in some strange way it is beautiful and stirring". (*Im Westen*, p.56) But, overwhelmingly, the war is bereft of all beauty; and it is significant that even the aspirant poet and dramatist Bäumer cannot share with an artist like Paul Nash a sense of awe at "these wonderful trenches at night, at dawn, at sundown".[53] Nothing can compensate for the destructiveness and horror of this war, because it has cut them off from beauty and all that it represents. Nash may observe and paint with all the "inspired egotism of the artist who is sure of his vocation",[54] but for Bäumer and his comrades such sublimation of the experiences of war is an impossibility.

Alongside the butterfly, poplar trees also represent the unattainability of the lost world; these are the trees of Bäumer's home town along the Pappelallee (Poplar Avenue; the equivalent in Osnabrück is Am Pappelgraben, and poplars find frequent mention throughout Remarque's novels). There Bäumer and his schoolfriends used to catch sticklebacks in the brook running the length of the avenue, but it is all now no more than a golden memory of a hopelessly lost time. And, significantly, the sight and sound of the poplars occur again on the last page of the novel as symbolic of Bäumer's vain aspiration to find his way back to his past and to make use of the foundation laid in those early years to build himself a positive future.

Remarque also employs the repetition of certain key words, of which "Erde" (earth) and "Stille" (tranquillity) are the most significant, in order to express certain central concepts. We have already encountered "earth" as representing the source of the life force, of the energy that flows through Bäumer when he is overwhelmed by the recognition that he is alive, and Kemmerich dead; and, ultimately, it is to the earth that man finally returns. The notion of "tranquillity" is associated with the lost past, and in the last lines of the novel both these key terms are stressed once again: the day of Bäumer's death is "quiet and tranquil", and his body lies "as if in sleep on the earth". (*Im Westen*, p. 263)

Bäumer dies on one of those days in the final stages of the war when military activity is on such a relatively subdued level that the report from the front line states merely that all is quiet on the Western front. Death and suffering have become so routine that it requires a major offensive or a particularly gory occurrence to force the war back into the headlines.

As a result, language too is alienated, words are stripped of their true import, and the most horrific experiences are depicted in flat, matter-of-fact terms, just as in Kafka's chilling fantasies. Again and again, Bäumer admits the inadequacy of mere words such as attack, counter-attack, mines, gas, machine-guns and the rest to encompass the terrors they purport to describe. This does not only hold true for his experiences in the front line: when he is at home on leave, words also come to him only with great difficulty, and he finds that the words of his books fail to reach him any more. He is unable to explain what things are like in action; and, when he pays a visit to Kemmerich's mother, he admits his total inability to put down on paper words adequate to depict the sufferings of the bereaved mother.

Bäumer's only recourse is to state quite baldly what happens when, for example, raw recruits — whom the comrades describe as children even though they are scarcely a few months younger than the majority of them — dying under a gas attack, failing to take cover at the right moment, or going beserk with fear.

So everthing is reduced to a numbing routine: in the descriptions of battle, of waiting behind the lines, thinking of home, enjoying the basic pleasures of food and sleep, the same formulae appear time and again to stress the sameness of every aspect of their lives, the treadmill of war from which there is no escape. Feeling and emotion dare not be allowed any room for expression, or insanity would inevitably result; and equally the words used describe the surface of the life to which they have been reduced, a string of bare utterances, an Expressionist sequence of substantives, as here:

> Grenades, gas clouds and flotillas of tanks — crushing, corrosion, death. Dysentery, influenza, typhus — throttling, incineration, death. Graves, field hospital, mass grave — no more possibilities exist. (*Im Westen* pp. 252-53)

This routine of suffering and the necessity for the suppression of feeling and emotion are to become a key motif in Remarque's later novels under the guise of the cliché, of which more later.

The recurrent motifs that express the lives of the comrades also stress the basic essentials of the life to which their animal existence has reduced them. They concentrate, as we have seen, on food and defecation. Only fleeting reference is made to tobacco, although it is stressed as vital to the soldier, and there is also relatively little emphasis on alcohol, a state of affairs that is more than remedied in Remarque's subsequent novels. Surprisingly, perhaps, there is not very much in the way of references to sexual matters (especially for those who have read the reviewers and the critics rather than the novel itself). Early critics claimed that *Im Westen nichts Neues* was read by some for its questionable aspects, but it is far from being a rich stamping-ground for those in pursuit of titillation, even by the standards of the 1920's. There is little to cause linguistic offense, apart from references to a certain portion of the anatomy and its defecatory rôle, and there is no specific reference to details of the sexual act. There are a couple of allusions to adolescent curiosity about sex, and to Leer's fascination with girls from the officers' brothels, who are supposedly under orders to wear silk chemises and to bathe themselves before receiving visitors from the rank of captain upwards. The episode of the passionate Lewandowski in hospital has already been mentioned in the context of Remarque's supposed mendacity in relation to life in the military hospital where he was a patient with Peter Kropp; this is described in matter-of-fact terms, as a basic element of life, rather than as an opportunity for obscene allusion or adolescent voyeurism. And the important sequence when some of the comrades cross the canal to visit the three Frenchwomen translates Bäumer's love-making with one of the girls into terms of the vague aspirations towards unattainable fulfilment which stalk the pages of his *Jugendstil* works. This comes across most forcibly when the comrades are gazing at a poster advertising an army theatrical performance, which portrays a man in a blue jacket and white trousers, and a girl who fascinates them, clad in a bright summer dress, white stockings and shoes, and holding a straw hat in one hand. They regard the girl as a "miracle", and their immediate reaction is to go off to have themselves deloused in a kind of ritual (as well as actual!) cleansing of their animal natures in response to such perfection and purity. When Bäumer embraces the French girl, he too is in search of a "miracle": "I press myself deeper into the arms which are holding me, perhaps a miracle will happen . . ." (*Im Westen,* p.140) Similarly, Bäumer is reluctant to climb into the bunk on the hospital train which is repatriating him, since it is made up with snow-white sheets.

But the miracle will never come; the comrades are either doomed to die, cut off from their former lives, from reality and even from their own true selves, or doomed to live on in a peacetime environment to which they will never be able properly to adjust, not least on the paradoxical grounds that, once an individual has existed for a period under the immediate threat of death, a return to "normal" life is an impossibility, since the senses have become so accustomed to being sharpened to the keenest edge by the experience of the front line that the comrades will in peacetime be in a constant state of frustration at the very lack of danger. So they and their generation are, in a very real sense of the term, spoiled for all time.

In all the debates about *Im Westen nichts Neues,* there is one common criticism made by defenders and detractors of the novel alike, from the National Socialists at one extreme, via the liberal pacifists in the middle, to the Marxists at the other end of the spectrum; and that is, that it does not succeed in providing a generally valid overall picture of the war. The novel's opponents argue that this one-sidedness constitutes a serious weakness in a work which has come to be regarded as official war history, its supporters on the other hand congratulate Remarque on refraining from spoon-feeding his readers, but instead assuming that they are sufficiently intelligent to make up their own minds about what happened in the trenches and to the rear. Interestingly, Remarque himself seems to fall into line with this view of *Im Westen nichts Neues;* in the Eggebrecht interview, he admits that he was seeking to do no more than simply put down on paper a "worm's eye view" of the war.[55]

But to argue that Remarque is either a weak-kneed pacifist gnawing away at the nation's vitals, or a mature writer probing fearlessly at the heart of his generation's tragic fate, or again a bourgeois liberal who recognizes the disease and fails to point to a cure, is to miss the point entirely. Nor is it enough to indicate that the limitations of the work are attributable to the fact that Bäumer is a relatively unsophisticated young man who would in any event be incapable of comprehending the wider historical perspective into which his individual life fits. (There is, in any event, no inevitable correlation between the intelligence, insight or whatever of the author's mouthpiece and the quality or complexity of the narrative.)

The truth of the matter is that, in *Im Westen nichts Neues,* Remarque is proposing the view that human existence can no longer be regarded as having any ultimate meaning. Bäumer and his comrades cannot make sense of the world at large for the simple reason that it is no longer possible to do so, not just for this group of ordinary soldiers, but for a substantial proportion of his entire generation. Remarque refuses to lull his reader into a false sense of security, into thinking that God is in his heaven and all is right with the world — all that is amiss is that we as individuals are too limited in vision to be able to recognize the existence of a grand design. On the contrary, he demonstrates that the holocaust of the First World War has destroyed, not only any semblance of meaningfulness that the universe may seem to have possessed in the past, but that even the continuity of the individual existence has been shattered.

The largest unit of significance that remains is the individual life, sustained by the "life force" pulsing within, which holds the individual for the brief span of his existence and then releases him into death.

Philosophers, sociologists and all the rest may argue that this adherence to the notion of the "life principle" is a dangerous aberration and a distortion of all the received dogma of Western civilization; but this is how Remarque experienced life in the Great War with all its contradictions, pleasures and sufferings, and, fortunately for the reader, authors are under no obligation to construct internally consistent philosophical systems which conform to certain predetermined moral and ethical principles. It is for this reason, we would argue, that *Im Westen nichts Neues* captured the imagination of so many millions of readers, and why it continues to be one of the greatest bestsellers of all time. It refuses to inject a consoling but essentially illusory pattern of causality and meaningfulness into human existence.

Not only has the war destroyed any possibility for Bäumer and his like of reaching out beyond his individual existence and grasping at the myth of a meaningful universe, it has also shattered what was formerly a genuine reality, namely, the experience of a human life as a continuous single entity, an onward and upward progression through the years. Now even the individual life has lost its overall significance: it has become alienated from itself, and the knowledge and experiences gained at one stage are demonstrably inapplicable to the next phase. All that can be rescued from the tangle of the lives of Bäumer and his comrades is a profound desire to hold on to life itself, a blind instinct not to let slip the life force, and an equally blind hope for the future. As we have seen, when that hope fades in the closing sequence of the novel, Bäumer's end cannot be far distant. These themes are developed and explored further by Remarque in his subsequent works, especially in the two novels which deal with aspects of the

Second World War; *Der Funke Leben* and *Zeit zu leben,* as will be seen when the time comes to discuss them in a later chapter. Nor is it coincidental that the word "Leben" (life) figures prominently in both titles.

Remarque's refusal to simulate meaning where he sees none is probably the cause of so many statements on the part of critics to the effect that *Im Westen nichts Neues* comes close "to being all things to all men"[56] — which it certainly is not, unless "all things" include anathema and "all men" the Nazis. Behind such statements, however, there lies at least a partial recognition of the fact that Remarque has succeeded in distilling the common experience of ordinary individuals in the First World War and beyond, and that he has not set out with any false moralizing or philosophical preconceptions, but has sought honestly to convey his experience of life (and that of countless others), however unpleasant and negative his conclusions may be. Nor is he trying to seek refuge in any new dogma, or sidling towards any existing unorthodoxy, such as existentialism. Remarque is essentially a non-intellectual writer who prefers to express rather than to explain his experience of life, and in *Im Westen nichts Neues* he was able to come to terms with his own full realization of what the experiences of the war meant for him and for so many of his generation; this is why the novel was for him, and for so many others, an "Erlösung", a release.

In his excellent but solitary study, Claude Cockburn defines as one of the qualities essential to a bestselling novel the presentation in an acceptable fictional form of "certain attitudes, prejudices, aspirations, etc., in the reader's conscious or subconscious mind".[57] In this respect, as we have seen, *Im Westen nichts Neues* is remarkably successful. It is nonsense to assert, as the Marxist critic tends to do, that Remarque has become so totally identified with the "little man", the petty bourgeois, that he is incapable of objectivizing him.[58] Anyone with a nodding acquaintanceship with Remarque's own predilection for the good life would hardly brand him as a defender of drab middle-class mediocrity. Remarque is simply being descriptive rather than prescriptive, to borrow a turn of phrase from the grammarian; and his fictionalized emotional experiences were recognized by millions of people as something with which they had a great deal in common.

If *Im Westen nichts Neues* is regarded in this light, then questions like the accuracy of his presentation of the "lost generation" (the credit goes to Gertrude Stein for inventing the term) cease to seem so vital. It does not really matter that

Remarque said that "our generation has grown up differently from any other before or since".[59] Many a critic has pounced gleefully on this assertion with pronouncements like: "Ample evidence shows that the heroes of Remarque are not representative of a whole generation but only of a certain type".[60] Remarque is not so lacking in perception as to be unaware of the truism, and it is disingenuous of his detractors to level this kind of accusation against him. What Remarque is asserting in his novel is that, so extreme were the experiences of Bäumer and his comrades that they were utterly devastated by their recognition of the discontinuity of life and the absence of any ultimate meaning in the universe. The majority of Remarque's readers, however, have not been eighteen-year-old front-line soldiers in the First World War; but they have, consciously or subconsciously, grown aware of a similar kind of insight in their own lives and experiences. As Cockburn suggests as a principle quality of the bestseller, Remarque has given literary expression to attitudes widely felt by ordinary people at large.

This does not, of course, mean that everyone reads Remarque for the same reasons: just as the pit watched Shakespeare for the farce and the fighting, some of Remarque's readers may have scanned the novel for bloodthirsty battle scenes, the prurient passages (in which they will have been more than a little disappointed), its supposed political and sociological significance, and so on. None of these misreadings should be allowed to be taken as invalidating the novel itself, especially since so many have wilfully distorted it and sought to reduce it to the level of a debating point in some campaign or other.

Cockburn stresses that it is not enough for the writer to touch on a nerve of his time; he must also write with consummate skill. In the words of Meyer:

> It is far more difficult to write a really absorbing book than to concoct a clever experimental one; it is far more difficult to tell a good story or to invent a memorable character that stays for a while in the human brain of millions or even of thousands than to fabricate Kunstgewerbe in the medium of words, so clever, so original that it can have any passing meaning we want to find there. This fashion will go, for it has come; and everything that is a fashion comes and goes, but the Odyssey has remained and so has Conan Doyle.[61]

Meyer overstates the case, but that does not impair its validity; as we have seen already, Remarque constructs his novel with considerable skill, employing balanced episodes (happy and tragic alternate with almost excessive inevitability), recurrent motifs and other devices. There is no doubt that the style of Im Westen nichts Neues marks a substantial advance on Remarque's previous work, his *Jugendstil* writings as well as the rather indifferent journalism of his Continental days, and indeed it sets the pattern for the rest of his novels. Apart from the major techniques already discussed, there are a number of detailed stylistic devices employed by Remarque which all conspire to enhance the overall impact of the novel. Chief among these are the preference for similes rather than metaphors, which helps to highlight the latter when they appear at key points in the text; the emphatic use of inversion at the beginning of the sentence which, although a not uncommon phenomenon in German, is adopted by Remarque with particular effect at moments of emotional tension; his sparing but striking use of anaphora, which is most impressive in the sequence of short paragraphs each beginning "O mother" in which Bäumer reflects on his leave and his previous life (*Im Westen,* p. 131f); the tendency for concrete substantives to dominate at crisis moments; the occasional very long sentence contrasting strongly with the predominant pattern of short, simple sentences; and so on. In *Im Westen nichts Neues* there is no doubt that Remarque suddenly found his own stylistic voice, so to speak; the language is shorn of all but the occasional trace of his erstwhile sentimentality, and like most of his subsequent writing it is compulsively readable. Remarque owes his success as a writer almost as much to his stylistic craftmanship as to his ability to express in narrative terms the sentiments of millions of his contemporaries. From both aspects, the novel

satisfied a need, and expressed and realized emotions and attitudes to life which the buyers and borrowers did not find expressed elsewhere.[62]

One of the worse fates that can befall a writer is to have a runaway bestseller with his first book; everything that follows will be held up against it, and sequels are notoriously disappointing. One critic at least has insisted — quite wrongly — that Remarque is a "one-book" author, despite the more than modest success of others of his works.[63] Remarque did in fact regard *Im Westen nichts Neues* as his "first" novel — *Die Traumbude* he considered as part of his juvenilia and something of an embarrassment, and *Station am Horizont* as a journalistic exercise; in a letter to Rabe, he replies to the latter's invitation to come and give a lecture on his new novel in these terms:

I have conned your arabesques with much amusement, but you will understand for all that, that at the moment I'd personally prefer to keep myself out of the limelight for a bit. It is only my first book, and one ought really to hide behind one's work for a while and only come to the surface if and when the second turns out good as well.[64]

Remarque was determined to let *Im Westen nichts Neues* find its own feet; and, in refusing to be dragged into the publicity and controversy which surrounded it, he demonstrated considerable restraint and good sense.

There is no doubt that Remarque was more than a little overwhelmed by the reception accorded to *Im Westen nichts Neues*, and was determined to write a sequel which would not only explore the fate of those returning from the front line in search of a land fit for heroes to live in but which would also be a more substantial literary achievement.

CHAPTER THREE

THE AFTERMATH AND THE INFLATION YEARS

That sequel was *Der Weg zurück*. In contrast to the speed and relative ease with which Remarque had written *Im Westen nichts Neues*, his "second" novel proved much more problematical. Hounded by press and public alike, he found it almost impossible to work in Berlin, and eventually took refuge in Osnabrück, which serves as the background for the greater part of the work. Choice of subject-matter also presented its difficulties: Remarque was anxious to preserve a measure of continuity with *Im Westen nichts Neues*, but he was equally determined not to "re-write" his bestseller. His declared intention was that his new work should offer some kind of hope for the future after the pessimism of *Im Westen nichts Neues*:

> We want to begin once again to believe in life. This will be the aim of my future work. He who has pointed out the danger must also point out the road onward.[1]

In writing this novel, Remarque felt that he more or less had to begin anew. Life would have been relatively simple, he suggested, if he had — as many critics maintained — merely invented the material for *Im Westen nichts Neues*: had that been the case, he would have felt more confident in his ability as a writer and could have gone on to "invent" new subject-matter.[2] However, having succeeded with a work which, in its emotional content at least, was semi-autobiographical, Remarque felt compelled to continue in similar vein, and evidently experienced difficulty in marshalling his thoughts at a time when he felt he was being pressurized on all sides to produce a worthy successor to *Im Westen nichts Neues* as rapidly as possible. *Der Weg zurück*, already under way in 1928, was finally published in 1931, and its reception was as mixed, though not as violent, as that accorded to *Im Westen nichts Neues*.

In company with his American critics, Remarque himself considered *Der Weg zurück* to be a far better novel than *Im Westen nichts Neues*. Concerned, as he himself has stated, with the "problems of the present",[3] *Der Weg zurück* certainly has a far broader perspective than *Im Westen nichts Neues*, examining as it does the problems facing the "lost generation" of soldiers upon their return from the war. Most of his German critics, however, have found *Der Weg zurück* wanting in almost every respect. Benno Reifenberg, not one of the greatest admirers of *Im Westen nichts Neues,* does at least accord the war novel the merit of being well written — even this mitigating feature, he asserts, is lacking in *Der Weg zurück*.[4]   Its worst fault in Reifenberg's eyes, however, is its "vagueness": he finds this defect both in Remarque's time-scheme, being unclear as to what "present" he is referring to, whether to 1919 or to 1923, and also in his characterization. Nor is Reifenberg satisfied by Remarque's attempt to generalize the fate which befell the "heroes" on their return from the front. He suggests — ironically in view of the general critical response to *Im Westen nichts Neues* — that Remarque might have given his book greater authenticity by making it more autobiographical.

One Marxist critic, Antkowiak, likewise maintains that the artistic merit of *Der Weg zurück* is inferior to that of *Im Westen nichts Neues,* and finds a total lack of unity in style and atmosphere: "In a word, *Der Weg zurück* as a book is a linguistic and artistic failure".[5]   Such a sweeping condemnatory statement, as well as being inaccurate, is oddly out of place in a study which aspires to examine the text in depth; what is all the more surprising, major errors occur in Antkowiak's account of the novel's plot. He states that one of the main characters, Ludwig Breyer, having discovered that he has contracted syphilis during the war years, eventually shoots himself: in fact, Remarque emphasises that Breyer, obsessed with the thought of his poisoned blood, slashes his wrists in order to let the poison flow from his body. Antkowiak also claims that the farmer Bethke shoots his adulterous wife out of jealousy and is punished for his crime by the court. In fact Bethke does no such thing, and Antkowiak has presumably confused Bethke with a totally different character Albert Trosske, who is brought to trial for shooting his girlfriend's lover. Not only does Antkowiak advance these toally erroneous statements,[6] he even repeats them a few pages later in his text.[7] Given elementary blunders of this nature, one is led to wonder just how close a study of Remarque's text has been made before it is condemned as a complete failure.

Antkowiak and another Marxist critic, Irene Wegner, advance the further criticism that Remarque has failed to face up to the full historical and social import of the November revolution (which was hardly his aim). Wegner, rather puzzlingly, takes Remarque to task for making war the sole experience of the "lost generation" (which quite evidently *was* Remarque's aim in writing the novel):

Birkholz and his comrades know nothing but the war, and they create the impression that they can no longer do anything but what they have learnt in the war.[8]

This is indeed the theme of *Der Weg zurück;* namely all that these ex-soldiers had experienced was war, and all their skills and accomplishments were inextricably bound up with war. Now these skills and experiences are not only entirely inappropriate to their present needs in a post-war society, they even prove a positive hindrance to any adaptation to civilian life. Wegner's accusation seems to indicate that she has somehow missed the entire point of the novel, and has fallen victim to the same error as that so prevalent among critics of *Im Westen nichts Neues* by seeking to hold up Remarque's novels against an external political, nationalistic or social yardstick.

The troubles of the young soldiers did not cease with the end of hostilities in 1918; on the contrary, their difficulties were in many respects only just beginning. In the words of Löhrke,

the war has been blamed for many things, perhaps for too much; but in many respects the aftermath was worse than the actual conflict.[9]

Upon their return home, the men found that they were expected to take up the thread of their lives as if there had never been a war, and this they were unable to do, since all their thoughts and reactions were still completely conditioned by their war-time experiences. "This", says Lörke, "is the war's least understood tragedy".[10]   Tragedy it indeed turns out to be in *Der Weg zurück*, with two of the comrades committing suicide, one shooting another, and a fourth ending up in prison after killing his girlfriend's lover. Remarque's readers were obviously looking for something much more positive from him in his second novel, and were disappointed to find it almost as depressing as *Im Westen nichts Neues*. Ludwig Marcuse summarizes the general impression created by *Der Weg zurück* in the following terms:

This book is full of horror like the war-book: there the bodies twitched beneath the clods of earth raining down upon them, here souls twitch under the pressure of an alien reality, of a life with which the soldiers from the front cannot come to terms.[11]

Although the closing pages of *Der Weg zurück* have generally been interpreted as positive and even optimistic, the overall tone of the major part of the book is without doubt one of bitter disillusionment, and demonstrates how the hopeful "road onward" of which

Remarque wrote failed to measure up to its promise of a brighter future.

After an introductory section portraying the final days of action in World War One, with some of the surviving characters from *Im Westen nichts Neues* present, and with a couple of references to less fortunate comrades such as Kat, Bäumer and Haie, (*Weg*, p.21) Remarque describes the coming of peace and the return of the soldiers to their home-town. Despite the longing to be back home, there are hints in the opening pages of a less than euphoric attitude towards the approaching peace. The vague hopes associated with peace and the resurgence of happy memories of pre-war days, a happiness which the men hope to recapture, are accompanied by a strange uneasiness, almost fear, engendered by the uncertainty of what peace will bring.

When a lull in the firing occurs during the final days of the conflict, the soldiers are at a loss to understand what has happened: they feel instinctively that something is amiss, but are unable to account for the situation. Finally the truth dawns upon them: "It has simply become still. Quite still". (*Weg*, p.13) The soldiers are almost relieved when the silence is broken by "the familiar sounds of death". (*Weg*, p.14) They are suspicious of the unaccustomed silence after years of almost ceaseless din of battle, and they are distrustful of the concept of peace, which is described as "Dreck" (dirt). (*Weg*, p.21) In many respects they have come to regard the front as their real home and feel a profound sorrow when the time comes for them to leave it. This sadness is partly attributable to the fact that they are leaving so many dead comrades behind them, but Remarque also speaks of a feeling that they are somehow leaving their "lost years" behind them. (*Weg*, p.22)

Even the title of the book is not entirely positive: although Remarque at one stage amplifies the words of the title to "the road back into life", (*Weg*, p.23) it is worthy of note that the phrase "going back" also implies a retreat. During the final stages of battle, when the troops are forced to withdraw, Remarque employs words which point strongly to the novel's title: "We are going back. Back". (*Weg*, p.17) In many respects, the soldiers' return to civilian life could be interpreted as a permanent retreat from the intensity of life at the front rather than as a new beginning, and instead of a "road onward" it seems that the soldiers are taking a retrograde step into the drab routine of civilian life. Boredom, it appears, is one of the chief associations which peacetime now has for them. When speculation arises as to where the comrades will be in a year's time, one of them replies "on our backsides". (*Weg*, p.54)

Indeed, the ex-soldiers find little outlet for their heightened senses and lightning reactions once the fighting has ceased, and life inevitably seems dull once the stimulus of imminent danger is no longer with them. As Ludwig Breyer remarks to Georg Rahe, who is so disillusioned with civilian life that he determines to re-enlist:

> In the field our nerves were always stretched to the limit because it was a question of life and death. Now they flutter about like sails in a dead calm.
> (*Weg*, pp. 194-95)

Birkholz and his comrades have developed their nervous reactions to such a pitch that they cannot simply switch them off once the war is over. Like Bäumer home on leave in *Im Westen nichts Neues*, Willy Homeyer and Ernst Birkholz spring into the air at the grenade-like sound of a tram, and when Birkholz tries to recapture his lost youth by revisiting Am Pappelgraben, he suddenly realizes that he is standing in an exposed position and runs for cover, trying to locate suitable sites for digging trenches. Each fresh attempt to pick up the threads of his former life is bedevilled in one way or another by the war, and Birkholz is led to ask: "Have the years out there completely burned down the bridge back to earlier days?" (*Weg*, p.140)

The "road back" does indeed prove difficult to find, most noticeably in the relationships between the former soldiers and their families, for the transition from "boy" to "man" has taken place on the battle-field, far removed from the parental home. When Birkholz's mother comments upon how much he has changed, he suddenly realizes that he and his mother have exchanged rôles, and she has now become the child. Instead of this being a new relationship, however, Birkholz feels that he can never again be close to his mother as he had been, and is overwhelmed by a sensation of loneliness: "Haven't I lost her? All at once I feel how strange and alone I really am". (*Weg*, p.14) Distinctions of age and respect for social position were equally obliterated for the soldiers, and consequently Birkholz finds that he has lost all sense of awe before his elders, including his parents: "Fear of older people was lost in the trenches. There all of us were equal". (*Weg*, p.66) Birkholz remains completely unmoved by his father's reproachful attitude towards his smoking, or by his concern for his son's future when Birkholz gives up his teaching post.

The gulf between the soldiers and their families is further widened by their inability to discuss their war-time experiences with them. When Birkholz's family ply him with questions upon his return from the war, he cannot think of anything to say, despite the fact that it is the war which dominates his every thought and action. He comments: "One cannot talk about the things out there with civilians". (*Weg*, pp. 62-63) Adolf Bethke makes a similar remark to Birkholz: "You understand me, Ernst, and I you, but with them it seems as if there is a wall between us". (*Weg* p.125) There is a certain degree of pride in this attitude of exclusive comradeship and — one cannot help feeling — some condescension towards the "civilians" who have not shared the all-important experiences of the war.

Certainly the ex-soldiers receive far less understanding from the rest of society than they would like to feel they had earned. When those of them who have not completed their studies are compelled to return to school, they are horrified to discover — as Remarque himself was — that their teachers continue to treat them as children and expect them to conform to the discipline of men to whom they now feel superior in many respects:

> We know life better than them now; we have acquired a different know-
> ledge, hard, bloody, horrible and remorseless. Today we could teach them,
> but who wants to! (*Weg*, pp.112-13)

Again there is a reversal of rôles, as the soldiers, equating experience in war with experience in life, regard the circumscribed world of their parents and teachers as a second-rate reality.

In the opening pages of his novel, Remarque states that each of the comrades — unlike many in *Im Westen nichts Neues* — has something from his former civilian life to sustain his spirits during the war: for one it is his wife, for another his business, and one cherishes the idiosyncratic ambition of once more eating "bacon with beans". (*Weg*, p.6) But now that peace has come, the contrary appears to be the case: finding their cherished hopes disappointed, the men cling to their war-time memories as the only true reality. This contributes to the violence of their reaction when the well-meaning headmaster embarks upon a speech eulogizing the sacrifice of their dead comrades, whom he envisages as heroes now sleeping beneath the green turf of a distant land. He is interrupted by mocking laughter, and Homeyer quickly disabuses him by describing in graphic detail the far from glorious circumstances in which some of their former school-fellows met their end. As well as regarding the headmaster's words as a grotesque defamation of their dead comrades, the surviving soldiers are reacting against the false picture which society is seeking to build up of *their* experiences.

Yet in many respects the view which the young men have of civilian life is just as false as that which society has of them. No attempt is made to bend established rules to accommodate the behaviour and attitudes of the soldiers, but they for their part are equally unwilling to alter their ways in order to conform to the standards demanded by society. "In the field it was easier", says Birkholz, "there, if one was simply alive everything was all right". (*Weg*, p.129) During the months and years of war, it was an idealized picture of the civilian world which had formed in the soldiers' minds, just as the people back home were idealizing the soldiers' achievements, and it soon becomes evident that the soldiers are completely unversed in the practicalities of everyday life. While the horrific intensity of the war obliterated all that they had learnt at home and in school, their present life-style cannot as quickly eradicate what has been learnt at the front, as two humorous episodes from *Der Weg zurück* demonstrate.

The Kat-like Willy Homeyer, renowned for his foraging abilities and his love of food, incurs his mother's wrath shortly after his return home by appropriating a neighbour's hen. Homeyer, supported by Birkholz, is quite unable to regard "foraging for food" as theft and is utterly bewildered when his mother insists upon returning the hen:

> Stolen? . . . It was requisitioned! Acquired! Found! — Stolen! If people take money, then one can speak of stealing, but not if they catch something to eat. (*Weg*, p.72)

It has become second nature to the soldiers to keep their eyes open for possible edibles, and Homeyer's skill in the art of noise-lessly despatching stray animals has rendered him the object of great admiration from his comrades. It is difficult for him to reconcile this with the horrified reaction of his mother, which is not diminished when Homeyer, undaunted by a lack of fuel with which to heat the stove, proposes that they chop up an old chair to supply the heat necessary to cook the bird.

Birkholz himself encounters similar problems when dining out at the home of some affluent relatives; halfway through the meal he forgets himself in memories of the war and is aroused by a giggle from the young lady seated beside him to find that he is eating a chop with his fingers, elbows propped on the table, while the rest of the guests, suitably provided with knives and forks, are staring at him in horrified silence. Birkholz's embarrassment at having lapsed back into the coarser eating habits of the field is mingled with rage at the fact that social niceties are considered so important, whereas in wartime the soldiers were concerned with the more fundamental issues of life and death, and instead of regarding eating as a social experience, treated it as one of the more enjoyable basic human needs. Birkholz rushes from the house to his waiting army dog, Wolf,[12] and says:

> Come, Wolf, ... these people are not for us! ... We'll go to our comrades.
> It's better there, even if they do eat with their hands and burp! (*Weg*,
> p.108)

Once again the implication is that life as a soldier was far more
real, if not more worthwhile, than the civilian existence which
Birkholz and his friends are now expected to lead, and they find
great difficulty in coming to terms with what they regard as
artificial values imposed by society on everyday life.

Hardly surprisingly, Birkholz and his comrades begin to feel
that they are not equipped to be anything other than soldiers. For
years they have been longing for the chance to "begin to live";
yet, once they have been given that chance, they feel unequal to
the demands of peacetime. "Each of them is a perfect soldier, no
more and no less" (*Weg*, p.121) — this is Birkholz's comment on
his colleagues as he surveys them in the unaccustomed surround-
ings of the schoolroom. As each of them endeavours to make his
way through life, the unifying bond of comradeship — a theme
first developed in *Im Westen nichts Neues* — remains the one thing
of value which they all hope to retrieve from their experiences.
The men realize from the outset that their lives have now come to
depend upon preserving at least this ideal, and feel that in order to
do so they must stick together: "We must stay together, how can
we live otherwise?" (*Weg*, p.47) On his first evening home, after
only a few hours' separation, Birkholz rushes out of his parents'
home to be reunited with his comrades — all of whom are equally
glad of an excuse to be together again. Later, having left each of
his comrades at his respective home, Birkholz again has a sensation
of unreality:

> It's strange: now my comrades are no longer with me everything around
> me is beginning to become unsteady and unreal. (*Weg*, p.78)

This sensation is shared even by the older men who have wives and
families, notably by Adolf Bethke, who looked after Birkholz
when he was a raw recruit. So accustomed has Birkholz grown to
the company and guidance of Bethke that he finds it impossible to
imagine life without him; and Bethke, much as he is longing to see
his wife and return to his home in the country, is equally reluctant
to part from his comrades. When Birkholz later visits Bethke, he
finds that this man to whom he had continually looked for advice
and who had been an excellent soldier is totally unable to cope
with civilian life. His wife, it transpires, has had a lover while
Bethke was at the front, and he is completely at a loss as to how
to react.

At first he sends his wife away, partly out of jealousy and anger, but partly also because of the reaction of the small community in which he lives. He is totally unprepared for the situation, and cannot rely on his own judgement as he would have done in a battle, because he has no experience on which to base possible courses of action. He therefore acts according to the dictates of society and his wounded honour, but is finally overcome with loneliness and takes her back again. Even so, Bethke is unable to recapture the happiness which he had so eagerly anticipated during the war years; the malicious gossip of their neighbours leads him and his wife to sell their beloved country home and move into a dingy town-house, only to find that the root cause of their unhappiness is, after all, within them; that it was really the four years of separation which had caused the gulf between them, rather than the wife's infidelity.

Seeing Bethke drowning his sorrows in a pub, Birkholz contrasts the sad, broken figure before him with the faithful comrade and courageous soldier who saved so many in the trenches and calmed all their fears. Bethke, too, harks back to the days of his greatness. As he sadly says to Birkholz: "If only we had stayed out there — at least we were together there". (*Weg*, p. 258) It is no longer possible for the two men to reforge the bond of the war-years, for in their civilian rôles they have both become quite different people, and at the end of the novel we are informed that Bethke has "moved away". (*Weg*, p.304)

The more youthful Albert Trosske also seeks to combat his isolation with the love and companionship of a woman, with equally disastrous results. All of the ex-soldiers have the feeling of not belonging anywhere, and after yet another evening spent aimlessly wandering around together, Trosske says: "Funny that one never wants to be alone, isn't it?" (*Weg*, p.148) Agreeing, Birkholz suggests that a career would be something to pin one's hopes on, but Trosske has different ideas; he wants a living person, a woman: "One must have something to hold on to, don't you understand that?" (*Weg*, p.149) Much as he cherishes his companionship with Birkholz and his other friends, Trosske wants someone more, someone who really belongs to him and who will love him; and above all he wants children, who will have experienced nothing of the war.

Trosske succeeds in finding a young lady by the name of Lucie, and a relationship quickly develops between them. This relationship soon becomes the most important thing in his life, and even his closest comrades are neglected for the girl. However, it eventually becomes clear that Lucie does not reciprocate Trosske's feelings and is not bestowing her favours upon him alone. Acting on a tip-off, Trosske goes one night to a café with his friends and surprises Lucie with her lover in a private cubicle. Reacting in the only way of which he is capable, Trosske shoots the man dead, scarcely needing to take aim, so good a marksman has he become. Although his friends try to get him away from the scene of the crime, Trosske insists on giving himself up to the police. Speaking in his friend's defence at the trial, Birkholz explains why Trosske reacted so violently:

> He wanted to marry because he couldn't find his bearings again after the war, because he was afraid of himself and kept remembering and was looking for something to hold on to. (*Weg*, p.291)

Horrified that he does not regret his act, the prosecution points out that killing a man is a very serious offence. Trosske calmly replies that he has killed many men, and when asked if he is trying to equate fighting for his fatherland with what he has just done, he makes this splendid reply: "No, ... the people I killed then (in the war) had done nothing against me". (*Weg*, p.292) Birkholz points out too that if Trosske had not been taught to shoot by his country, then he would not have committed murder now.

The sense of comradeship which they feel is clearly demonstrated at Trosske's trial, as each of them obviously takes the view that it could be any one of them in the dock now, facing charges for something which the war has taught him to do. They all do their utmost to save Trosske, and Birkholz's empassioned cry: "You're dealing with our comrade ... don't condemn him!" (*Weg*, p.295) is really a *cri de coeur* on behalf of them all. They care little about what he has done; the important factor is that he is their comrade, a part of themselves.

Along with the tragedies which overtake the individual soldiers comes the ultimate tragedy of Remarque's novel, the disintegration of the concept of comradeship itself. Bound together in war by common aims and shared misfortune, they discover that a variety of conflicting peace-time interests is sufficient to undermine the one positive value which they had discovered in the war. When Homeyer and Birkholz join other soldiers in an abortive revolutionary march to the house of the area commander, Birkholz experiences a resurgence of the old bond between them: "Soldiers don't need to know anything of each other. They are comrades, that is enough". (*Weg*, p.75) It transpires, however, that it is not enough for peace-time, and while the soldiers had inquired little of each other's personal lives in the years of war, it is these — and in particular social distinctions — which now become all-important. It is not surprising that the fashion-conscious Remarque uses clothes in *Der Weg zurück* to draw attention to the different social positions of the various soldiers. Understandably, social standing and military skill rarely correspond. Adolf Bethke and Ludwig Breyer, both "giants" on the battle-field, respected by all, are "small men" from the social point of view, and at a soldiers' reunion are completely outshadowed by men to whom they have frequently given orders and whose soldiering skills are nothing in comparison with their own. And men who cared nothing for their personal appearance on the battle-field are now deeply offended if their attire is the object of scorn.

It is not only in appearance that the men have changed; they are indeed different people, for it is their function in society and their family circumstances which are now the important things in their lives. The shock of this realization is completely unnerving for the soldiers, both individually and collectively. Valentin Laher, an impoverished former acrobat, one day encounters two comrades on the street and greets each of them joyfully. The first, the smartly dressed Arthur Ledderhose, is evidently prospering in his business and can scarcely spare the time to talk; the second, formerly a close friend of Laher's, addresses him formally and pretends that he hardly recognizes him. Both men are ashamed to be seen in the company of the scruffy Valentin, and are only too ready to forget all that they have been through together. At the reunion, Birkholz contrasts Laher and Ledderhose:

> Valentin is wearing an old blue and white sweater under his torn, open uniform, and looks like a tramp — but what a soldier! —, and Ledderhose, the twisted hound, sits there haughtily... in a canary-yellow mackintosh, smoking English cigarettes. Everything is topsy-turvy. (*Weg*, p.183)

In addition, many of the soldiers appear to have undergone complete changes of character: those who previously had little to say are now talking volubly, apparently gaining confidence from their well-groomed appearances; those who showed fear of their superior officers in the field now slap them on the back and enquire condescendingly about their exams. Unwillingly, Birkholz has to concede that their last hope of salvaging something from the war is vanishing before their eyes:

> Everything else was destroyed in the war, but we had believed in comradeship. And now we see that what death hasn't accomplished, life is succeeding in doing: it is separating us. (*Weg*, p.184)

As this realization dawns upon the comrades, each of them reacts in a different way. Tjaden, with whom much of the novel's humour is associated, is transformed from one of the great unwashed into a clean and neatly dressed citizen when he succeeds in becoming engaged to a local butcher's daughter, whose chief charm lies in her father's chosen trade. The energetic and good-natured Willy Homeyer, perpertrator of a multitude of daring exploits, also succumbs to the attractions of a way of life which will ensure that he is well-fed, and settles for the relatively mundane occupation of schoolteacher. But Georg Rahe, a former schoolfriend of Birkholz,[13] tries to rediscover comradeship by re-enlisting in the army. The comradeship which he hoped to find again proves to be just as illusory as the new civilian life he thought he had been fighting for during his first stint as a soldier, and Rahe leaves the army again. The final blow came when he found himself obliged to fight against fellow countrymen, supposed Communists, who to Rahe were only former comrades whom he was now expected to kill as enemies. Convinced that they have all fought in vain and that life holds nothing for him, Rahe returns to the scenes of former battles and with a final cry: "Comrades! We have been betrayed!" (*Weg,* p.301) he shoots himself. Like the soldiers leaving the battle scene at the beginning of the novel, Rahe feels that he belongs here, alongside his dead comrades, for it was here that all their lives were destroyed.

Not only Rahe's experiences, but also the fate of two other characters in the novel, Max Weil and company leader Heel, clearly illustrate Remarque's own attitudes to the revolution or indeed to civil war of any kind. Although some left-wing critics have complained that Remarque underestimated the significance of the revolution, or rather failed to accord it the same degree of importance as did the Marxists, it is clear that for him the key feature of the revolution was that it set his fellow countrymen fighting against each other and brought war once again to the very doorstep of peaceful men and women. This he found abhorrent and unjustifiable.

Weil's fate marks the ultimate degradation of the notion of comradeship. Heel, a fearless soldier and in many ways an incipient Nazi, had always disliked the pacifist Jew, Max Weil, because of his hatred of war. He is angered by Weil's news of the Kaiser's flight and the revolution in Berlin, and at first refuses to give credence to the report. Later in the novel, when the revolution reaches his home town, Heel forms part of the defence force trying to quash the uprising, and has no hesitation in ordering his men to shoot the unarmed man who appears to be at the head of the procession. This man turns out to be Weil, who, in accordance with his principles of non-violence, had simply been trying to persuade the soldiers not to shoot at the crowd. It is typical irony on Remarque's part that it should be the pacifist Weil, who had been looking forward to days free from bloodshed, who is killed in peace-time. The wrong men, as is pointed out more than once in Remarque's novels, always suffer. The Nazi era is foreshadowed in this incident, not only because Weil is a Jew, but also because of Heel's whole attitude to the killing. Obviously in his element in a situation of war, where he can put his soldiering skills into practice with a clear conscience, Heel is curiously unmoved when he discovers that he has killed a former comrade: "That's not the point", he says, "all that matters is one goal: peace and order". (*Weg*, p.250) Heel regards the individual life as relatively unimportant.

The 'destruction of the concept of comradeship, both from outside and from within, leads Birkholz and his friends to look elsewhere for something in which to believe. One of the most sympathetic characters in the novel, and the one gifted with the greatest insight, is Ludwig Breyer. It is in him, and to some extent in Birkholz himself, that the hope of finding a "new beginning" is centered. Breyer, an excellent soldier and a respected lieutenant, popular because of his ability to be on friendly terms with his men without losing any of his dignity, is portrayed from the outset as a man of special qualities. He is brave, belittling his wounds and refusing to go to hospital — partly, admittedly, because of the low opinion he holds of these institutions (perhaps he had read *Im Westen nichts Neues!*), but partly also because he wishes to remain alongside his comrades. It is he who defies Heel after the shooting incident and marches into the line of fire in order to retrieve Weil's body. Breyer also serves as a calming influence, immediately quelling the noise in the school when he stands up to address the headmaster.

It is Ludwig Breyer, too, who acts as spokesman for the young soldiers, putting the feeling of his comrades into words. The siren voice of patriotism, which led himself and many others to volunteer for active service, was, Breyer suggests, propagated by ambitious diplomats and princes, who had no qualms about manipulating the youth of their country in order to attain their own selfish ends. Young men in their own country and elsewhere have, Breyer maintains, been deceived and misused, for instead of fighting for freedom as they believed, they have simply been destroying themselves and their own future:

> A generation has been destroyed! A generation of hope, faith, determin-
> ation, strength, ability, has been hypnotized, so that it came into conflict
> even though its goals were the same everywhere in the world! (*Weg*, p.199)

The bitterness which the "lost generation" feels is heightened by the fact that the ambitions which first sent the young men off to war are still preserved in the minds of those whose guidance they once sought, their parents and teachers.

Whereas Georg Rahe, who is equally aware of the mis-spent potential of his generation, opts for a form of escape in returning to the army, relinquishing any hope of being able to lead a successful life in post-war society, Breyer advocates working towards a new life. They are all determined that some good shall be salvaged from their experiences, but while the others cling to the concept of comradeship, an ideal which was engendered by the war to replace that of patriotism, Breyer sees the necessity of breaking away completely from anything directly associated with the war:

> "I think we are ill, Georg. We still have the war in our bones". Rahe nods. "And we'll never get rid of it again". "Yes we will", replies Ludwig, "because otherwise it would all have been in vain". (*Weg*, p.196)

Instead of looking back to the war, Breyer advocates working within society towards a new future. The real battles of life, he realizes, are not fought with guns: "There is only one single battle: that against lies, half-measures, compromises, old age!" (*Weg*, p.198) They had at first believed that their heroic efforts in the war would help to create a bright new future, but Breyer suggests that instead they were, in fact, engaged in upholding the very qualities which they despised and wished to eradicate.

However, it proves no easy task to turn one's back resolutely upon the war and bravely face the future. Somehow the war manages to intrude into every new beginning initiated by the men. When Trosske's bid to build a secure existence, free from the taint of the war, comes to such a disastrous end, even Breyer begins to despair:

> I think we are all lost . . . Everything is in vain, Ernst. We are finished, but the world goes on as if the war had never been. (*Weg*, p.270)

Even Breyer, with the best will in the world, is unable to escape the pernicious influence of the war, and he himself falls victim to its far-reaching consequences. He had contracted syphilis during his time as a soldier and, obsessed by the thought that he is unclean, he despairs of ever recovering. The tragedy of Trosske is the final blow, and after reminiscing with Birkholz about the Romantic literature which they read during their younger days and which contrasts so starkly with the harsh reality they have known, Breyer commits suicide by slashing his wrists.

As well as being one of his closest friends, Breyer represented to Birkholz the one hope of finding a way out of an intolerable situation, and the news of Breyer's death causes him to suffer a nervous breakdown. One of his first acts upon recovering is to visit Breyer's grave, where he experiences for the first time since the war a resurgence of life within him. The sensation is caused quite simply by a sudden appreciation of the peace and beauty of Nature, which is, as ever, oblivious to the sufferings of man. A gentle breeze is blowing over the graves, the sky is golden, and a blackbird is singing in a tree. For Birkholz, this represents the essence of life:

> Ludwig, for the first time I have felt today something like home and peace, and you are no longer with me. I still don't dare to believe it, I still think it must be weakness and tiredness — but perhaps it will one day become surrender, perhaps we only have to wait and be silent and it will come to us of its own accord; perhaps the only things which have not left us are our bodies and the earth, and perhaps we don't need to do anything but listen and follow them. (*Weg*, p.281)

Birkholz now concludes that instead of rushing frantically around trying to find goals in which to believe, a stance of patient acceptance should be adopted. Although he is as yet too disillusioned to believe fully in anything, he does tell Rahe that he felt something of the new beginning which Breyer seemed to have found but was prevented from developing because of his illness.

Birkholz's appreciation of Nature's indefatigable life-force is by no means a new one. Even in the midst of war, he had been aware that the same earth which formed men's graves was the source of an abundance of life, and his first sight of a peaceful landscape at the end of the war arouses both thankfulness and amazement that Nature has continued its course in spite of the traumatic events in the world of man:

> That there should still be all this: these colourful trees, the woods enveloped in a blue haze — woods, no longer tree stumps eaten away by grenades; this wind over the fields, without the smell of gunpowder and the stench of gas. (*Weg*, p.123)

The sight and smell of the earth feature prominently in *Der Weg zurück*, as in *Im Westen nichts Neues*, largely because the soldiers spent so much of their time in close proximity to the earth, pressed against it when under enemy fire. It also holds happier memories, however — memories from childhood, which Birkholz attempts to recapture by returning to Am Pappelgraben, Remarque's own favourite childhood haunt, where he, like Birkholz, caught sticklebacks and butterflies and lay dreaming under the trees.

Although the relationship between the life-force of Nature and that in man is no longer to be found in the haunts of childhood, whose magic has been destroyed by the war's rude interruption of Birkholz's youthful happiness, it is eventually re-established; and in the passage describing Birkholz's visit to Breyer's grave, where the word "earth" features seven times, he describes himself — by analogy with the graves — as "a hill without a name, meadow, earth". After this association with death, the earth seems to fill Birkholz with new life; he undergoes a kind of "rebirth", described in visionary terms:

> The silent streams of the earth circle up and down, and my blood circles with them; it is carried off and participates in everything . . . It circles and circles; it takes more and more of me with it. and washes it into the earth and the underground streams, slowly and without pain my body disappears, it's gone . . . But the movement increases. It becomes more regular, it passes into my breath and pulses . . . The earth washes against my body again — I open my eyes. (*Weg*, p.279)

This interflow of life between his body and the earth gives Birkholz new hope, and is the dominant theme of the final part of the novel.

The final chapter opens with a reference to spring and new growth:

> The earth smells of March and violets. Primroses peep out from under the damp foliage. The furrows in the fields are shimmering violet. (*Weg*, p.303)

The few remaining comrades are meeting, but the bond between them is no longer strong. Their peaceful walk is disturbed too by the sound of members of the German youth movement playing at soldiers, and they feel that all had indeed been in vain, that the war is about to start all over again.

The friends do, however, manage to find a refuge in the form of a peaceful country inn — a motif which recurs with variations in several of Remarque's later novels. Birkholz returns alone to the inn and spends a night there. He no longer fears the past, but feels a new assurance and sense of purpose. He had expected something dramatic to occur which would erase the dominance of the war, but instead it was simply the passage of time which gave him a new perspective. In spite of all the destruction which he has witnessed, he still has his own life, and has now learnt to value that and all the processes of growth which aid its development. Birkholz has now come to terms with the fact that life will not contain the kind of fulfilment which he had expected in his youth and that the "way back" will be a "way of work" which he will have to tread alone. There will be many obstacles along this path, but he will never again despair, he says, because there will always be something, "even if it's only my hands or a tree or the breathing earth". (*Weg*, p.311)

Drei Kameraden, begun in Berlin and completed during the first years of Remarque's enforced exile, pursues the fate of members of the "lost generation" through the inflationary years of the late 'twenties. Although critics once more complain that both the time-scheme and location of the novel are unclear, the many references to riots, unemployment, inflation, and the profusion of political parties holding clandestine meetings enable the reader to draw the conclusion that we are dealing with the Berlin of the 'twenties which Remarque knew at first hand.[14]

Again Remarque adheres to the by now established principle of including a fair measure of autobiographical material. The narrator's account of his early years includes a number of details from Remarque's own life. Robert Lohkamp recounts that his "real life" began in 1916 when, at the age of 18, he became a recruit; in 1917 he went to Flanders with Middendorf; in 1918 he was taken wounded to a field hospital; his mother died of cancer shortly after the end of the war; and in 1923 he became publicity manager for a rubber manufacturer. Lohkamp also shares Remarque's musical talent: he is employed in the evenings as pianist in a café frequented by a group of prostitutes headed by Rosa, know as the "Iron Horse". According to Rabe, this personage, who figures more prominently in *Der schwarze Obelisk,* actually did exist, nickname and all:

> The prostitute known as the "Horse" is well drawn; she really did live in the brothel at No. 75.[15]

And, hot on the heels of the Alsatian in *Der Weg zurück*, the Irish Setter which accompanied Remarque during his stay in the Hoberg house in Osnabrück where *Der Weg zurück* was written[16] finds his way into *Drei Kameraden.* "Billy" is a present from Lohkamp to his girlfriend, Pat, and keeps her company during her lengthy illness.

As its title suggests, *Drei Kameraden* continues to explore the theme of comradeship which figures so prominently in Remarque's two previous novels. In one sense, *Drei Kameraden* begins where *Der Weg zurück* ended: namely, with the realization that comradeship, while precious in itself, cannot restore to life the sense of purpose which the young soldiers lost during their years of active service in the First World War. As in *Der Weg zurück,* Remarque dwells upon the disillusionment of the young men who marched out full of ideals but returned

> without beliefs, like miners returning from a shaft which had caved in . . . We had become hard, with no trust in anything but the comrade next to us and in the only other things which had never deceived us: objects — sky, tobacco, trees and bread and earth — but what had become of that? Everything had collapsed, become falsified and forgotten. And for anyone who couldn't forget, there only remained impotence, despair, indifference and schnapps. (*Kameraden,* p.38)

Even that faith in natural objects which was regarded as a means of countering despair at the close of *Der Weg zurück* has now been abandoned, it seems, and only alchohol remains as an aid to oblivion.

Given this point of departure, it is hardly surprising to find the majority of critics again taking Remarque to task for his negative approach. Antkowiak indeed goes as far as accusing him of "nihilism", and finds more than an echo of Nietzsche in the narrator's assertion that the life of man has no particular purpose.[17] Although Antkowiak declares that Remarque's concept of comradeship has nothing in common with the Fascists' aggressive and fanatical interpretation of the term, if only because Remarque is so pessimistic,[18] he adopts a less charitable stance in an earlier review of Remarque's novel. Here Antkowiak claims that the concept of the Nietzschean Superman with its doctrine of murder and force originates in precisely the kind of hopelessness which Remarque presents. He further accuses Remarque — without any justification — of idealizing the rule of the mob instead of portraying a purposeful and progressive kind of comradeship:

> Remarque has never understood that true solidarity and comradeship can only flourish where a progressive common goal, life itself, forges mutual bonds.[19]

The only form of comradeship to be found in *Drei Kameraden,* according to Antkowiak, is completely negative, since it derives from an inability to cope with life.

Despite repeated assertions, Remarque was never able to convince his critics that his novels were not and did not aspire to be politically orientated. Adopting the same standpoint with *Drei Kameraden* as they did with *Der Weg zurück,* most critics take the view that if the novel is *not* political, then it ought to have been, given the time and place in which it was written. Antkowiak, who designates Remarque as "politically disorientated",[20] states that

Drei Kameraden must have come as a bitter disappointment to all the anti-Fascist German emigrants who shared Remarque's exile,[21] since it does not serve the anti-Nazi cause in the least: *"Drei Kameraden* is, so to speak, a perfect example of a literary work which avoids reacting to contemporary events".[22]

Remarque, it is true, does not name a single political party in the course of his novel, despite the fact that one of his main characters, Gottfried Lenz, regularly attends meetings of one undefined group. Indeed, it seems that even Lenz's two comrades are somewhat in the dark regarding his political activities, since they do not know which meeting he is attending when they wish to warn him of an impending police raid. Even when Lenz is murdered by a man from a rival party, we are told only that his murderer wears a uniform and yellow leggings. Antkowiak, after stating in his early review of *Drei Kameraden* that the killer (of Otto, he mistakenly writes, showing a similar confusion of characters as in his criticism of *Der Weg zurück*[23]) comes from a brawling Fascist gang,[24] in his book takes Ilja Fradkin to task for identifying the murderer as a Fascist: "How does Fradkin know that we are dealing with a Fascist murderer? It is certainly not evident from the text".[25]

Weiskopf, who finds such a lack of political awareness on Remarque's part equally infuriating, is wrong in asserting that Lenz's political interests are introduced out of the blue shortly before his murder:

> Suddenly we are surprised by the news that this main character is attending a political meeting — of what kind? — and is assassinated by opponents.[26]

We are, in fact, informed near the beginning of the novel that Lenz is attending a political meeting, rather to the surprise of his friends, who assume that he is attracted primarily by the novelty of the thing. Nor is it at all clear that Lenz is playing an active part at the meetings; his friends are concerned for his safety principally because his shock of red hair makes him such an easy target.

Remarque's strong aversion to nationalism is made clear, however, in his vignette of one of Lohkamp's fellow-lodgers, a civil servant, who makes trouble when a Russian — sympathetically drawn by Remarque — takes charge of a suicide victim in the lodging house. The civil servant declares that the Russian, as a foreigner, has no right to assume the responsibility in such a situation, particularly when he, a German national, is at hand. When Lohkamp suggests later that the official should apologize to the Russian for his rudeness, he receives the following outraged reply: "A German doesn't apologize! Especially to an Asiatic".

87

(*Kameraden*, p.201) By way of explanation for the transformation of this previously mild man into a fanatic who regards all foreigners as little better than vermin. Lohkamp is informed that the civil servant has in recent months been attending election meetings, again of an unspecified party, but clearly nationalistic in nature.

As for Remarque's avoidance of any direct political involvement, he had evidently made a conscious decision to stick to this policy, despite his own experiences at the hands of the Nazis during the writing of *Drei Kameraden*. As in *Der Weg zurück*, references to the revolution of 1919 express concern only for the fact that soldiers and comrades are taking up arms against each other, (*Kameraden*, p.9) and Remarque adopts an equally non-political stance with regard to the unrest described in *Drei Kameraden*:

> "Otto", I said to Köster, "now I know what the people want. They don't want politics. They want a substitute religion."
> He looked around. "Of course. They want to believe in something again. It doesn't matter what. That's why they're so fanatical."
> (*Kameraden*, p.232)

Remarque typically condemns fanaticism and extremism, whatever the political ideology that inspires it; his prime concern is with the cause of the unrest: namely, the loss of faith — religious as well as political — experienced during the war years. A chance encounter with a Catholic priest, who entreats Lohkamp to place his trust in God, leads the narrator to call to mind his many comrades from the war — again those like Katczinsky, Müller and Kemmerich from *Im Westen nichts Neues* — who were not helped by God in their hour of need: "Damn it all, rather too much blood has been shed in the world for this kind of belief in the heavenly Father!" (*Kameraden*, p.189) As well as making it impossible for Lohkamp to believe in a loving God, the memory of the gruesome deaths which his friends and millions like them have died also fills him with abhorrence at any continuation of the violence in the guise of political revolution.

Despite this pacifist viewpoint, however, it seems that there are, for Remarque, certain situations which call for violence as the only solution. In almost all his novels the motif of vengeance plays an important rôle. The beating which Himmelstoss receives in *Im Westen nichts Neues*[27] has a close parallel in *Der Weg zurück* with the thrashing of a former company sergeant — now the landlord of a pub — for his ill-treatment of a comrade. (*Weg*, pp. 96-97) In *Drei Kameraden* the motif occurs twice; first, in an altercation with a hotel porter, and secondly, in the avenging of Lenz's death. On both occasions the assistance of the authorities is spurned and revenge is made into a personal issue, for, in Remarque's view, the individual is ultimately responsible for his own destiny. Man, Lohkamp maintains, must fight for the things which he holds dear, and not simply submit to his fate:

> What's the point in being submissive? One has to pay for everything in life, twice and threefold. So why should one be submissive? . . . Submissive, I thought. What does that change? Fight, fight, that was the only way in this tussle, in which one was defeated in the end. Fight for the little that one loved. At seventy one could become submissive. (*Kameraden*, p.147)

In each of the vengeance episodes in *Drei Kameraden* a challenge to the dictates of fate plays some part. When Lohkamp has the opportunity of repaying in kind the beating he has received from a hotel porter, it is not only the thought of what he has suffered at the porter's hands which prompts him to unleash his anger, it is also the thought that the porter, a thoroughly despicable character, obviously enjoys the best of health and will probably never suffer from the tubercular disease which causes Lohkamp's girlfriend so much pain. His anger at this injustice becomes confused with his initial grievance, and Lohkamp has to be forcibly prevented from murdering the porter. After rendering his victim practically unconscious, Lohkamp announces that he now feels "much better". (*Kameraden*, p.164)

Similarly, when their comrade Lenz is killed, the reasons which prompt Lohkamp, and more particularly his friend Köster, to assume responsibility for avenging his death are by no means dictated solely by the bond of comradeship which had existed between the three. When Lohkamp proposes that they leave the matter in the hands of the police, Köster's reply recalls the attitude of Albert Trosske in *Der Weg zurück*. At his trial, Trosske had maintained that his shooting of his girlfriend's lover was far more justifiable than the killing he had been required to do during his time as a soldier because, while the men he had shot in the war had done nothing against him personally, the man who had stolen his girlfriend most decidedly had. In his reply to Lohkamp, Köster states that of all the men he killed during the war, he particularly recalls the frightened childlike face of a young Englishman:

> I didn't know the boy, and he had done nothing to me. It took longer than usual before I got over it and until I quietened my conscience with that damnable: war is war. But I tell you, if I don't also kill the man who killed Gottfried and who shot him down like a dog, then the incident with the Englishman was a terrible crime — do you understand that? (*Kameraden*, p.245)

Having once learnt the art of killing, in the cause of a remote and meaningless ideal, the ex-soldier Köster, like Trosske, regards it as natural and even essential to kill in defence of himself or his comrade — or as an act of revenge.

It has emerged from *Im Westen nichts Neues* and *Der Weg zurück* that the autonomous existence led by the soldiers during the war gave rise to a feeling of alienation from society and to a mistrust of civilian institutions. This attitude still prevails in *Drei Kameraden*: as Antkowiak and others have pointed out, the three comrades live a totally meaningless existence on the periphery of society.[28] All three work in the garage business which Köster owns, supplementing their income by driving an old taxi when times get hard — as they frequently do — and their sole ambition is to make enough money to meet their day-to-day needs. As another comrade, the painter Ferdinand Grau, explains to Lohkamp when the latter complains that everything they undertake seems doomed to failure, they all belong to a generation characterized by a futile longing but without real goals, to "the secret brotherhood which would rather go to the dogs than embark on a career", and would rather gamble life away than wipe out by hard work the memory of the days when all that mattered was the fact that they were still alive. (*Kameraden*, pp.217-18) Once again the war, during which life was lived so intensely, is held responsible for the present aimless existence the friends now lead, rejecting any aspiration towards a career and preferring instead to wander from bar to bar, consoling themselves with alcohol, which has by now become an inevitable feature of Remarque's novels. The "path of work" initiated in *Der Weg zurück* has now vanished without trace, and even Lenz, with his — presumably left-wing — political affiliations, scorns the very notion of knowing his way in life with the trite formula: "Goals render life bourgeois". (*Kameraden*, p.166) Even now, when the war is long since over, these men seek to justify their lack of direction by attributing it to a kind of euphoric gratitude that their own lives have been spared when so many others were lost. Grau's words make it evident that the comrades still have — and wish to retain — a pride in having lived through a "unique" experience which wrought such a fundamental change in their lives.

Valentin Hauser, another comrade from the war, spends his time in a state of more or less permanent inebriation, drinking toasts to various episodes from the war, all of which he recalls in minute detail. Lohkamp explains to his girlfriend that Hauser "no longer knows what he should do with his life — so he's just happy that he's still alive". (*Kameraden*, p.29) It is evident that Lenz shares this philosophy when he proposes the following toast:

Cheers, my friends! Because we're alive! Because we're breathing! Because we feel life so strongly that we no longer know what to do with it!
(*Kameraden*, p.218)

Early in the novel Lohkamp too dismisses a momentary sadness at the futility of his life with the words: "Nothing mattered – as long as one was alive"; (*Kameraden*, p.16) but it soon transpires that other things do matter, for the mere fact of being alive cannot compensate for the feeling of loneliness which is such a dominant theme in *Drei Kameraden*.

Ernst Birkholz, at the end of *Der Weg zurück*, realizes that, despite the bonds of friendship deepened by experiencing a common fate, the individual is in the last analysis thrown back upon his own resources. The optimism of *Der Weg zurück*, expressed in terms of man's relationship with Nature and the positive aspiration towards a new future, is lost in *Drei Kameraden*, where its place is taken by an uncompromising exploration of the individual's existential, as well as social, isolation. At the very outset of the novel, Lohkamp finds his solitude hard to endure, and longs for "a bit of warmth" in the shape of a female companion. (*Kameraden*, p.38) Each of the three comrades tries in his own way to escape from this sensation of loneliness: Lenz through politics, which results in his murder; Köster in his devotion to his car, which he finally has to sell; and Lohkamp through his love for Pat, who dies. Each attempt is abortive, and the end of *Drei Kameraden* is even gloomier than its opening, but Remarque explores each possibility with humour, sympathy, and a gift for engaging the emotions of his reader.

Only by taking life lightly, or by appearing to do so, can Lohkamp and his friends begin to overcome the feeling that human existence is absurd and futile:

If one didn't laugh about the twentieth century one would have to shoot oneself. But one couldn't laugh about it for long. Really it was enough to make one cry. (*Kameraden*, p.116)

Even the love between man and woman, which here emeges for the first time – but by no means the last – as a dominant theme, offers no hope of salvation. Indeed, it is his supposedly superficial treatment of this aspect of the novel which has attracted the bulk of the adverse criticism of *Drei Kameraden*. Weiskopf suggests that the influence of Hollywood has already penetrated into Remarque's world, since *Drei Kameraden* seems peopled with characters from the movie city and totally fails to reflect "real life", and, with more than a degree of hindsight, he describes the "heroine" Patrice Hollmann as "an improbable film-creature, half

Greta Garbo with consumption and half Elizabeth Bergner with lashings of cream".[29] Weiskopf does concede, however, that Pat's death scene reveals how much talent Remarque has, if only he would free himself from cheap sensationalism.[30]

Pat described by Remarque as "slight" and "elusive", "as if from another world", (*Kameraden*, p.27) certainly has an aura of unreality and insubstantiality, like all his subsequent heroines, but he has made her so with a particular intention in mind. Since the world he knows can offer no sense of purpose, Lohkamp turns to a woman who embodies a world which he has not previously encountered. Similarly Clerfayt, in *Der Himmel kennt keine Günstlinge,* is attracted to Lillian for precisely this reason: "You function according to different laws from the ones I know". (*Himmel*, p.166) The ephemeral beauty of Remarque's heroines in *Drei Kameraden* and *Der Himmel kennt keine Günstlinge* also heightens the poignancy of the illness which is eating their lives away. The contrast between their external glamour and the ugly disease within is underlined as Pat and Lillian carefully observe their decline in the mirror: their increasingly slender limbs may appear attractive, but each is aware that they mark the advance of disease.

Like most of Remarque's heroes, Lohkamp seeks in the love of a woman a means of escape from a drab existence. In an adroit turn of phrase, Lohkamp declares that "without love one is really just a corpse on leave". (*Kameraden*, p.65) However, the collapse of youthful ideals and the loss of so many friends in battle have generated a conviction that anything which promises happiness is inevitably suspect, and Lohkamp regards his love for Pat in the same light:

> The gap was too great; life had become too foul for happiness; it couldn't last; one no longer believed in it; it was a brief respite, but no haven. (*Kameraden*, p.185)

The fact that his relationship with Pat does bring him happiness, despite his cautious approach, only increases the fear that something will destroy what he has found:

> I knew only too well that all love has a desire for eternity and that this was its eternal torment. There was nothing which endured, nothing. (*Kameraden*, p.96)

The impermanence of human relationships is poignantly explored in *Drei Kameraden,* where Lohkamp's experiences in civilian life seem merely to underscore the lesson of the war; namely, that today's contentment can be overturned in a moment. Having once learnt to live from day to day, Lohkamp had become acutely aware of the tricks which time can play, and when Pat, in her dying hours, is disturbed by the sound of Lohkamp's watch ticking her life away, he flings it against a wall in a futile attempt to stop time altogether.

The passage of time, a dominant theme in Remarque's work, is often related to that of illness, which heightens man's consciousness of the brevity of life. In *Drei Kameraden*, and more particularly in the later *Der Himmel kennt keine Günstlinge,* illness also emphasizes the unreal and intangible qualities of the heroine, who inhabits the totally alien world of the invalid. In both *Drei Kameraden* and *Der Himmel kennt keine Günstlinge* this is symbolized by glimpses of life inside a sanatorium, which is both literally and figuratively far removed from the "average German town" where the main action takes place. The sanatorium high in the mountains has both a different climate and different habits and conventions from life elsewhere, and one cannot but recall Thomas Mann's *Der Zauberberg,* which undoubtedly influenced Remarque. Even the vocabulary employed by the patients has meanings unique to their own world; for example, the term "abgereist" ("gone away") is used (in both *Drei Kameraden* and *Der Himmel kennt keine Günstlinge*) when someone has died. The inhabitants of the sanatorium also behave very childishly, sneaking out behind the backs of their doctors for a night on the town, or playing silly pranks on the rare patient who recovers and is allowed to go home. The patients' perspective of life is often diametrically opposed to that of the healthy, and things normally regarded as trivial assume extraordinary importance, and vice versa. The point is also made in *Der Himmel kennt keine Güstlinge* that while tourists are attracted to the mountains and flock there for the skiing, the patients, ironically, are all longing to get out of their mountain prison, and would be happy never to see another snow-flake.

Illness serves a similar function to that of war in Remarque's novels, representing, as it does, a world apart, in which the constant threat of imminent death intensifies the individual's appreciation of life's simple pleasures and reduces his concern with the material problems which beset others. When Lohkamp expresses fears that his life-style is well below that which he feels Pat deserves, she merely throws her arms about his neck and exclaims: "Oh, you silly thing, how beautiful it is to be alive!" (*Kameraden,* p.120) Illness has the qualities which Grau attributed to war: a reduction of man's existence to the bare essentials of life and death. During a trip to Venice, where references to the river Styx and to gondolas resembling black coffins again suggest the influence of Thomas Mann,[31] the recovery of Lillian from a sudden illness leads her to make this observation:

> Someone who often escapes death is equally often born again, and each time with deeper gratitude, if only he gives up the illusion of having a claim on life. (*Himmel*, p.214)

This is scarcely a startling discovery, although Lillian appears to regard it as such, but it is certainly one which could easily have been made by one of the soldiers in *Im Westen nichts Neues* and *Der Weg zurück*. It is no coincidence that both Pat and Lillian contracted tuberculosis as a result of malnutrition during the war years. Like the male characters in the novels, they also suffer from the far-reaching effects of war.

In *Der Himmel kennt keine Günstlinge* the threat of death is doubly present as Clerfayt, a professional racing driver, also risks his life daily. Lillian leaves the sanatorium with Clerfayt to return to the "lost paradise" of the world outside (*Himmel*, p.34) although she knows that in so doing she is shortening her own life. The two of them are united by the desire to "live for the moment" and, in the words of Gresinger, the "message" of the novel appears to be that "the length of one's life matters less than the fact that it is lived with consciousness and mental activity".[32] The more cynical would doubtless find much to criticize in the particular form of "intense living" which the two adopt: Lillian devotes an inordinately large proportion of her few remaining weeks of life to choosing dresses in Paris, while food and drink — rarely absent for long in a Remarque novel — seem to occupy most of the waking hours of both Clerfayt and Lillian.

Although Lillian condemns motor racing for toying with the precious gift of life, it is really the fact that Clerfayt lives from one race to the next which attracts her to him, and when he begins to talk of giving up racing, marrying Lillian and settling down in a house in Toulouse, she decides that the time has come to leave him. She realizes too that her own life closely resembles one of Clerfayt's races in that it is a race against time from which she is trying to extract as much mileage as she can. (*Himmel*, p.254) With typical irony it is, in fact, the healthy Clerfayt who dies first and not the fatally ill Lillian. Clerfayt is killed in an accident immediately after he has made up his mind to give up racing and build a secure future for himself with Lillian, not knowing that she is intending to leave him. The irony is complete when Lillian, returning to the sanatorium at the end of the novel, meets Clerfayt's former partner Hollmann (who shares his surname with

Pat of *Drei Kameraden*), now cured of his illness, leaving the sanatorium to take Clerfayt's place as a racing driver.

Remarque's interest in motor racing derives from his days with Conti, mentioned *en passant* in *Der Himmel kennt keine Günstlinge* as one of the teams taking part in a race. (*Himmel*, p.256) Although *Der Himmel kennt keine Günstlinge* (dedicated to Paulette Goddard Remarque) was published in 1961, it is generally regarded as a reworking of *Station am Horizont.* Antkowiak, for example, states that it seems to belong to the period *before Im Westen nichts Neues,* despite the fact that the events described supposedly take place after the Second World War,[33] and Sieburg summarizes the general critical response when he writes: "This novel is the weakest of all the feeble books which the world-famous author has published".[34] Although Remarque's dialogue in *Der Himmel kennt keine Günstlinge* is masterly and he manages to end almost every short section of the novel with a well-turned phrase, it is true that a charge of superficiality would on this occasion be difficult to refute.

While Clerfayt's own car, "Guiseppe", has only a minor part in *Der Himmel kennt keine Günstlinge,* its counterpart in *Drei Kameraden,* named "Karl", plays quite an important rôle. "Karl" is a strange-looking hybrid which Köster has converted into a racing car and in which he and his friends delight in challenging more orthodox machines to races on the public highway As well as consoling the comrades when things are going badly, the car also fulfils a number of specific functions. "Karl" is the means whereby they encounter Pat (she is a passenger in a rival car); it brings medical aid to Pat when her life is in danger; it carries Lenz to hospital, then assists in the hunt for his killer; and finally it furnishes the money to prolong Pat's stay in the sanatorium. The car's fate is carefully plotted: we are informed at the outset of the novel that a business man named Bollwies, having witnessed the performance of the car, is very keen to buy it, but that Köster "wouldn't sell it for any money on earth". (*Kameraden*, p.11) Remarque describes with obvious relish the private races — invariably won by "Karl" — and the dramatic chase through the fog when Köster brings a rather frightened medical specialist to the aid of Pat. The car participates in all the major events of the novel and rapidly assumes the proportions of a fourth comrade. Shortly after the death of Lenz "Karl" too is sacrificed (to Bollwies) in order to raise money for Pat and Lohkamp to stay in the sanatorium, even though Köster knows that Pat will not recover and that his gesture is, therefore, futile. The garage business flounders, and at the end of the novel Lohkamp and Köster are left penniless and alone.

When Lohkamp inveighs against God, "Karl" is even included (somewhat improbably) alongside Lohkamp's dead friend and sick girlfriend:

> Lenz was dead. Karl was gone. And Pat? With blinded eyes I stared into the heavens, those grey, endless heavens of an insane God, who had invented life and death to amuse himself. (*Kameraden*, p.263)

Lohkamp's remarks are scarcely calculated to reassure those readers still searching for something positive in Remarque, and his discussion with Pat on the subject of life after death is equally unlikely to prove a source of inspiration. Even Nature's rich pattern of growth, eulogized in *Der Weg zurück*, now seems to have lost any meaning it may have possessed. When Lohkamp suggests that the world cannot come to an end because it is so badly made, Pat points to a bush of yellow roses:

> "That's just it," I replied. "The details are wonderful, but the whole has no meaning. As if it's made by someone who could think of nothing else to do with the wonderful variety of life but to destroy it again."
> "And to create it anew," said Pat.
> "I don't see any sense there either," I replied.
> "It's not become any the better for it up to now." (*Kameraden*, p.273)

Instead of the possibility of a bond existing between man and Nature, as in *Der Weg zurück*, Nature's beauty now seems only to offer a contrast, and to portray a form of eternal life which is denied to humanity. While mankind is the plaything of God, the birds in the branches of the trees in the cemetry sing "like tiny silver pipes of the dear Lord". (*Kameraden*, pp.17-18) It is no coincidence that Lohkamp first learns of Pat's illness during an idyllic week's holiday in a beautiful natural setting: it almost seems as if there is one God for Nature, and another, more malicious, for man.

The weighty subject of man's relationship with the Almighty and the bearing which this has on the life and death of the individual is explored in greater depth in one of Remarque's most significant novels, *Der schwarze Obelisk*, which was published in 1956, but is set in the Germany of the early 'twenties. Like the image of the black coffins in *Der Himmel kennt keine Günstlinge*, the black obelisk (in fact, a memorial stone) is a symbol of death, and furnishes the novel with a *leitmotif* which provides much of the humour characteristic of the work. Remarque's style and technique are here at their keenest, and his cynical humour has been compared — with more than a little justification — with that of Oscar Wilde.[35] Nor could anyone complain, on this occasion, of any lack of precision on Remarque's part in regard to time and place: the first sentence of the novel sets the scene in the monumental masons' Heinrich Kroll and Sons (the fictional parallel to the Vogt firm in Osnabrück where Remarque was employed for a time), and the second informs the reader that it is April 1923.

Der schwarze Obelisk is Remarque's most overtly autobiographical novel: the age of the first person narrator is given as twenty-five, Remarque's own age in 1923; (*Obelisk,* p.24) reference is made to his birth in the town's charity maternity unit and to the poverty of his family; (*Obelisk,* pp.358-59) his time as a schoolmaster is mentioned twice; (*Obelisk,* p.29 and p.265) and various of Remarque's possessions — notably his piano and his butterfly collection — also find their way into the novel. Remarque's various literary activities too play their part in *Der schwarze Obelisk*: the narrator, Ludwig Bodmer, is a member of a literary circle, and has had some poems published in the local newspaper. Like Remarque too, Bodmer leaves his job at the monumental masons' when he is offered a job with a newspaper.

Remarque makes little attempt to disguise Osnabrück (Werdenbrück in the novel).[36] As well as a description of the Süsterstrasse, the location of the Vogt firm and the house of the Hoberg family (called Hohmann in the novel), street-names like the Hakenstrasse and the Grosse Strasse, already familiar from *Der Weg zurück,* reappear in *Der schwarze Obelisk.*

Like many of his other novels, *Der schwarze Obelisk* has two parallel settings, this time the town and a mental institution on the outskirts of Werdenbrück where Bodmer — again like Remarque — plays the organ at Sunday church services. The distinction between the town and the institution (which, like the sanatorium in *Drei Kameraden* and *Der Himmel kennt keine Günstlinge,* is far removed from such worldly considerations as the dollar crisis) is underlined by the fact that Remarque adopts a far more serious tone in the sequences in the mental institution than in the rest of the novel. At the institution Bodmer has many a discussion with the priest and *bon viveur* Bodendiek,[37] and also learns something of the inmates from the doctor, Wernicke. Remarque's portrayal of mental sickness is extremely sympathetic, and, according to one psychiatrist at least, also very accurate.[38]

The principal love-theme in *Der schwarze Obelisk* takes the form of a relationship between Bodmer and one of the patients in the mental home, a schizophrenic who goes by the name of Isabelle, and who is another elusive beauty along the lines of Pat and Lillian. Once again, the relationship proves doomed, ending, on this occasion, not in death but, ironically, with the recovery of the heroine, who then forgets all that has passed between herself and Bodmer.

The "rarefied" atmosphere of the mental institution furnishes a backcloth for Remarque's most philosophical observations on life, death and religion, primarily in conversations between Bodmer and Bodendiek, or between Bodmer and Isabelle. However, the narrator's questioning of the meaning of life is an underlying theme throughout the novel, despite his deceptive lightness of touch.

Although a lack of direction in the lives of the narrator and his associates is as evident in *Der schwarze Obelisk* as in Remarque's earlier novels, Bodmer shows a far more active desire to find some kind of purpose for his existence. Indeed, he questions everyone, from the coffin-maker Wilke to the bookseller Arthur Bauer, about the meaning of life, but — hardly surprisingly perhaps — receives no satisfactory answer:

> It seems to be the same with "truth" and the meaning of life as with hair tonics — each firm praises its product as the only true one . . . If there were really a hair tonic which made hair grow, then there would only be the one, and the others would have gone bankrupt long since. (*Obelisk*, p.104)

Bodmer half envies and half despises those who do have clearly defined patterns of existence, such as the bookseller's self-imposed rôle of shop-keeper, husband and father, or the doctor and priest at the mental home with their respective scientific and theological interpretations of life's problems. In an organized existence, says Bodmer, even the horrific can be classified and thereby rendered less dangerous, for "only the Nameless kills", (*Obelisk*, p.91) and yet Bodmer find himself unable to accept any of the philosophies of life with which he is confronted.

References to a "nameless fear" abound in Remarque's work, and particularly in *Der schwarze Obelisk*, where Bodmer seeks salvation both in a woman and also in religion. Like all of Remarque's central figures, Bodmer has a dread of being alone, and he greatly values the companionship of a woman. He is also aware, however, that the individual is ultimately thrown back on his own resources:

> "Come, Isabelle. No one knows what he is or where he is going — but we are together, that is all that we can know" . . .
> Perhaps there really is nothing else, I think, when everything falls into decay, but the bit of being together; and even that is a gentle deception, for when the other person really needs you, you can't follow them . . . Everyone has his own death and has to die it alone, and no one can help. (*Obelisk*, pp.82-83)

The mystical nature of these observations sets the tone for the relationship between Bodmer and Isabelle, which is far more spiritual than any other man-woman relationship in Remarque's work.

Discussions between Isabelle and Bodmer often turn to religion, and the schizophrenic Isabelle shares Bodmer's intangible fears as well as his scepticism of the religious establishment. The priests, says Isabelle, have nailed God on the cross and locked Him up in the chapel so that they can live off His wealth. (*Obelisk*, p.253) If they ever let Him out, she adds, they would have to nail Him to the cross again:

> "Yes", I say, "I believe that too. They would kill Him again; the same who pray to Him today. They would kill Him just as they have killed many in His name. In the name of justice and brotherly love". (*Obelisk*, p.255)

Bodmer, like Remarque, finds it difficult to reconcile the Church's doctrine of brotherly love with its evident condoning of killing in the name of war, and elsewhere rebukes the Catholic priest Bodendiek for having — with his Protestant colleagues — given the blessing of the Church to the Great War instead of condemning it. (*Obelisk*, p.170)

Bodmer also discusses, with both Isabelle and Bodendiek, the age-old problem of reconciling the concept of a loving God with human suffering, both in war and in illness. Bodmer becomes particularly bitter when talking with Bodendiek about the painful illness and death of his mother (another autobiographical reference by Remarque). When she lost two of her children, Bodmer says, she eventually came to doubt in God, and therefore, in the eyes of the Catholic Church, she died in a state of sin. (*Obelisk*, p.87) God may be the God of love, he adds, but it is

> a love which is filled with sadism. A love which torments and causes misery and thinks it can correct the terrible injustice in the world with the promise of an imaginary heaven. (*Obelisk*, p.88)

The sight of the kindly but complacent priest calmly enjoying his food and wine serves only to fuel Bodmer's anger. Bodendiek, on the other hand, remains imperturbable and appears to have an answer to everything. Like generals, says Bodmer, priests are without the doubts and fears of ordinary men and consequently live to a ripe old age. (*Obelisk*, p.239)

It seems to Bodmer that the mental patients, with all their neuroses, are often far closer to the truth in their observations on life than either their priest or their equally self-assured doctor. While the priest and doctor are still very much a part of the world outside the institution, the patients' circumscribed world, together with their illness, leads them to question the fundamental problems of man's existence, (*Obelisk*, p.188) and — with typical irony — Remarque frequently makes the ramblings of the insane appear far more meaningful than much that happens in the supposedly "normal" society outside. Indeed, Isabelle frequently makes such astute observations that Bodmer finds it difficult to believe that she is ill at all.

It is also significant that during her illness Isabelle gives up going to chapel, refusing to believe that the man there depicted with a beard and bleeding limbs is really God. After her recovery, however, she goes to mass every day, also reverting to her real name of Geneviève Terhoven. Both the doctor and the priest are delighted with her recovery, therefore, but Bodmer's attitude is quite different:

> Isabelle! I think. She knew once that God was still hanging on the cross and that not only the unbelievers martyred Him. She knew and despised the smug believers who made a fat sinecure from His sufferings. (*Obelisk*, pp.339-40)

As far as he is concerned, Isabelle, who once represented life, has now died: "Farewell, Isabelle . . . Farewell, life!" (*Obelisk*, p.344) For Bodmer, bidding farewell to Isabelle means that he is also bidding farewell to his own youth, but he does feel that he has also learnt something from the experience. In fact, when asked shortly after Isabelle's recovery by the ever-optimistic Bodendiek whether he has been "looking for God", Bodmer replies: "No. I've found Him". (*Obelisk*, p.345) The "God" he has found is not the God of Bodendiek, however, but a concept of eternity similar to that expressed in Remarque's earlier works. Bodmer had earlier told Isabelle:

> "Nothing which is there can be lost. Never."
> "Do you believe that?"
> "There's nothing left for us but to believe it."
>
> (*Obelisk*, p.248)

And now that she has gone, he addresses the following words to her in his imagination:

> You have suddenly become invisible like the old gods, a wavelength has altered, you are still there, but you cannot be held any more, you are still there and will never be lost; everything is still there, nothing is ever lost; it is just that light and shade pass over; it is still there, the face before birth and after death, and sometimes it shines through in that which we call life, and blinds us for a second and we are never the same afterwards.
>
> (*Obelisk*, p.344)

The image of light as a symbol of the eternal is touched upon again when, at a farewell party given by his literary circle just before Bodmer leaves for Berlin, a fellow-poet asks him as what he will go into the world. Bodmer's reply incorporates the title of another of Remarque's novels (*Der Funke Leben*): "As a small spark of life which will try not to go out". (*Obelisk*, p.370)

As far as the more orthodox religions are concerned, Bodmer appears to cherish a certain sympathy with the Gnostics, and when Bodendiek asks him, in astonishment, what he knows of them, Bodmer replies:

> Enough to suspect that they were the more tolerant part of Christianity. And all that I have so far learnt in my life is to value tolerance. (*Obelisk*, p.170)

Remarque too always prized tolerance above all else and there is no doubt that Bodmer is speaking for him when, in the course of the same conversation with Bodendiek, he comments upon the intolerance prevalent in Germany at the time. (*Obelisk*, p.171) Bodmer's main quarrel with the established Churches is their lack of sympathy for the viewpoint of others, and he accuses the Catholic Church in particular of being a dictatorship. (ibid.) Dr Wernicke, who holds similar views about Catholicism, later remarks to Bodmer: "Don't undervalue the wisdom of the Church! It's the only dictatorship which hasn't been toppled for two thousand years." (*Obelisk*, p.177)

Watching a Catholic and a Protestant priest blessing a war monument, "each for his God", (*Obelisk*, p.114) Bodmer reflects upon the dilemma of God, to whom prayers for victory in war would be directed from a variety of countries and faiths:

> I imagined God as a kind of distraught Club Chairman in a hurry, particularly when two enemy lands of the same faith were praying. Which should He decide in favour of? For the one with the most inhabitants? Or the one with the most churches? Or where was His justice, if He let one land win but not the other, although they had prayed there just as assiduously? (*Obelisk*, p.114)

Bodmer imagines God as an overworked old emperor, rapidly changing robes from one religion to another, according to which kind of service is being held at any one time.

Remarque highlights the rivalry between the Protestant and Catholic Churches in an episode which has a characteristic blend of "black" humour and social criticism. A woman whose twins have recently died asks for a double coffin for them, but problems arise over the funeral because of the different religions of the parents — one twin has been christened a Catholic and the other a

Protestant. The coffin-maker Wilke predicts that the priests concerned will be unwilling to take part in the same funeral service: "They are more jealous of the dear Lord than we are of our women". (*Obelisk*, p.263) Although the woman eventually succeeds in having the twins buried together, it is only after she has gone to the expense of purchasing another grave in the town cemetry, as she is refused permission to bury the Protestant twin in the Catholic burial ground. Bodmer is horrified too when he discovers that a Catholic suicide victim, whose poverty has driven him to take his own life, cannot be buried in consecrated ground. Bodmer tries to console the distraught widow who, having been told by the priest that her husband died in a state of mortal sin, has visions of him burning in Hell for eternity. He tells her: "God is much more merciful than the priests". (*Obelisk*, p.66)

Although Remarque has been much criticized for not making adequate reference to contemporary events, he is certainly not guilty in regard to the problems of Germany in the inflation years of the 'twenties. The poverty of Remarque's own early years had impressed upon him the value of money and the privations caused by its absence. Some of the consequences of the inflation are touched upon in *Drei Kameraden*, where, for example, the marriage of two of Lohkamp's fellow lodgers is wrecked for want of money, which causes the wife to leave home and the husband to commit suicide:

> It was the need for a measure of security and a little money which was destroying this marriage and this gentle, modest life. I reflected that there were millions of such people and that it was only ever the little bit of security and the little bit of money. Life was bound up in a terrifying way with the miserable battle for bare existence. (*Kameraden*, p.185)

Equally pitiful is the spectacle of crowds of unemployed in the betting shops, engaged in a pathetic attempt at making their fortunes and instead fainting with hunger. (*Kameraden*, p.178) Similarly, when Pat and Lohkamp visit a museum one Sunday — to indulge in one of Remarque's own passions, viewing an exhibition of Persian carpets — they likewise encounter a crowd of the unemployed, who are seeking shelter and a little diversion there. Lohkamp is struck by the contrast between the great artistic achievements of mankind and his inability to ensure that his fellows can enjoy the means of day-to-day subsistance. (*Kameraden*, pp.195-96)

Inflation in Germany inevitably plays an even greater rôle in *Der schwarze Obelisk*, and one of Bodmer's first acts is to set fire to a ten Mark note in order to light a cigar, so worthless has the money become. (*Obelisk*, p.8) Bodmer, like many others, is obliged to request a daily pay-rise in order to meet the rapidly escalating cost of living, and Georg Kroll brings a suitcase full of notes as petty cash for a couple of days, and tosses over bundles of notes to Bodmer so that he can buy a new tie. (*Obelisk*, pp.11-12) Remarque does not fail to touch on inflation's more tragic sides too, the suicides and the strikes:

> There was only one suicide yesterday, but two strikes. After long negotiations the officials have received a wage-rise which in the meanwhile has already been devalued so much that they can now scarcely buy a litre of milk a week with it. Next week it'll probably just be a box of matches. The number of unemployed has risen by another 150,000.
> (*Obelisk*, pp.195-96)

Things finally reach such a peak that the bank-rate changes hourly, (*Obelisk*, p.207) and the workers are paid twice a day, then given half an hour off to buy food before the value of their money depreciates further. (*Obelisk*, p.241)

As a result of his occupation, Bodmer is frequently brought face to face with widows who cannot afford to pay funeral expenses or with the tragic situation of suicide victims like an old couple who, finding their attempt to commit suicide by gas thwarted because the gas has been turned off due to unpaid bills, hang themselves with lengths of clothes line, leaving an apologetic note to the man who has bought the wardrobe in which their bodies are found. (*Obelisk*, p.140) But for Bodmer, the saddest victims of the inflation are the war-wounded, whose pensions have become practically worthhless, despite occasional belated supplementation by the government. (*Obelisk*, p.241) Bodmer contrasts their sad procession of protest with the war profiteers who sound the horns of their luxurious limousines in impatience at the cripples in their path. (*Obelisk*, pp.241-42) Bodmer accuses the government of deliberately allowing inflation to run its course as a means of wiping out its own debts, despite the toll it takes in human lives. (*Obelisk*, p.213)

Indeed, it oftens appears to Bodmer and his friends that things are even worse in the days of post-war inflation than they were during the war itself. Georg Kroll comments:

> The war has been over four and a half years . . . At that time we became human beings through terrible misfortune. Today the shameless hunt for possessions has made us robbers again. (*Obelisk*, pp.10-11)

Peace, it seems, is merely the continuation of war by other means. In his preamble to *Der schwarze Obelisk*, Remarque makes clear his own humanitarian and pacifist principles as he gives his reasons for returning to the days of the 1920's. Maintaining that the twentieth century has heard more discussion of peace than any other, but to less effect, Remarque adds:

> So don't complain if I return to the legendary years when hope still wafted over us like a flag and we believed in things as suspect as humanity, justice and tolerance — and also believed that *one* world war must be sufficient lesson for a generation.

Remarque further expresses his amazement that, even after two world wars, factories should be producing, in the name of upholding the peace, weapons which could destroy the whole world many times over.

To the undoubted dismay of Marxist critics, Remarque continues to regard the 1918 revolution as an extension of the war, and cynically observes that the revolutionaries themselves were so frightened that they enlisted the aid of generals from their former regiments who proceeded to kill large numbers of people and were given pensions for doing so. (*Obelisk*, p.24) The novel contains several passages condemning any form of war, notably a description of a ceremony attending the erection of a war-memorial to those who had fallen in the 1914-1918 war. The severest criticism is reserved for Major Wolkenstein, and anti-Semitist who only reluctantly agrees to the inclusion of the names of two Jewish soldiers on the memorial, and even then places them at the very bottom of the stone, where "the dogs will probably piss on it". (*Obelisk*, p.112) The ex-servicemen's association, of which Wolkenstein is the head, was a pacifist organization in 1918, but is now distinctly nationalistic in tone. Wolkenstein himself appears at the ceremony in full imperial dress, asserting that anyone who is not nationalistic is betraying the memory of the fallen heroes. Bodmer, on the other hand, maintains that these same dead heroes would gladly knock Wolkenstein from his podium, were they in a position to do so. He bitterly resents the fact that the defenceless dead have become "the property of thousands of Wolkensteins", who exploit them to their own ends, which are dressed up in terms like "patriotism":

> Patriotism! Wolkenstein understands by that wearing a uniform again, becoming a colonel, and once more sending people to their deaths.
> (*Obelisk*, p.113)

Bodmer's comments upon the way in which the attitudes of many soldiers towards the war have changed cannot but recall the experiences of Remarque's own "heroes" in *Der Weg zurück* and *Drei Kameraden*:

> The war, which almost all soldiers hated in 1918, has gradually been transformed into the biggest adventure of their lives for those who survived it. (*Obelisk*, p.112)

Everyday life, he adds, seemed like paradise when they were at war; now, in peace-time, war is similarly endowed with charms it did not possess and seems glorious in the abstract.

Heinrich Kroll, Georg's brother and a partner in the firm, is another nationalist of the Wolkenstein school, and is equally unsympathetically portrayed by Remarque. Heinrich Kroll subscribes to the Wolkenstein view that the Jews were largely responsible for Germany's defeat in the Great War, though he also apportions some blame to the likes of Bodmer:

> "There you see it," says Heinrich bitterly to Riesenfeld. "That's how we lost the war. Through the slovenliness of the intellectuals and through the Jews."
> "And the cyclists," adds Riesenfeld.
> "Why the cyclists?" asks Heinrich in astonishment.
> "Why the Jews?" retorts Riesenfeld. (*Obelisk*, p.232)

As well as making Heinrich the butt of other characters in the novel, as a result of which his political opinions appear as ridiculous as Heinrich himself, Remarque also invites criticism of the nationalist cause by portraying its followers as ruthless exploiters of the innocent.

In one episode, for example, Heinrich and his National Socialist friends take advantage of a postman whose mind has become deranged by continually having to deliver tragic news during the war, the final blow coming when the postman's own two sons were killed. To compensate for all the sad news he has brought, the postman now collects and delivers all the letters and postcards he can find, imagining them to be from Russian concentration camps, where soldiers supposed dead are, in fact, still alive and will soon be returning to their families. Heinrich and his friends use the unfortunate postman to send abusive letters to their political opponents and also to send obscene missives to various women in their neighbourhood. However, when Bodendiek receives one of the obscene letters in error, he lies in wait for the culprits at the rendezvous designated in the note, knocks together the heads of the two men who turn up to keep the appointment, and then forces them to go to confession each week, on pain of excommunication. Every week he extracts promises from them that they will follow the path of virtue, and eventually succeeds in completely reforming them. A third man, however, avoids the priest's wrath, and he — it is none other then the infamous Wolkenstein — far from repenting of his behaviour, goes from bad to worse and eventually becomes a Nazi stalwart.

The terrorism and intimidation which accompanied the rise to power of the National Socialists is vividly portrayed in *Der schwarze Obelisk*. After the dedication of the war memorial, a joiner who displays a Republican flag is condemned by Wolkenstein as a traitor, despite the fact that he was wounded in the war defending his country. The joiner is later attacked and severely injured by Wolkenstein's party, and even when the man dies as a result of these injuries, none of the witnesses to the crime has the courage to tell the police who has done it, so great is the fear of retribution.

A favourite ploy of the young National Socialists is to request the national anthem from restaurant bands at thirty minute intervals and demand that everyone stands up. When Bodmer and his friends refuse to do so, they too are branded as Bolshevists and are only able to escape uninjured from a restaurant under the escort of a choral society similar to the one referred to in *Drei Kameraden* whose leader is a certain Bodo Ledderhose. On another occasion, Bodmer and a few friends, among them a war-cripple, are again attacked by a large procession of the same young National Socialists, who are attired in para-military uniforms. Once again the National Socialists are put to flight with the assistance of the choral society, after having been thoroughly scared by the spectacle of the cripple swinging his artificial arm around his head. One of the attackers turns out to be the butcher, Watzeck, who lives opposite the Krolls' stonemasonry. Like Wolkenstein, Watzeck subsequently becomes a staunch Nazi in the Second World War, and, having discovered that his wife, Lisa, had once had an affair with Georg Kroll, he exploits his authority to have him placed in a concentration camp, where he dies. (*Obelisk*, p.383)

In general, however, the theme of revenge in *Der schwarze Obelisk* is treated in a far more light-hearted vein than in most of Remarque's other novels. In the opening pages we meet Ludwig Bodmer incorporating the names of people he dislikes — usually officers from his war-days — into his drawings of gravestones, complete with mourning widows. A certain Karl Flümer is accorded a particularly nasty death:

> That was not without justification. The man had treated me very badly and in the field had twice sent me on patrols from which I'd only by chance come back alive. (*Obelisk*, p.17)

Bodmer's friend Willy (red-headed like the Willy in *Der Weg zurück*) entertains similar feelings towards the unfortunate

Flümer, but has a different way of avenging himself. Willy's girlfriend, Renée de la Tour, has the unusual gift of being able to imitate an army officer giving a command, and Willy — extending the army image — imagines when he makes love to Renée that he is violating Flümer (*Obelisk*, p.109) or a lieutenant Helle, who also made his army life a misery. (*Obelisk*, p.211)

Renée also comes in useful in the "Walhalla" restaurant belonging to the former soldier Eduard Knobloch.[39] Bodmer and Georg Kroll, having bought up hundreds of meal vouchers from the "Walhalla" before the inflation rendered them impractical, are now obtaining meals at the prices of several months ago, and Knobloch is naturally reluctant to serve food at such a loss to himself. He has therefore instructed his waiters to ignore them, but a booming baritone command from Renée fetches not only the waiter but also Knobloch himself, who is completely mystified about where the voice has come from.

Der schwarze Obelisk is full of colourful characters, and a lady who possesses an even more bizarre talent than Renée de la Tour is Frau Beckmann, housekeeper and mistress of the shoemaker Karl Brill. To a piano accompaniment by Bodmer, Frau Beckmann extracts a nail from a wall with her ample buttocks, while Brill takes bets against her being able to perform the feat. (*Obelisk*, pp.177-83 and pp.332-36)

Another colourful personality is a near neighbour of Bodmer's, sergeant Knopf, who has the habit of relieving himself against the black obelisk of the book's title when he returns from his local bar. Bodmer's constant battle to preserve the obelisk forms a *leitmotif* throughout the novel. When reasoning and buckets of water have no effect, Bodmer adopts a more dramatic course of action and instills the fear of God into Knopf by speaking to him through lengths of drain-pipe. Terrified by the apparently subterranean voice, Knopf returns home leaving the obelisk unsullied. (*Obelisk*, p.197)

This is not the end of the matter, however, as Knopf returns — rather cautiously — only to hear a disembodied voice announce the worst of all fates, his demotion: "A true Teuton would rather have a finger cut off than have his title taken from him". (*Obelisk*, p.259) Shortly afterwards, Knopf becomes ill, and when it seems as if he is going to die, Bodmer contemplates putting the obelisk on his grave. However, after his wife and daughters have spent days making mourning clothes, Knopf — who continues drinking despite his doctor's orders — suddenly gets up and walks downstairs, furious that money has been wasted on black clothes:

Since no one had told him that he was mortally sick, and his wife, out of

> fear of him, hadn't fetched a priest who could have prepared him for
> eternal blessedness, it hadn't occurred to Knopf to die. (*Obelisk*, p.324)

When Bodmer and his colleagues reassure Knopf that, because of
the inflation, he has in fact gained over the mourning clothes, he
also tries to do business with his gravestone — which his wife had
ordered, but not paid for. Knopf buys the gravestone, then tries
(unsuccessfully) to sell it back immediately at a profit. When
Knopf later makes a further assault on the obelisk, Bodmer tells
him to use his own gravestone. Knopf is scandalized that something so valuable should be employed for such a purpose, and
from then on is cured:

> What no one had succeeded in doing, the simple concept of ownership
> had achieved! The sergeant uses his own toilet. Let some Communist
> try and interfere with that! Ownership gives a sense of order! (*Obelisk*,
> p.337)

As for the obelisk, Bodmer — very fittingly — sells the stone,
which had long been considered unsaleable, on his last day with
the Kroll firm, thus marking the end of an era in his life.
Appropriately enough, the obelisk finds a home on the grave of
the celebrated prostitute, the Iron Horse. The prostitutes are again
depicted in a very positive light. As schoolboys Bodmer and his
friends had often visited the brothel, under the impression that it
was a bar, and had drunk lemonade with the prostitutes, who had
helped them with their homework and, according to Bodmer, been
far more strict with them than their own parents. Years later,
when Bodmer and Willy go to the brothel with the intention of
availing themselves of the prostitutes' more usual services, the
women are horrified when they recognize the young men and
refuse to have anything to do with them, saying it would be like
the boys violating their own mothers. Again, unlike many of the
bereaved, whose newspaper notices often belie actual sentiments,
the prostitutes are genuinely grieved at the death of their colleague,
the Iron Horse, and Bodmer comments: "I have never seen such
loyalty and faith as here". (*Obelisk*, p.376) For Remarque, the
prostitutes represent the poor and oppressed, who earn a living the
only way they can, and who never really profit from life.

It is a characteristic feature of many of Remarque's novels that
it is the most humane who are the ones to suffer while the villains
live on, and this is underlined at the end of *Der schwarze Obelisk*,
when Remarque gives a brief synopsis of the fates of some of the
main characters. Most of Bodmer's friends end up in concentration

camps, while people of Wolkenstein's ilk not only become prominent Nazis but also evade prosecution after the war and live on in prosperity. The fate of the town itself is similar: most of Werdenbrück — like Osnabrück — is destroyed by bombs in the Second World War, leaving very few of the places Bodmer loved; but two buildings escape completely — the mental home and the maternity home, both of which subsequently have to be extended.

CHAPTER FOUR

THE EMIGRÉ NOVELS

What distinguishes the twentieth-century refugees is the increasing difficulty of fleeing and, even more important, the immense difficulty, often impossibility, of gaining entrance elsewhere. The rise of modern totalitarianism, especially in Nazi Germany and Soviet Russia, brought in its train the closing of national boundaries, and the problem of getting in became as great as the problem of getting out. The result was the stateless refugee, shunted from border to border, dependent on charity and chance rather than the law, a modern "man without a country".[1]

These words from Stressinger on the ever topical subject of unwanted refugees summarize Remarque's treatment of a theme which occupies the greater part of his work from the 'forties onward. The survivors of the "lost generation", whose stint in the trenches wrought such estrangement from the rest of society have now been forced into a new rôle, that of the itinerant emigré, compelled, for one reason or another, to flee from Germany and, as a consequence, completely cut off — now in a literal as well as a spiritual sense — from family, friends and homeland. The "man without a country" then, is doubly "lost": he is at odds with the ideology of the political party ruling his native country, separated from the land, and often the people, that he loves, yet he has nowhere to go, for, as Stressinger indicates, dissidents were often hounded just as much outside Germany as in the Reich itself. At the beginning of *Liebe deinen Nächsten,* a number of emigrés arrested in Vienna are brutally mishandled by the police on their way to prison, and the equally unsympathetic attitude of the civilian population is demonstrated by the cry of a passer-by: "Beat the whole pack of emigrés to death!" (*Liebe,* p.596) Classed almost as criminals — the only person in the cell to which the emigrés are taken who is in possession of a valid passport is "a respectable pickpocket and cardsharp with full rights as a citizen" (*Liebe,* p.602) — the refugees are pitied but unwanted, and the general attitude of the authorities seems to be that the tales of torture from Germany are vastly exaggerated. (*Arc,* p.431)

Much play has been made of the fact that Remarque himself was not in anything like the dire straits of his central figures during his own enforced exile, since he was one of the priviliged few whose name was sufficiently well-known to ensure him a rather warmer welcome than that accorded to many of his compatriots, particularly his fellow non-Jews, who were frequently regarded with great suspicion when they applied for asylum. It is clear, however, that Remarque was deeply hurt at being deprived of his German citizenship, and his continuing love for the Germany of his youth is reflected in his choice of an Osnabrück setting for *Zeit zu leben und Zeit zu sterben*, *Der schwarze Obelisk*, and *Die Nacht von Lissabon*.

It will be clear from the preceding chapters that Remarque's work draws heavily on the journalistic principle that "good news is no news", and the pattern of suicides and fatal illnesses established in the early novels is continued without respite in *Liebe deinen Nächsten*, *Arc de Triomphe* and *Die Nacht von Lissabon*. The formula of the emigré novels is, in fact, much the same as that of *Drei Kameraden;* namely, a hero drawn temporarily from the lethargy of a drifting existence by a love-affair or by a desire for revenge, or both. A tragic outcome to the love-affair is balanced out by a successful act of vengeance, and at the end the hero is as solitary and even more cynical than he had been at the opening of the novel. Although Antkowiak is able to find — for the first time in Remarque's writing — some development in the character of Ravic in *Arc de Triomphe*,[2] there is little evidence that either he or any other of Remarque's protagonists undergo any kind of evolutionary process or find any salvation from the misery of the world.

It is only a small step from the restless ex-soldier in the aftermath of the First World War to the German emigré in the days of Nazism. Remarque's heroes are still as isolated and as lacking in purpose as ever, but rather more mature than Birkholz of *Der Weg zurück* or Lohkamp in *Drei Kameraden*: they do have at least a more warmhearted response to their fellow-men and a greater desire to serve them. This is especially true of Ravic in *Arc de Triomphe*, who, as a surgeon operating illegally in Paris, often finds himself assisting the poor and the suffering at great personal risk. On one occasion he is actually deported from France when he goes to the aid of an accident victim. Like Remarque's earlier heroes, the central figures of *Liebe deinen Nächsten*, *Arc de Triomphe* and *Die Nacht von Lissabon* are semi-autobiographical: in *Arc de Triomphe*, which is set in 1938, Remarque gives Ravic's age as forty, his own age at that time, and in *Die Nacht von Lissabon*, in addition to making Schwarz an erstwhile citizen of Osnabrück, he even goes so far as to give Schwarz's date of birth as 22 June 1898 (Remarque's own birthdate). Other personal details are incorporated too, including references in *Liebe deinen Nächsten* to characters with the names Rabe and Vogt, a reference in *Arc de Triomphe* to someone by the name of Zambona, the maiden name of Remarque's first wife, and at the end of *Die Nacht von Lissabon* the first person narrator who is divorced from his wife soon after arriving in America, refers to the ironical fact that in order to make the divorce legal he first had to remarry his wife. (*Nacht,* p.302) Porto Ronco also receives a passing mention in *Die Nacht von Lissabon,* and all three novels contain references to collectors of Impressionist paintings.

When asked about the character of Ravic, whose surgical operations are described in some detail, Remarque replied:

> The figure of Ravic contains characteristics of three people. I have given something of myself and something of my friends, doctors, who like myself lived in Paris incognito. One of them treated me after my first heart attack . . . As you know, I have never studied medicine and this man helped me to write the passages dealing with medicine.[3]

Despite the inclusion of autobiographical detail, however — or in the case of the consciously elusive Remarque, perhaps because of it — his heroes remain sketchily drawn and out of focus. His heroines fare even worse, for, in addition to their extremely high mortality rate, they are colourless individuals indistinguishable from Pat of *Drei Kameraden* or Lillian of *Der Himmel kennt keine Günstlinge* and are similarly endowed with a suntan and an English-sounding Christian name. The only really colourful characters are, in fact, the minor ones, such as the prostitutes in *Arc de Triomphe* (bearing a striking resemblance to those of *Drei Kameraden* and *Der schwarze Obelisk*) or the old Jewish emigré "Vater Moritz" in *Liebe deinen Nächsten.* Part and parcel of the emigré novels, including the later *Schatten im Paradies*, is a sympathetically drawn chess-playing white Russian typifying the other main stream of refugees at the time. As Schwarz points out in *Nacht von Lissabon,* the Russians have had fifteen more years experience at being emigrés than the Germans, and some of them were also fortunate enough to receive a little sympathy and Nansen passports — an absolute luxury to the likes of Schwarz. (*Nacht,* p. 39) A Russian with one of the cherished Nansen passports makes a fleeting appearance in *Liebe deinen Nächsten,* (*Liebe,* p. 602) but it is in *Arc de Triomphe* that the chess-playing white Russian (without a Nansen passport) first comes into his own, as Ravic's close companion and fellow lodger. He later fills a similar rôle in *Schatten im Paradies* as the landlord of the hotel which for a long time is the home of the refugee Ross.

The rather shadowy nature of his emigré heroes is closely related to a change in perspective on Remarque's part. From *Im Westen nichts Neues* onwards, most of Remarque's novels are based closely on his own experiences in Germany during and after the First World War and, as a consequence, are written in the first person singular, a technique which Remarque resumes for the even more closely autobiographical *Der schwarze Obelisk*. With the first of the emigré novels, however, *Liebe deinen Nächsten,* Remarque reverts to the third person narrator he had employed in *Die Traumbude* and *Station am Horizont*. Not only that, he also divides the interests between two main protagonists, the mature emigré Steiner, and the twenty-one-year-old Ludwig Kern (whose Christian name forms a link with Ludwig Breyer in *Der Weg zurück*, and with Ludwig Bodmer of *Der schwarze Obelisk* — and also, in a sense, with Ravic in *Arc de Triomphe*, whose real name is Ludwig Fresenburg).[4] As regards personality, it is Steiner who is the prototype for Ravic in *Arc de Triomphe*, which is also written in the third person, and for Schwarz in *Die Nacht von Lissabon*. Although *Die Nacht von Lissabon* (written some time after the other two emigré novels) has a first person narrator, or to be precise two first person narrators, the story is given a remoteness by Remarque's adoption of a framework technique. A man arriving at the port of Lisbon hoping to get tickets for a boat to America is stopped by the "Ancient Non-Mariner" figure of Schwarz and offered two tickets for the journey, if he will only listen to his story and save him from being alone that night. Throughout the ensuing narrative, the reader has none of the impression of direct involvement which characterizes the earlier first-person novels.

In *Liebe deinen Nächsten* and *Die Nacht von Lissabon*, Remarque gives a further sense of remoteness to his narrative by his frequent employment of the flashback. In *Die Nacht von Lissabon* this is done in a fairly straightforward and very effective manner: the narrative present is Lisbon in 1942, and Schwarz's tale within the tale, narrated in the course of a single night, takes place in 1939, when he returns to Osnabrück to seek out his wife. Schwarz's story is well-placed, and additional information concerning his original expulsion from Germany due to the hatred borne him by his Nazi brother-in-law is introduced without disrupting the main thread of the narrative. In *Liebe deinen Nächsten*, however, the flashback technique is rather overstretched, being used not only for the main protagonists, Steiner, his young protégé Kern, and Kern's girlfriend Ruth Holland (whose name recalls both the Ruth who is the narrator's wife in *Die Nacht von Lissabon* and Pat Hollmann of *Drei Kameraden*), but also for several secondary characters. This involves uncomfortably frequent switches of narrative viewpoint, and inevitably detracts from the main thread of the action, or rather the two interwoven threads centring on Kern and Steiner. This is all the more serious since *Liebe deinen Nächsten* leans more heavily in plot than most of Remarque's novels.

Although the greater part of *Die Nacht von Lissabon* is devoted to Schwarz's story, it does resemble *Liebe deinen Nächsten* in that it follows the fates of two individuals. Remarque's resumption of a first person narrator may be due to the fact that the story again incorporates much autobiographical material, in particular some very accurate descriptions of Osnabrück, which this time appears under its own name, as do most of the streets named by Remarque in the novel. The Lotterstrasse, for example, which Schwarz sees mentioned in a newspaper, (*Nacht*, p.35) is given a precise and accurate location, and it is coincidentally just off this street that Remarque's friend Rabe now lives. However, the framework technique in *Die Nacht von Lissabon* detaches the reader from Schwarz's return, and this becomes especially clear if one compares Schwarz's clandestine return from exile with Bäumer's return home on leave in *Im Westen nichts Neues*. The two situations are in many ways parallel: the exile, like the soldier, has been forced to leave his home and family and to live a hand-to-mouth existence which is constantly fraught with danger. Outside the confines of "normal" society he develops new skills and new priorities – particularly important is his ability to react speedily in moments of danger, an attribute, it will be recalled, which the World War One soldiers retained long after the end of hostilities.

Schwarz's emotions on seeing Osnabrück again, though bound up with memories of childhood like those of Bäumer and those of Birkholz in *Der Weg zurück*, have none of the immediacy and poignancy conveyed by the earlier novels. We are, in fact, often left with the impression that Remarque is using Schwarz to express at one remove his own self-indulgent emotionality. Remarque's greatest failing as a writer is this tendency towards oversentimentality, emotional self-indulgence, and pretentiousness. *Liebe deinen Nächsten*, not one of his better novels, is particularly marred by this latter failing, one of the more outstanding examples being the deathless line: "Dawn came on blue feet and filled the room"! (*Liebe*, p.818) In *Die Nacht von Lissabon*, however, any cosmic or oversentimental utterances are deliberately detached from the narrator of the framework, and thus doubly removed from Remarque himself, by being placed in the mouth of Schwarz. By contrast, some of Remarque's most brilliant atmospheric writing – in particular the opening paragraphs of the novel which describe the boat lying in Lisbon harbour ready for the voyage to the refugees' ideal of America – is placed in the mouth of the first person narrator of the framework.

Liebe deinen Nächsten, undoubtedly the weakest of the three novels under consideration here, is not only far more contrived and artificial than any other Remarque novel – with the possible exception of *Der Himmel kennt keine Günstlinge* – it is also simplistic in the extreme. Almost without exception, each of the characters encountered by Kern in the course of his wanderings from town to town and border to border is either wholly good or wholly bad, in true fairytale tradition. It is typical of Remarque that people frequently condemned by society, for example, the prostitutes in *Arc de Triomphe*, or the cardsharp in *Liebe deinen Nächsten*, are fundamentally good, while the more respected members of society show little sympathy for those in need. Kern himself, a twenty-one-year-old half-Jew is, on the one hand, amazingly naïve, being taken in by the simplest ruses and showing very little ability to judge character, despite the continual awareness of danger which his time as a refugee has supposedly taught him; yet, on the other hand, he is depicted as being intelligent, quick-witted and, like the young soldiers in *Im Westen nichts Neues*, although he learns from the more experienced Steiner (who fulfils the rôle of Kat) he himself is able to give advice to those who have had less experience in the ways of being an emigré than he has. It is typical of Remarque's predilection for the ironic turn of the screw that one of the people to whom Kern gives advice is his former Professor, his superior of former days, but his inferior in the emigré world.

The history of Kern, to which rather more pages are devoted than to the fate of the more typical Remarque hero Steiner, is primarily intended to mark out the fate of the average refugee. Although Kern does form a lasting relationship with another young refugee, Ruth Holland (an untypical relationship in that it does not end in disaster), the main emphasis is on the misery of the existence of the refugee, about which Remarque clearly feels very deeply. Much play is made of the fact that the refugees have done no wrong and yet spend a large proportion of their time either in prison or evading the police. In *Die Nacht von Lissabon*, Schwarz's wife Helen comments: "Don't you realize yet that innocence in this century is a crime which is always punished most severely?". (*Nacht*, p.183) While Steiner has allegedly been involved in some kind of political opposition to the Nazi regime – a factor which helps to endear *Liebe deinen Nächsten* to the Marxist critic Antkowiak, who announces that Remarque has "awoken from his political lethargy"[5] – Kern has left Germany, as did countless others, simply as a result of his father's religion. Kern himself declares his religion to be "evangelical", and one of the ironies of his "mixed" religion is that he finds himself in a "Catch 22" situation: he is forced to flee Germany because he has a Jewish father, but is refused aid from the Jewish emigré association because he has a Christian mother. (*Liebe*, p.706) Remarque also demonstrates the unwillingness of many of the wealthier German emigrés to involve themselves with helping people like Kern, even by buying any of the goods which Kern touts round in a suitcase. Fearing to jeopardize their own positions, they prefer to remain what Remarque in *Die Nacht von Lissabon* calls "the spectator":

> It was the age-old scene of humanity — the servants of power, the victim, and the ever-present third party, the spectator, who doesn't raise his hands and doesn't defend the victim and doesn't try to free him because he is afraid for his own safety and whose own safety is in jeopardy for that very reason. (*Nacht*, pp.116-17)

Stressinger makes the point that the emigrés depended to a large extent on luck, since none of the countries in which they found themselves were willing to do anything positive to help the refugees, for fear of being overrun by them. Chance is particularly prominent in the emigré novels, where repeated reference is made to the fact that the emigrés need a "miracle" — a Remarquian keyword — if they are to achieve anything worthwhile. In *Liebe deinen Nächsten*, however, there are rather too many "miracles" and the narrative soon degenerates into implausibility. It is "by chance", for example, that Kern is reunited with his father, happening to enter the very chemist's shop where his father, formerly a manufacturer of perfumes and the like, had been trying to sell the formula for a particular brand of toilet water. Equally coincidental are Kern's three encounters with a refugee who has a passion for chicken, but always happens to be arrested just after he has purchased one and is on the point of consuming it, as is the fact that Kern's prison guard was once helped by Steiner. Kern is reunited in various countries with a surprisingly large number of his acquaintances, and one cannot help but feel that the law of chance is here used as an excuse for all these coincidences. As Ravic comments in *Arc de Triomphe* when a golden opportunity arises to dispose of his old enemy Haake without being arrested himself: "So much chance is impossible". (*Arc*, p.541)

Die Nacht von Lissabon, where the "miracle" motif is equally prominent, is not without its blemishes either. Schwarz escapes with remarkable — or "remarquable" perhaps — facility from a concentration camp and gains access to his wife's camp just as easily in order to rescue her, and at one point the two of them are very opportunely assisted by an influential American. The ultimate miracle, of course, is that of being able to obtain a passage across the Atlantic, and in both *Liebe deinen Nächsten* and *Die Nacht von Lissabon* this is rendered possible by the death of another emigré. In *Die Nacht von Lissabon* it is the death of Schwarz's wife Helen which deprives him of his will to escape and prompts him to offer the tickets to the narrator and his wife, Ruth, and in *Liebe deinen Nächsten* it is the death of Steiner which gives Kern and his Ruth sufficient funds for their passage to Mexico. This proves the point made in *Liebe deinen Nächsten* that the only help which a refugee receives comes from the dead — usually in the form of a still valid passport, whose useful life often spans several human lives. (*Liebe,* p.646) While the narrator of *Die Nacht von Lissabon* derives little happiness from his legacy, since his wife leaves him in America, the ending of *Liebe deinen Nächsten* is, despite the death of Steiner, the nearest Remarque ever comes to a happy ending, although we are told nothing of the life Kern and Ruth lead once they have arrived in Mexico.

Of the many similarities between *Liebe deinen Nächsten* and *Die Nacht von Lissabon*, the most striking is that of the basic plot involving two heroes who share a common Christian name, Josef Steiner and Josef Schwarz. Both men return, at great personal risk, to Nazi Germany for the sake of their wives, who have been left behind. Steiner's wife, Marie, is dying in a hospital, and he goes, in response to a letter from her, to be with her in her last few days of life. Schwarz's wife too is soon revealed to be ill, although this is not the reason for Schwarz's return, and her ultimate death leaves Schwarz with as little will to live as Steiner. In each case the wife had refused to divorce her husband, although in the case of *Die Nacht von Lissabon*, Helen's refusal was more to spite her Nazi brother than out of love for Schwarz. In fact, of the two relationships, that between Steiner and Marie seems to be the closer, despite — or possibly as a result of — the fact that they are apart for most of the narrative.

In both novels the return to Germany involves not only a reunion with a loved wife but also an act of vengeance. Steiner's is the more dramatic, and perhaps the more satisfying of the two from a literary viewpoint. His old enemy has the highly appropriate name of Steinbrenner (stone-*burner*) and himself comments upon the similarity between his name and that of Steiner. (*Liebe*, pp.826-27) Arrested by Steinbrenner in the hospital where his wife has just died, Steiner pushes Steinbrenner through a window and falls with him to his death. In *Die Nacht von Lissabon*, the enemy is Helen's Nazi brother, and here the actual details of the avenging murder more closely resemble Ravic's murder of Haake in *Arc de*

Triomphe, since both murder victims are lured into a car and then killed.

The importance of the revenge theme in Remarque's work will be evident from the previous chapters, and in the emigré novels it assumes a significance almost equal to that of the love motif. In addition to Steiner's dramatic act of vengeance, *Liebe deinen Nächsten* contains a couple of minor variations on the same theme, in connection with Kern's treatment at the hands of the rich German Ammers, who purports to be a friend to the emigrés, but is in fact working for the Nazis, and has Kern arrested when he calls at his house. First Kern himself exacts what might be termed psychological revenge on Ammers by giving him the benefit of his two semesters of medical training and informing him that he is suffering from cancer of the liver. Kern is most gratified when he later learns that Ammers is indeed undergoing treatment for a liver complaint. Steiner tackles the same Ammers in a different way: disguised as a Nazi agent, he persuades Ammers to hand over a substantial amount of money "for the Nazi cause", after expressing his disapprovel at the furore allegedly caused by Ammers in connection with Kern and ordering him to have nothing more to do with emigrés. It is with *Arc de Triomphe*, however, the best of Remarque's emigré novels, that new dimensions are given to the concept of revenge. In Remarque's novels we are accustomed to love rekindling the "spark of life" which is man's existence, but in *Arc de Triomphe*, the love for one individual is set against hatred for another, both emotions infusing into Ravic renewed vigour and a *raison d'être*. Not only are the two threads of the narrative interwoven in terms of plot, they are consciously linked in an antithetical pattern. At the end of the novel, when Ravic has lost Joan — first to another man and then through her death — and murdered Haake, the man who had tortured him and his friends, including his then girlfriend, in a concentration camp, he is indifferent to the fate which will befall him now that France is openly at war with Germany: "He had experienced revenge and love. That was enough. It was not everything, but it was as much as a man could ask for". (*Arc*, p.560) Each experience is somehow regarded as a purging of the emotions and a form of liberation:

> He had loved one person and lost her. He had hated another and killed him. Both experiences had freed him. One had allowed his feelings to break out again, the other had wiped out his past. Nothing had remained unfulfilled. He no longer had any desires: no hatreds and no complaints. (*Arc*, pp.569-70)

Like the novels concerned with war and its aftermath, it is the intensity of life which is important and, it seems, more important than the question of happiness or unhappiness. At the height of his relationship with Joan, Ravic's emotions are described as follows:

> Suddenly he didn't know any longer whether he was ridiculous or miserable, whether he was suffering or not — he only knew that he was alive. He was alive! He was there ... he was no longer a spectator, no longer an outsider ... it was almost a matter of indifference whether he was happy or unhappy; he was alive and felt fully that he was alive, and that was enough!
> (*Arc*, p.487)

As in all the man-woman relationships in Remarque's novels, Ravic's love for Joan is accompanied by a fear of losing her, and it is this fear which gives an added intensity to his affair with Joan as well as to his planned act of vengeance on Haake, whom Ravic is equally afraid of letting slip from his clutches. What is described in *Die Nacht von Lissabon* as a "feeling for life intensified by the presence of danger" (*Nacht*, p.138) is the *modus vivendi* of the Remarque emigré just as it was of the soldier. The constant preoccupation with day-to-day survival brings out the fundamental instincts of love for a woman (who is often compared to an animal), a bond of comradeship with those in the same plight as oneself, a constant search for food and warmth, and a primitive desire to kill one's enemies.

Philosophical questions on the meaning of life and death are raised from time to time, but these are generally shelved in favour of more immediate concerns. One of Schwarz's first questions to the narrator in *Die Nacht von Lissabon* is whether he believes in life after death. The narrator's reply sums up the philosophy of the emigré: "In recent years I've been too preoccupied with survival before death". (*Nacht*, p.14) The emigré dares not look into the future but, even more important, he must not look back. For all their inexperience, Kern and Ruth in *Liebe deinen Nächsten* soon become aware of this and sell all the books from their student days in order to buy more practical things, and give up any idea of holding on to their past lives. Such resolutions do not, of course, prevent the emigrés from reminiscing about their past, as the many flashbacks demonstrate, but these are always accompanied by an awareness that illusions are all that one can hold on to in life. Like the young men of *Der Weg zurück*, there is no road back to normality for the emigrés. Schwarz, who does attempt a return of a kind, discusses this problem with Helen in terms which clearly parallel Remarque's own sentiments:

> "My fatherland made me a cosmopolitan against my will. Now I must remain so. One can never go back."

119

"Not even to a person," I said. "Even the earth leads a rolling-stone existence. It is an emigrant of the sun. One can never go back, or one cracks
up." (*Nacht*, p.83)

The world of the emigré is very much one of fleeting relationships
and sudden departures. The joy with which the emigrés greet one
another when chance encounters bring them together is
accompanied by a fear of never seeing each other again, which is
especially intense in the case of a man-woman relationship, where
the ultimate fear is that death will take away the loved one for
ever. This is particularly so since Remarque's heroines are such
frail and sickly creatures — even one of the few to survive the end
of the novel, Ruth Holland, has a fairly serious illness in the course
of *Liebe deinen Nächsten*. In *Die Nacht von Lissabon* and *Arc de
Triomphe*, where the heroines die, Helen of cancer, and Joan of a
gun-shot wound, both Schwarz and Ravic express (like Lohkamp
in *Drei Kameraden)* disbelief that someone one loves so intensely
can be taken away, as if the bond of love and that of life are one
and the same.

The transient nature of even the most passionate relationship
is highlighted in the recurrent motif of the mirror, which is linked
with sickness. In the previous chapter it was noted that Pat and
Lillian measured the insidious progress of their illness by regarding
their wasting limbs in the mirror, and Helen in *Die Nacht von
Lissabon* does the same. When Schwarz returns home to find her
dead, all the mirrors in the room lie broken and her evening dress
is torn to shreds. But the mirror image also demonstrates that the
imagined security of holding on to another person is as illusory as
anything else. Repeated references to the loved one as a Fata
Morgana, especially frequent in *Arc de Triomphe*, further empha-
size the transitory nature of human relationships.

Remarque's preoccupation with sickness and death leads inevitably to an interest in medical matters. As early as *Im Westen
nichts Neues*, hospitals played an important — and fairly notorious
— part, and doctors are rarely long absent from the scene in any of
the subsequent novels. Almost all of Remarque's doctors are
depicted as caring individuals doing their utmost to alleviate
human suffering and never able to come to terms with the inescapable fact that their continual battle against death is never
successful in the end. Such a man is Dr Ravic in *Arc de Triomphe*,
where the medical theme comes into its own. *Liebe deinen
Nächsten*, the immediate predecessor of *Arc de Triomphe*, paves
the way for this concentrated study of Ravic: Kern had been a
medical student before his departure from Germany, and a number
of kindly and dedicated doctors make an appearance in the course
of the novel. The closing pages of *Liebe deinen Nächsten* are also

set in Paris, where many of the refugees — like Ravic — find a rather more permanent abode, and reference is made in *Liebe deinen Nächsten* to the Hôtel International, which is to be Ravic's Paris home. The title "Liebe deinen Nächsten" (love thy neighbour) also foreshadows Ravic's caring and altruistic approach to his fellow man, a cast of mind which Remarque himself both admired and cultivated.

Reference has already been made to the accuracy of Remarque's descriptions of the various operations which Ravic performs — like the portrayal of psychological illness in *Der schwarze Obelisk*, these are the product of careful research by Remarque. Although the French laws prohibit Ravic from legally practising his profession, his considerable skills as a surgeon are appreciated and exploited by two French doctors for whom Ravic performs the more difficult operations, receiving little money and no recognition for doing so. One of the doctors, in fact, is so anxious to preserve all the credit for himself that he only allows Ravic to have sight of the patients when they are under the anaesthetic, so that frequently all Ravic sees of his patient is the part of the body on which he is to operate. Ravic is quite happy with the arrangement, however, for his surgical work, in which he can become completely absorbed, offers him at least the satisfaction of spending some of his time in a worthwhile way.

Although Joan is not suffering from any disease — in this novel another female character assumes the rôle of the cancer victim — she does find herself in desperate need of Ravic's medical skills when one of her lovers shoots her in a fit of jealousy. Ironically, Ravic, whose skilful hands have saved so many lives, finds that Joan's wound is such that his medical knowledge is powerless to save her, and he is forced to watch the woman who, as he says, has given him life, (*Arc*, p.488) die before his eyes. The situation is doubly ironical since at the beginning of the novel Ravic does, in fact, save Joan's life, but not in his capacity as a doctor: he meets her one night on a bridge in Paris and dissuades her from committing suicide. Their love-affair, then, ends as dramatically as it had begun, and this makes it all the more surprising that *Arc de Triomphe* should have been regarded as "uninteresting" by an American publisher.[6]

Like the black obelisk, the "Arc de Triomphe" of the title has a symbolic rôle in the novel: it looms darkly above Joan and Ravic as they make their way from the bridge where they meet to an all-night café for their first drink of Calvados, and a couple of pages later it is compared to the gateway to Hades. (*Arc*, p.287) Various meetings with Joan as well as Ravic's encounter with Haake take place in the shadow of the famous Arch, and at the close of the novel, when both Joan and Haake are dead and Ravic surrenders to the French authorities as war with Germany is declared, the Arch is hidden from his sight by the darkness.

It is typical of Remarque's novels that the people the hero would most like to live are those that die — usually in a most painful way — while those he wishes dead, like Haake, have to be actively disposed of. As Ruth comments in *Liebe deinen Nächsten*: "Evil is harder, it is more resilient". (*Liebe*, p.653) Yet, however impermanent the love-affairs of Remarque's heroes may be, they do, for a time at least, restore the homeless emigré to an awareness of himself as a human being. One of the most significant points which Remarque makes in his emigré novels is that the refugee leads an almost dehumanized existence. From the official viewpoint he quite simply does not exist — deprived of status and nationality alike by the government of his own country, he is merely an unwanted statistic in any other land. At the beginning of *Die Nacht von Lissabon*, the narrator remarks: "A human being was nothing any more at this time: a valid passport was everything", (*Nacht*, p.8) and in *Liebe deinen Nächsten* Steiner tells Kern: "A man without a passport is a corpse on leave". (*Liebe*, p.600) It may be remembered that Lohkamp used this same expression with regard to love in *Drei Kameraden*, and Ravic too employs the same image — of which Remarque seems to have been inordinately fond — when he describes the way in which Joan has breathed new life into him:

> Here I stand, no longer like a corpse on leave with a little bit of cynicism, sarcasm and some courage, no longer cold; living again, suffering perhaps, but open again to the storms of life. (*Arc*, p.488)

It should be noted too that Remarque does not confine his interest solely to those who — like himself — were refugees of the Nazi regime; as well as including references to refugees from other countries, notably from Russia and Spain, he seems to regard the emigré existence as a twentieth-century disease. Schwarz tells Helen: "There are ... more emigrants than one thinks. Including some who have never moved from the spot", (*Nacht*, p.82) and at the end of the novel the narrator, who has inherited the passports of Schwarz and Helen, hands them on in his turn to a Russian emigré, and refers to "a new wave of emigrants", (*Nacht*, p.303) pointing to the fact that the problem is an on-going one.

At the close of *Die Nacht von Lissabon*, the ship which was lying in the harbour at the beginning of the novel is still there, the "ark" which will carry those to be rescued from the flood of Nazism sweeping Europe to the ideal of all refugees, the "paradise" of the United States of America, which Remarque explores in *Schatten im Paradies*. But before then the Second World War — whose outbreak is seen in the emigré novels — supervenes, an international catastrophe which produced some of Remarque's very finest fiction.

CHAPTER FIVE

THE SECOND WORLD WAR NOVELS

Remarque wrote two novels which take as their subject aspects of the Second World War; each is penned with that fine sense of literary craftsmanship which characterizes him at his best, and, taken together, both seem to mark the beginnings of a change of direction in his concept of the human condition. *Zeit zu leben und Zeit zu sterben* and *Der Funke Leben* make an outstanding pair of novels, but the latter is particularly exceptional because of Remarque's skill and restraint in handling a theme which, German critics have told us with monotonous regularity, it is impossible for German creative art to portray with any measure of success. None the less, in his account of life—and death—in a Nazi concentration camp, Remarque has matched in the sphere of narrative fiction what Celan achieved in poetry with "Todesfuge", (Fugue of Death) or Rolf Hochhuth in his drama *Der Stellvertreter* (The Representative).

Zeit zu leben is concerned with a soldier on leave from the Russian front during the closing stages of the war, whilst *Der Funke Leben* deals in the main with the sufferings of the inmates of a concentration camp inside Germany, and concludes with their liberation by the Americans. In certain respects, the two novels are complementary: in the town where Graeber spends his leave, prisoners from the nearby concentration camp are drafted to help shovel away the debris from bomb-damaged buildings; and, in *Der Funke Leben,* working parties are sent out to engage in similar labour. In both, Remarque has drawn on the same fictionalized location, although it is viewed from entirely different standpoints.

Surprisingly, though, the differences are less significant than the similarities: the titles of both novels contain the word "Leben" (life), and both are preoccupied with the theme of survival under conditions of extreme emotional and physical stress, in which human existence is under constant threat. To this extent, these two works continue to explore the basic issues of *Im Westen nichts Neues* in a Second World War setting, and it is no coincidence that all three deal with the closing stages of the armed conflict fought out in a growing recognition of the inevitability of

German defeat. But equally surprisingly, Remarque appears to have become less, rather than more, pessimistic, despite his own experiences of National Socialism and his enforced exile from Germany.

Controversy has never been far away from Remarque and his work; and *Zeit zu leben* and *Der Funke Leben* are no exception to that rule, but on this occasion there is also some doubt as to the proper identity of *Zeit zu leben* itself, as we shall see shortly. The familiar arguments are paraded by the various vested interests among the critical fraternity, especially by the Marxists. Once again, too, Remarque paints his canvas with such compelling *trompe l'œil* authenticity that many commentators experience the same sense of having been cheated when they realize that, far from having been the result of personal experiences in a concentration camp or at the Russian front, these novels were penned in cosy exile a continent away in America. The old cry goes up that the worse defect of these novels is that their author "was not there",[1] and even if it is accepted that the fact that he was not there is not a culpable offence, the suspicion remains that they must be documentary, and that their author must have "worked his way through mountains of personal reports".[2]

One cannot help but sympathize with such views when confronted with the chilling verisimilitude of Remarque's depiction of the snow melting along the Russian front to reveal the previous winter's corpses; first those who died in January emerge, stiff as boards, to be followed by the December dead, among whom

> were found the weapons which belonged to the January dead. The guns and hand grenades had sunk deeper than the bodies . . . With these corpses it was easier to cut out the identification marks from under their uniforms; the melting snow had already softened the material. (*Zeit*, p.6)

For the hundredth time the reader is convinced that only a man with the keenest eye who had actually been there could have noted and recorded such details. Equally authentic is his description of the camp crematorium in *Der Funke Leben,* where the bodies come tumbling down a chute into the building:

> They fell on top of one another and got entangled together. One of them came down feet first and remained standing upright. He leaned against the chute, eyes wide open, mouth twisted to one side. The hands were half clenched into a gnarled fist, and a medallion hung down out of his open shirt. He stood there like that for a little while. (*Der Funke Leben*, p. 194)

The dead are stripped, searched for gold fillings or other valuables and thrust into the furnace where Remarque describes their bodies as arching up for a moment in the intense heat as if struggling for a a brief instant to regain their lost hold on life.

The Marxist commentators dredge up all the tedious old arguments about Remarque failing to do what he clearly does not set out to do in the first place; namely, to recognize that bourgeois democracy is no answer to Fascist dictatorship. (In contrast to the avowedly non-political *Im Westen nichts Neues*, however, Remarque does take a clear political stand in these two novels.) One critic even goes so far as to accuse him of contributing to the deterioration of East-West relations in *Der Funke Leben*:

> When this novel came out, the Cold War had reached a pretty hysterical pitch, and Remarque has always been particularly susceptible to the influence of current opinion.[3]

By a nice ironical twist, Remarque does get the better of one of his Marxist detractors, who brings forward this strangely familiar line of argument in relation to the supposedly negative stance of the inmates of the concentration camp:

> Whilst the Communist resistance fighters in Bruno Apitz's novel *Nackt unter Wölfen* (Naked among Wolves), inwardly hardened by their concentration camp experiences, are to number among those who will play an active part in determining the kind of life to be led after their liberation from Fascism, the concentration camp experiences of Remarque's heroes have undermined them and have not furnished them with the grit and determination to fight actively for a better world.[4]

Exactly the same arguments were brought to bear against *Im Westen nichts Neues* — by the very National Socialist critics that the Marxists so utterly condemn; and this very neatly underscores precisely the political point which Remarque is seeking to put across; namely, that extremism of any kind, whether of the left or the right, inevitably leads to a tyranny of identical evils: intolerance of political opponents, inhuman acts in the name of humanity, torture regrettably essential in the pursuit of the highest ideals, whether at the hands of an SS interrogator or of the Secret Police of a Communist state.

To a man, the Marxist critics avert their eyes and fail to meet Remarque's challenge when, in the course of an attempt to win one of the prisoners over to the Communist cause, he causes the following exchange to take place:

> "We shall win our wars. We conduct them differently. From within."
> "Yes, from within and inwards. Then you could just keep the camp right here. And fill it."
> "We can," said Wagner with total seriousness. "Why don't you come over to our side?" he repeated.
> "For that very reason. If you came to power, you would have me liquidated. But I wouldn't do the same to you. That's my reason." (*Der Funke Leben*, p.310)

126

By and large, on the other hand, such non-partisan reviewers and critics as have deigned to glance in the direction of these two novels have stressed their positive qualities, praising Remarque's discipline in his depiction of harrowing scenes in the concentration camp,[5] and even the Marxist Antkowiak recognizes that

> despite all its inner contradictions, *Zeit zu leben* is a significant work of contemporary German literature and there is no doubt that, from the artistic point of view as well, this novel represents Remarque's most mature achievement as a writer.[6]

This is high praise indeed from the representative of a culture in which the state ordains that aesthetic quality is strictly subordinated to the transmission of the socialist message.

But what of the question of identity referred to earlier? It relates to *Zeit zu leben,* and gave certain among the critics a field-day, a heaven-sent opportunity to launch an onslaught against the political establishment in the Federal Republic.

The novel first appeared in print in English, at the end of May 1954, in an American edition, ably translated by Denver Lindley, under the slightly modified title of *A Time To Love and a Time To Die.* The German text was to be published by the respected firm of Kiepenheuer & Witsch, but publication was held back by a number of proposals for alterations which the firm put to Remarque, "which had nothing to do with toning the book down, but which related to questions of the setting, the terminology and similar factors, which were not in their proper historical context".[7] The final manuscript landed on the desk of the publishers on 10 April 1954, but there was a further delay occasioned by the serialization of the novel in the magazine *Münchener Illustrierte.* When it finally saw the light of day, it was also published in the German Democratic Republic by the Aufbau Verlag under licence.

It seems that the Scandinavians were the first to light on the differences between the English language and other versions of *Zeit zu leben* (the novel had also been rendered into Norwegian and Danish), and these seemed to be both substantial and politically motivated. The attack against Remarque and his publisher was launched in Norway by the newspaper *Information,* and the cudgels were eagerly taken up by Marxist critics in East Germany, notably by the periodical *Neue Deutsche Literatur,* in whose pages Dr FC Weiskopf pilloried what he regarded as blatant acts of political censorship perpetrated by the capitalist publishing barons. Remarque, he claims, had succumbed to pressure from Dr Witsch of Kiepenheuer & Witsch, publishers and henchmen of the "Adenauer state", who were both fearful of offending the countless former Nazis who had insinuated themselves into positions of power in the Federal Republic, and also anxious to suppress the unacknowledged heroism of the Communist underground during the war, which Weiskopf regards as "the leading, best-organized and most courageous of all the opposition movements".[8] The hero Graeber, we read, has been thoroughly "verwitscht" (in English "be-Witsched", or perhaps "white-Witsched"). And the author of *Zeit zu leben,* Weiskopf thunders, was first "castrated" and then caused to "prostitute himself", a feat which is not only physically implausible but metaphorically remote, given Remarque's stature in the bestseller lists. As the editor of Dr JC Witsch's correspondence, Kristian Witsch, writes in a letter to the present authors:

> It is possible that the author himself suggested and delivered a different version for publication in Germany, but one thing is clear: the German publishers have certainly not "doctored" the text without authorization because Remarque would have spotted that at once and this would have been the end of their relationship.[9]

Weiskopf claims that political references are excised, and it is indeed true that allusions to the SS are toned down, and that a former Communist in the American edition changes his political allegiance in the German. Two sections relating to a Jewish soldier are also cut; and the emphasis in the concluding pages is shifted by means of two significant insertions.

All these claims are perfectly true, as far as they go. It is interesting to note that the argument is loaded by the omission of any reference to alterations which do not strengthen the case. A curious piece of censorship (if such it be) is passed over in silence: in the American edition, a soldier is made to belch (quietly) at one juncture; in the German version, he unbuttons his flies and relieves himself, passing in addition to water a stream of caustic observations about army life.

That these emendations were made by Remarque himself —or at the very least, with his full knowledge and assent— is stressed by a note which Remarque attached to a German version of the novel based on the American edition, which the East German Aufbau Verlag wanted to publish. In it he states:

> Tell them your edition is the latest version authorized by the author, no other will be printed, and that foreign publishers have also been informed of this fact for any subsequent editions.[10]

Could Remarque, then, be guilty of covering up Nazi excesses and moderating the tone of his novel? Clearly, the answer is a resounding no. All the changes he made served two ends: either.

to increase the level of plausibility, by not having Jews and Communists serving on the Russian front, or to improve the balance of the work by cutting out two longish sequences which unnecessarily divert attention from the main thread of the narrative.

In any event, Weiskopf's arguments are revealed in all their implausibility by the simple fact that, two years previously, Remarque had published the other novel under consideration in this chapter, *Der Funke Leben,* which contains the most explicit and outspoken portrayal of the horrors of life in a Nazi concentration camp. (Differences between the American and German versions of this novel amount to no more than those minor punctuation changes and inconsistencies which attend any translated work.)

Apart from the general vendetta conducted against Remarque and his supposed espousal of woolly liberalism, there is just a suspicion that the onslaught on him was really directed at his publishers in Germany, Kiepenheuer & Witsch, strong opponents of the East German regime and publishers of many works attacking the Communists in the other half of Germany.

It is clear that *Zeit zu leben* and *Der Funke Leben* belong together, but no one among the mixed bag of reviewers and critics who have commented on them has lighted on one central factor that links the two works; namely, that a principal character kills a fanatical Nazi and then himself dies. *Zeit zu leben* concludes with Graeber killing Steinbrenner (both name and political affiliations are borrowed from *Liebe Deinen Nächsten*), who was on the point of shooting down a group of Russian prisoners, and then himself being shot. In *Der Funke Leben,* prisoner 509, the main figure of the first part of the novel, shoots an SS man and then dies. This officer is not called Steinbrenner himself, but his companion bears that name.

At the end of *Im Westen nichts Neues,* Bäumer also dies, but his death is seen in entirely negative and pessimistic terms. In *Zeit zu leben* there is at least a suggestion of hope for the future, both in that a meaningful act against the Nazi regime has been committed by an individual who has come to realize the necessity for involving himself in wider issues than his own personal survival and also in the fact that his wife Elisabeth may be pregnant. Discussing what is to come after the war, she says:

What is to become of us if those who are against all that is going on now refuse to have any children? Are only the barbarians to have any? And, if so, who would put the world to rights again? (*Zeit,* p. 327)

She then expresses the desire to have a child by him, and there is the strong suggestion that her letter to Graeber may contain some information in that direction. The hope is at least expressed, and that in itself marks a huge advance on the bleak negativity of *Im Westen nichts Neues*.

In *Der Funke Leben* a much more concrete step forward is taken: the two lovers, Bucher and Ruth Holland (another Ruth Holland!) both survive the war and have a chance of building a future for themselves, although it is stressed that they are inevitably setting out with nothing; and in a real sense they have less than nothing, because they first have to overcome the psychological and physiological effects of their years of imprisonment. Ironically, Bäumer's futile attempt to recapture a lost past is translated into a determined effort to do the opposite, to *forget* what has gone before.

There are many such cross-references between *Im Westen nichts Neues* and the two Second World War novels. In a number of ways, Graeber in *Zeit zu leben* can be regarded as a slightly older and wiser version of Bäumer; and the sequence with the Russian POW's anticipates some of the scenes in *Der Funke Leben*. And, once more, Graeber's home town and the Mellen of *Der Funke Leben* are fictionalized representations of Osnabrück. There are the by now familiar references to real street names, such as the Haken-strasse and the Luisenstrasse (which, absorbingly, are allowed to run into one another in fiction although they do not do so in fact), to the Café Germania, the Domschule and the Marienkirche. Remarque even casts his geographical net a little wider to embrace Locarno and Porto Ronco, which, however, are only referred to, not actually visited as in *Die Nacht von Lissabon*.

The officer Rahe, resurrected from *Der Weg zurück*, is a parallel to Remarque's friend Rabe, but only, it must be stressed, in regard to the name; the figure in the novel is depicted as a remote individual at best, and at worst as one who exploits his position ruthlessly. There is also a scattering of other autobiographical references, among them the inevitable reference to someone — in this instance, Elisabeth's father — being put into a concentration camp because he expressed the view that the war could no longer be won. Also in *Zeit zu leben,* there are personal autobiographical echoes in the sequence in which Graeber assumes a non-commissioned officer's uniform in order to be able to take Elisabeth out to dine in the exclusive Café Germania: he impresses the waiter with borrowed gourmet knowledge of wine and food, but there is more than a streak of self-irony in the fact that the waiter gently lets slip that he knows Graeber is not entitled to the uniform he is sporting. By implication, however, the waiter indicates his admiration of a man who can carry off a deception with such panache.

There are numerous other parallels, major and minor, between fact and fiction, as well as between the Second World War novels and *Im Westen nichts Neues:* in this latter context, the fact that the soldier lives by chance, the shrinking band of comrades at the front, the gradual build-up of expectation as the train brings the soldier nearer to home and a spell of leave, the field kitchens, the artillery fire, the advances and retreats, the episode in which the hero fails to salute a major when on leave, the unchanging routine of deprivation and suffering in the front line, and so on. But there is one dimension entirely absent from *Im Westen nichts Neues,* which is a dominant theme in both these Second World War novels, namely, the exploration of a deep love relationship and the possibility that it may survive not only the specific horrors of war or the inhuman conditions of internment under the Nazis, but also the inescapable facts of life themselves. And for anyone having even a nodding acquaintance with Remarque's other novels, the outcome in each case is the exact opposite of what might have been expected.

Zeit zu leben is typical of Remarque's narrative technique in that it follows the fortunes of one individual, Graeber, who returns on leave from the Russian front to find that his parents' house has been destroyed by bombs and his parents themselves are missing. In searching for them, Graeber calls on their medical practitioner, a certain Doctor Kruse, only to find that he has been removed to a concentration camp. A relationship rapidly develops between Graeber and Elisabeth, the doctor's daughter; they marry, and spend the remaining days of Graeber's leave together.

Der Funke Leben, on the other hand, is a much more stylistically complex work. There is no one central dominant character holding the stage throughout the action. It is primarily concerned with the sufferings of the men in the "Little Camp", the enclosure inside the main compound in which those too ill or too weak to work any more are left to die. Attention is first focussed on 509, who has been in the camp since before the war broke out. Along with a fellow prisoner, he refuses to "volunteer" as a medical guinea pig for a local doctor, and, although brutally tortured for his defiance, he manages to retain a hold on life, and when he emerges from the torture cells, he is hailed by the other prisoners as a heroic figure, living proof — but only just — that it is possible to challenge the system and survive. This, coupled with the first bombing raid on the nearby town, constitutes the first real indication that the tide has indeed turned, that, after more than a decade of tyranny, the Nazi system is on the brink of defeat.

The novel pivots about a central point at which 509 realizes that, although he may not survive the war himself, he can reach out beyond his own personal existence and invest his aspirations towards a better future in a younger man, Bucher, and it is at this juncture, when human values are once again beginning to assert themselves in the face of Nazi bestiality, that a relationship begins to develop between Bucher and Ruth Holland, one of the women prisoners. 509 does die, but Bucher and Ruth are liberated by the Americans.

In *Der Funke Leben,* we are also allowed to cross the barbed wire and follow the activities of Neubauer, the camp's commandant, an obsessive and neurotic individual, whose wife Selma is a superbly drawn caricature of the hysterical wife. The widely ranging episodes in the novel are handled in a masterful manner by Remarque, and, by comparison, the scene changes in *Im Westen nichts Neues* appear more than a little obvious.

Both novels are concerned with death and suffering, and it is all the more surprising that they should both be concerned with the depiction of "love stories" in the old-fashioned sense of the term: neither with sucrose escapism à la Barbara Cartland, nor lurid scenes of physical passion explicit down to the last detail, but with a restrained account of the growth of positive relationships which begin to point the way beyond either the selfish pursuit of individual destinies or the equally negative exclusivity of the closed circle of comrades which had dominated the lives of so many of his previous characters. In raising his sights to encompass the larger totality of society and to contemplate the promise of the future, Remarque prefers to tread a middle path: there is none of the melancholic aspiration towards an elusive ecstasy which tainted his accounts of his transient amours in the *Schönheit* days. The women may be of flesh and blood, but the atmosphere is certainly not one of "burning eroticism" (the reviewer in *Die Welt* must have read yet another different version of *Zeit zu leben*). Love is seen as neither an ever-receding goal nor as an end in itself, but as a means towards readjusting individual conceptions of society and the passage of history.

The courtship and marriage of Graeber and Elisabeth unfolds against a background of air raids on their home town, of Graeber's search for his parents, who are missing after their home had been bombed out, and of Elisabeth's despairing hope that her father may still be alive in the concentration camp to which he had been taken. The love between Bucher and Ruth in *Der Funke Leben* is only taken up in the latter part of the novel: it evolves more slowly and is depicted only in its earlier phases, progressing in parallel with the growing awareness on the part of the internees in the concentration camp that the end of their years of suffering is in sight, and that once again there is room for hope, for beginning to believe in a life which has more to it than a mere grim struggle for personal survival in the present moment.

Like *Im Westen nichts Neues,* these two Second World War novels concentrate on the closing stages of the armed conflict, but — in contrast to the story of Bäumer — they both recognize the possibility of making a new beginning when the war is over, of building a bridge of humanity across the years of tyranny. As the German defeat approaches, life and love begin to reassert themselves, although there are no illusions about the difficulty of the task ahead.

The problems confronting Elisabeth and Graeber are highlighted in a curious episode which closely parallels (and may well be borrowed from) the sequence in the story *Romeo und Julia auf dem Dorfe* by the nineteenth-century Swiss writer Gottfried Keller, made famous by the instrumental interlude, "The Walk to the Paradise Garden", in the opera by Delius, *The Village Romeo and Juliet.* There the two doomed lovers, Sali and Vrenchen, unable to achieve their goal of a respectable bourgeois marriage because of their fathers' feuding, spend a last evening together dancing in the grounds of a tumbledown inn, the *Paradiesgärtlein* (Paradise Garden), in a heightened magical atmosphere remote from the insoluble problems of the real world.

In *Zeit zu leben,* Graeber stumbles on a similar idyll, and takes Elisabeth there. It is an inn called Witte's Restaurant which has been miraculously preserved in the midst of the bombing and destruction, an island — the term is applied to it more than once — of peace, a link with the past. There is no picture of Hitler gracing the wall, and its tranquillity and the sense of permanence with which it is imbued carry the two back in their minds to the magic and timeless innocence of childhood.

Like Sali and Vrenchen, Elisabeth and Graeber have very little time together and are almost certainly doomed, but Witte's Restaurant permits them, as did the *Paradiesgärtlein,* to affirm the positive qualities of life, despite the fact that their own individual futures are under serious threat.

It is this positive affirmation of life which marks a distinct move on Remarque's part away from the bleak pessimism of his earlier novels, a shift which has been entirely ignored by his critics. No longer is life conceived of entirely in terms of selfish individual survivial; no longer are enduring values and permanent relationships shunned; no longer, either, do the central figures of these

Second World War novels, unlike the disillusioned young men of the Great War, express fear at the prospect of returning normality.

For the maturer figures of Bucher and Graeber, the fear of boredom which peace brings is banished, and its place is taken by a willing acceptance of normality, the decency and uneventful respectability for which the unfortunate Sali and Vrenchen so hopelessly yearned. And in Elisabeth's possible pregnancy there lies a hope of continuity, of a new and more secure generation able to face the future with confident hope of a reasonable measure of happiness and stability. The transition, however, will not come easily, nor will the past be readily forgotten. A large measure of bitterness remains:

> We have lost all our standards. For ten years on end we've been isolated... We have been declared the Master Race... And, as always, the innocent are harder hit than the guilty. (*Zeit*, p. 38)

One significant contributory factor in this shift in a positive direction is, of course, the fact that the figures in these two novels are older than the young men of *Im Westen nichts Neues*, and have a strong point of reference outside their immediate circumstances with which they can identify and to which they can cling in the midst of their present sufferings. Here, as elsewhere in his novels, Remarque again stresses the key theme of home as that point of reference. For the young men of *Im Westen nichts Neues*, this was not a possibility, since they were in the middle of the process of growing up, were deliberately freeing themselves from home when they went to war, and so had not the time to gain a proper awareness of its true significance.

When Graeber returns on leave, his first thought is that the bombing has destroyed the distinctive features of the town of his birth; it "no longer looked like the home which he had expected; it looked as if it might have been in the middle of Russia". (*Zeit*, p. 83). Associated with home, love and normality is the motif of light: when Graeber first sees Elisabeth, she is haloed in a bright beam of light; in the same novel, love is described as being like lights coming on in the windows of a house; and, inevitably in wartime, the lights of non-combatant Switzerland shining in the darkness symbolize peace and normality.

All of these motifs are poignantly captured in the brightness of a white-fronted house shining from a hillside opposite the concentration camp in *Der Funke Leben,* beckoning to Bucher and Ruth and instilling into them hope for the future. The white house is a symbol of peace, home, and love: and it is there that they will make their way as soon as the war is over and they are released from the camp.

Significantly, the first reference to the white house does not come until the middle of *Der Funke Leben*, when the tide has turned against the Nazi captors. 509 has defied an order and, to the surprise of all the inmates, he has not been tortured to death. The ray of hope, the spark of life, begins to flicker a little more strongly, and they can now look out beyond their immediate misery towards the white facade in the distance which encapsulates all their aspirations.

But when they are liberated and make their way up the hillside, they find that the future will not be so easy as they had hoped:

> The garden bloomed; but when they came up to the white house, they saw that a bomb had fallen at the back of it. It had destroyed all the rear portion of the building; only the house front had remained undamaged.
> *(Der Funke Leben, p.382)*

Recognizing that the house had sustained them, even though its wholeness had proven an illusion, like the sense of indestructible permanence Graeber and Elisabeth found in Witte's Restáurant, enables them to keep their hopes alive and face the future with a measure of confidence.

Another significant change marked by these two novels comes in the context of characterization. For the most part, Remarque is not concerned with drawing character in depth; his figures tend to be sketchy and generalized.

It is true that none of the protagonists in *Im Westen nichts Neues* merit the title of fully rounded, developing characters. They are indeed generalized figures, and even those which are depicted in greater detail can be more accurately described in terms of a collection of characteristics rather than as complete characters. This is, however, entirely consonant with the subjective lyricism of the novel, a feature which — like its tendency towards effusiveness and extravagance of expression — both reflects the extreme youth of Bäumer, the first-person narrator, and also points to the fact that Remarque was still endeavouring to shake himself free from the contrived affectations of his *Traumbude* days.

For a variety of reasons (none of which are connected with his ability to portray it), character does not play a dominant rôle. Strong personalities are present, like the bibulous Sergeant Knopf in *Der schwarze Obelisk*, but there is nothing in the way of character development. Even the profoundly moving portrayal of Ravic in *Arc de Triomphe* is more a cumulative portrait than a dynamic depiction of character.

As early as *Im Westen nichts Neues*, Remarque presented a situation in which the causal bond between character and the external environment, which is a key feature of mainstream European literature, was shattered by the facts of war in the front line. Meaningful development of personality in a vacuum in which chance is the only law has become impossible; and, in addition, characters exposed to extreme situations are forced back on to the basic elements of life in order to be able to survive at all; self-enrichment and personal development are something of a luxury under heavy bombardment in the trenches, or for an illegal immigrant living from hand to mouth, or again a skeletal figure hanging on to the last spark of life in a concentration camp.

But in *Der Funke Leben* and *Zeit zu leben*, a distinct break in this pattern occurs, and this comes about for one very important reason, namely, that the shattered causal bond is beginning to mend. Despite all the meaningless sufferings of war, Graeber does emerge as a developing personality, because his love for Elisabeth enables him to make a measure of progress away from living entirely selfishly for the present moment to an awareness that there is something above and beyond the individual life, although this is almost cancelled out in his gesture of humanity at the end of the novel, when he releases the Russian prisoners, only to find that one of them turns a gun against him and shoots him down.

Equally, in *Der Funke Leben*, 509 emerges from his torpor, challenges the system and survives; this causes him to cast his mind back to the days before he was brought into the concentration camp, days which he had hitherto deliberately excluded from his mind. He recalls his own name, and thus re-establishes the broken link with the past. A link with the future also emerges: he recognizes that he will not survive the war, but transfers his hopes for the future to the younger Bucher. At the same time, too, many of the prisoners begin to be dimly aware of the possibility of the survival of justice and humanity despite all the suffering they have undergone: "We have been subjected to degradation. But it's not us who've been degraded. It's the others who have done it to us." (*Der Funke Leben*, p.314)

But it is none the less true that none of these characters are drawn in any real depth, and that the emphasis remains elsewhere than in characterization. However, there is one very significant exception to this general rule in the figure of Neubauer, the Nazi camp commandant in *Der Funke Leben*. His character is explored in considerable detail, since it is only through character that Remarque is able to explore the paradoxical nature of the Nazi party member seeking to reconcile strongly conflicting elements within him.

Before the Nazi seizure of power, Neubauer was an ordinary clerk performing a humdrum job; but when he joined the party, he found himself rapidly catapulted into a position of power and privilege which enabled him to amass considerable wealth at the expense of his fellow citizens. In 1933, a block of business property in the town had belonged to the Jew Josef Blank. Neubauer was desirous of owning this property, and Blank offered it to him at half its real value. A fortnight in the local concentration camp persuaded him to reduce the asking price to a mere 5,000 Marks. In the course of his internment, Blank had unfortunately "lost his footing", and in the process had broken an arm, been blinded in one eye, and sustained other injuries.

Neubauer, however, is not one of the fanatical extremist Nazis who delight in the brutal assertion of their superiority over lesser beings for its own sake; on the contrary, it is clear that he, like countless other nonentities, entered the ranks of the Party out of sheer opportunism. He found himself incapable of making any impact on the strength of his own unaided and diminuitive talents, so he climbed on the band-waggon as did so many thousands of other little people at the time.

The property he acquired from Blank underlines the fact that Neubauer is inspired, not by sadism, but by the desire to become a big businessman. This is why he actually *paid* for the property, which was duly and legally signed over to him by Blank, whereas in fact he could have confiscated the building without having to part with a single Pfennig. Although the price was vastly below the true current market value of the property, it was still beyond the financial means of Neubauer, so he actually found himself in the Gilbertian situation of purchasing the building from its erstwhile owner by instalments, paying Blank out of rental income. This "business instinct", the desire to do deals, amass wealth and exploit the system to the limit — even to the point of stepping beyond the bounds of legality — is deeply rooted in Remarque's characters. He is clearly fascinated by this entrepreneurial facet of man's personality, the desire on the part of the individual to become more than a cog in the machine, to be able to exercise a positive and controlling rôle within society, which in the last analysis, bolsters the illusion that one is capable not only of beating the system, but also of overcoming the basic facts of life and death.

Neubauer, however, has no real functions within society which would permit him to assert himself on the basis of his own merits. Before the Nazis seized power, he was performing a humdrum job like countless other faceless thousands. His whole existence was a drab cliché. Thus it is that he exploits the new status accorded him by his membership of the Nazi party in order to graft on to himself, as it were, the rôle of businessman.

Neubauer is inordinately proud of his acquisitions: he owns business premises, a cigar shop, and a part share in the local newspaper. At the same time, however, he is inspired with a profound sense of fear, not just in regard to his newly-won rôle as a local businessman, but especially his position as commandant of the camp, a task for which he has neither the ability nor personality. He is under constant threat of being shown up in his true light as an inadequate and immature individual, and he goes to extreme lengths in an attempt to mask his ineptitude.

But there is a further strand to Neubauer's character which is reflected in his inadequacies in his assumed rôle as the tough Nazi: Neubauer is abjectly terrified of being punished for his own brutality. Over many years, he has accumulated in his office secret files "proving" his mildness and generosity; it is not the threat of imminent defeat for Germany that has driven him to this course of action.

And, in Neubauer's fears, Remarque reflects one of the less happy aspects of the German national character, as he sees it: namely, a tendency to fall in with a strict hierarchical system, which allows Neubauer to convince himself that he is doing no more than his duty, and that he is acting under orders. Whatever he does, it is in the name of the Führer, and Hitler himself stated that he assumed responsibility for all that has happened, including the less pleasant actions which have been regrettably essential in order to further the cause of National Socialism.

Neubauer's self-delusion borders on schizophrenia. As Graeber in *Zeit zu leben* stresses on more than one occasion, the Germans under Hitler have learned to become past masters in deception and duplicity; but Neubauer has actually reached — and passed — the point at which he comes to believe in his own rationalization of his actions.

One clear illustration of his ability for self-deception is the cigar shop which he now owns. It had belonged to a Jewish firm, but had been "acquired" by Sturmführer Freiberg. In 1936, Neubauer had overheard Freiberg in his cups making tactless observations about the Führer, and out of a sense of the purest duty, he had reported his indiscretions. Freiberg disappeared, and Neubauer purchased the shop for a quarter of its true value from Freiberg's widow.

> He told her that he had information that Freiberg's property was to be confiscated. Money, he went on, was easier to conceal than a shop. She had been grateful. Had sold up... He had acted with propriety. Duty was duty, after all — and the shop really could have been confiscated.
> (*Der Funke Leben*, p.42)

The extreme pressures building up within Neubauer cause him to seek refuge in his own private idyll, a negative version of the "white house" or Witte's restaurant. The latter are recognized by the respective lovers for the symbols and ideals which they represent, but Neubauer becomes totally and obsessively immersed in his own little paradise garden, a plot of land in the suburbs (paid for in full, it is stressed, in a straightforward business transaction), which he has transformed into an idyllic garden, not without assistance from forced labour from the camp. Among the flowers and vegetables there are some livestock, notably his two Angora rabbits, on which he dotes. Their smell reminds him of "a long-forgotten innocence", (*Der Funke Leben*, p.45) but equally forcibly of the privations of his own childhood, when he was allowed to have nothing he wanted:

> Even as a lad, he'd always wanted rabbits. His father had refused to allow it. Now he had some. . . . The security of those childhood memories. Forgotten dreams. Sometimes one was so damned alone. . . . The most he'd been given as a boy was 75 Pfennigs. Two days after, someone had stolen them. (*Der Funke Leben*, p.135)

The roots of his aspirations to rise above mediocrity lie in childhood, where he was refused love and never permitted to have what he wanted. But now he has created for himself a new childhood in his secluded garden.

Even into this sanctuary, however, harsh reality has infiltrated: ashes from the concentration camp crematorium are spread as fertilizer on the soil, and two Russian prisoners act as unpaid gardeners. When one of these men seemingly threatens Neubauer with his spade, the commandant assaults him, kicking him to the ground, all the while congratulating himself on his humanity, since, he argues, he could have shot the fellow out of hand.

In the majority of his novels, the very nature of his subject matter must, it seems, have sorely tempted Remarque to adopt an intrusive posture, to seek to preach to the reader about the horrors of war, the despair of the exile, or the precariousness of the human condition in general. And this temptation could never have been stronger than it was during the composition of *Der Funke Leben*; but, even here, Remarque refrains from judging Neubauer for the wall of self-delusion he has built up around himself. He simply portrays him without comment, as he is, contradictions and all. The temptation to caricature is equally avoided, as it is with Neubauer's hysterical wife Selma (a beautifully drawn vignette, this), who is terrified for her own safety, yet at the same time honest in her awareness of her own frailty and the qualities of others — including Jews.

The refusal on the part of human character to fit into neatly prescribed patterns of good and bad, right and wrong, is further highlighted in *Zeit zu leben*, in which Graeber, although a convinced anti-Nazi, accepts food and other favours from an erstwhile schoolfriend, Binding, now a prominent local SS man. Remarque even depicts Binding's housekeeper as a woman who adulates her employer, and states (without tongue in cheek): "Everyone was, it seemed, a good person to someone. And to someone else, the opposite." (*Zeit*, p.124)

That there is some good in all of us is indeed a tired old cliché, but, as Remarque constantly reminds his reader, it tends to be the tired old cliché which holds the truth in the midst of a confusing and contradictory world. The average reader may accept Remarque's assertion that the riddle of existence cannot be forced into the straitjacket of a neat ideology which sweeps all contradictions under the carpet, but nothing infuriates his politically committed critics more than his supposed "inability" to draw the "obvious" political lesson from the situations he depicts; but Remarque does not set out to attack any political stance, nor, indeed, to defend a party line, since in his eyes all extremes are bad, and all political manifestations equally corrupt.

These two novels, perhaps more than any others of his works, do, however, make unambiguously clear what Remarque is attacking as the great evil of the age. It is neither Communism nor Nazism as such, but the dehumanizing process that all totalitarian systems inevitably set in train, shifting the centre of concern away from the individual as a human being towards an impersonal set of rules and regulations to which humanity is forced to conform. Not even the Catholic Church escapes Remarque's strictures, when the beadle seeks to enforce his regulation about homeless or bombed-out married men and women sleeping in separate parts of the church because the house of God is no place for the pleasures of the flesh.

Shortly before, the closed logic of the bureaucrat presented itself in all its absurdity on the occasion of the civil wedding between Graeber and Elisabeth. The official demands two witnesses; and the next couple in line volunteer their services. When, however, Graeber and Elisabeth are pronounced man and wife and have been presented with their free copy of *Mein Kampf* (a gift from a benevolent state), the official refuses to permit them to reciprocate since, as he argues with impeccable logic, Graeber and Elisabeth cannot, as a married couple of some two minutes' standing, be regarded as two independent witnesses.

Such absurdities spill over into the grotesque in *Der Funke Leben*, when, during roll call, the inmates frantically scrabble round to collect together enough corpses and severed limbs to make up the requisite total. "The numbers at roll call had to tally. Bureaucracy did not draw back in the presence of corpses." (*Der Funke Leben*, p.46)

These and many other illustrations of the bureaucratic mind Remarque employs to underpin his thesis that all such attempts to escape the complexities and contradictions of life by hiding behind the skirts of a rigid established pattern of conduct; and he equally attacks any individual who employs similar devices to hide away from life.

Remarque does not preach anti-bureaucracy; in this, as in all else, he permits the characters and the action to speak for themselves, and this stance is aptly reflected in the narrative technique he employs in his two Second World War novels. In neither is the plot as such of very great import; particularly in *Der Funke Leben*, the emphasis is on a series of loosely-linked episodes, cumulative in effect, operating on the basis of theme and variation, antithesis, and recurrent motifs. This structural formula continues to reflect a world in which causality is absent, where human existence is disjunctive, and where the individual personality is subjected to alienation and fragmentation.

And it is indeed tempting to regard the Second World War novels as the mixture as before, reflecting the fact that life is just as bad as it was previously, if not a great deal worse. One of the key antitheses in *Im Westen nichts Neues* is that between the battlefield and the unspoilt world of home; but even this is shattered in *Zeit zu leben* and *Der Funke Leben*, for the bombs are now destroying civilian life and property (including that of the hapless Neubauer).

But, suprisingly, and apparently against all logic, both novels, as we have seen, hold a glimmering of hope. At the end of *Im Westen nichts Neues*, Bäumer dies in the midst of suffering and destruction that have become so routine that the despatches for the day reported "all quiet on the Western front"; but in the two Second World War novels, there is more than a hint of a new beginning. True, Graeber dies, but it is not an utterly pointless death. He has at least been able to make a personal stand against the mindless tyranny he has served for so long by seeking to ensure the humane treatment of some Russian prisoners.

Hope is also the keynote at the close of *Der Funke Leben*. The central figure of the first part of the novel, prisoner 509, the first man ever to defy the camp authorities and survive, dies, but envisages in the younger man Bucher a kind of successor, one who will carry the fight for humanity and moderation beyond the end of the war.

Still, the hint of optimism is hedged about by all manner of reservations. The ex-teacher Pohlmann, a liberal in imminent danger of arrest, is sought out by Graeber, who asks him to try and help him come to terms with an apparently meaningless world bent on self-destruction. Pohlmann concedes the validity of dreams of a better future, but the main weight of emphasis remains as before:

> Humanity has not progressed smoothly, but always in fits and starts, jerks and setbacks. (*Zeit*, p. 283).

And the same holds true for the individual life: when Graeber returns to the Russian front, it is as if he had always been there — but now at least he has the memory of his time with Elisabeth. As in the emigré novels, the spark of life flickers on against seemingly impossible odds, but now not just because it *is* the spark of life. Now there seems to be something concrete and positive to live for, even if that something is reserved for others to enjoy.

CHAPTER SIX

FALSE PARADISE

It is sad to record that a novelist who achieved such heights when writing at his peak should bow out from the literary scene, not with a bang, but a whimper. The signs of decline are already present in *Der Himmel kennt keine Günstlinge*, which all to readily slips into triteness and cheap sentimentality in a manner uncomfortably reminiscent of his early *Jugendstil* efforts and his journalistic work for *Echo-Continental*. Perhaps Remarque had exhausted his considerable creative talents; but, more likely, he was obstinately writing on in the face of fading health, impelled by the spark of life within him to seek to recreate and even excel the achievements of his earlier years and to cheat the shadow of death which loomed over him.

Schatten im Paradies was composed during the last six years of Remarque's life and published posthumously. The manuscript was clearly never completed to his satisfaction. It has been suggested that Remarque was of the opinion that the novel was his best work,[1] but it is hard indeed to see how this could be so. Not only does the text abound in inconsistencies (which Remarque, had he lived, would certainly have rectified), the narrative is lacking in conviction as, too, are the characters. Even Remarque's compelling readability has deserted him. Schwark is far from overstating the case when he claims that *Schatten im Paradies* does not — to put it mildly — compare favourably with Remarque's previous novels, and adds:

> Weariness sets in at the very latest just after half way through, interest in the characters and their cynically sentimental conversations fades away — in a different way from that which Remarque intended, they remain "shadows in paradise".[2]

The first person narrator, Robert Ross, is particularly insipid, and his girlfriend Natascha even more so. Their love-affair is singularly lacking in interest, the only real emotional response aroused in the reader being one of relief when the relationship between the two of them ultimately fizzles out when Ross returns to Germany, leaving Natascha behind in New York. Their conversations are even more inconsequential than those between Clerfayt and Lillian in *Der Himmel kennt keine Günstlinge*, and the well-worn topics of food, drink and clothing intrude excessively into both dialogue and action.

It may well be the case that Remarque himself was far from unaware of the blandness of the love theme since, for the very first time, he seems to feel constrained to spice the relationship with lurid accounts of the physical encounters between the two of them. Each of these little episodes represents an abrupt and embarrassingly unwelcome change of tone, one which is uncomfortably out of place both in terms of character development and the overall pattern of the narrative. Equally out of place are the two inadequately motivated explosions of anger on the part of Natascha; and time and again the reader is forced to the conclusion that Remarque's hitherto fertile imagination has quite simply run out of steam — the creative writer has, it appears, degenerated into a literary technician.

Ross's character gets off to a shaky start when he is caused to utter a number of somewhat contradictory statements. First of all, he declares — in common with many of Remarque's heroes — that he does not like to sleep unaccompanied. (*Schatten,* p.20) A handful of pages later, however, he appears to have changed his mind, when he declares: "It suddenly seemed important to me to sleep alone again". (*Schatten,* p.24) Some time later, he is constrained to readopt his original stance: "I didn't want to be alone". (*Schatten,* p.45)

A review of the novel in *Die Welt der Literatur* highlights inaccuracies in the chronology of the story of Ross's exploits during the Second World War, during which he spent a period in a German concentration camp, before being released as a non-Jew; then he sequestered for two years in hiding in a Brussels museum of art during the German occupation; subsequently he was interned in a French Camp, from which he escaped in the general confusion when France capitulated; and then he was for a time in a camp at Gurs, from which he escaped by bribing a guard.[3]

Many of the minor characters also behave inconsistently, especially in the closing chapters of the novel, which Remarque's deteriorating health presumably left him unable to bring up to the moderate standard of the rest of the novel. One of the more abrupt Jekyll-Hyde changes is undergone by Ross's boss, Silvers, who is portrayed as a shrewd, hard-headed businessman, whose glib tongue and agile brain normally enable him to get the better of everyone with whom he comes into contact. But in the course of a business visit to Hollywood, where he is seeking to cut a fine figure, Silvers suddenly confides in Ross, telling of a traumatic experience with a young starlet, who almost renders him impotent by calling him "Daddy". Leaving aside the irrelevance of the whole contrived episode to the main strand of the narrative, the idea of a man of Silvers's ilk revealing his own private weaknesses to an employee of a few weeks' standing is implausible in the extreme. From this juncture onwards, Remarque's depiction of Silvers steadily deteriorates and rapidly forfeits all credibility, despite efforts to reinstate his former image as a scheming business-man always bent on depriving Ross of the commission due to him.

An equally forced — and equally irrelevant — episode supervenes during Ross's time in Hollywood, and is shot through with all the worst aspects of Remarque's style and sentimental proclivities. During the night, a young girl enters Ross's room and asks if she might spend the remainder of the night on his sofa.

> I awoke quite late. The girl was no longer there. On a towel I found the lipstick impression of her mouth. She had probably left it as a silent saluta-tion... I remembered no more than that she had at some time stood before my bed and I thought I had felt her naked body, cool and smooth; but I wasn't sure if it had come to more. (*Schatten*, p.308)

The wheel, so its seems, has turned full circle, and Remarque has reverted to the ethereal sentimentality of his *Traumbude* days. Not a few inept turns of phrase also creep into the closing pages of the narrative, witness the following comment which Ross passes about one of his friends: "I saw that there was little to be done with him. He was going round in circles like a dog with constipa-tion." (*Schatten*, p.367) Remarque's technique of employing repeated phrases and images also becomes obtrusive in the latter part of the novel.

Perhaps it is unfair to attach all of the blame to Remarque, since he had not approved the text for publication, but surely his publishers could have arranged for the many blemishes to be ghosted out with a few strategic strokes of the blue pencil.

The chief source of regret, however, is that this final work could well have constituted a fitting culmination to the whole series of his mature novels. Not only does *Schatten im Paradies* represent a kind of sequel to *Arc de Triomphe* and *Die Nacht von Lissabon* (the emigré Robert Ross arrives in America via Paris and the port of Lisbon), it also contains numerous references — direct and indirect — to the earlier novels and to Remarque's own life.

The narrator's name (Ross) had earlier been used by Remarque in his drama *Die letzte Station*, and in *Schatten im Paradies* Robert Ross explains that his surname is an assumed one, borrowed from a dead emigré — the device of an acquired identity is familiar from *Die Nacht von Lissabon* and other novels. The name of the

homosexual Kiki echoes that of Kiki in *Drei Kameraden*; and the
celebrated Dr Ravic of *Arc de Triomphe* re-emerges in *Schatten im
Paradies* as an emigré, in which he tells Ross that he has now
resumed his real name of Fresenburg, although Ross, who had
known him in Paris, persists in referring to him by his adopted
name.

Many references from other novels seem to have made their way
almost unaltered into *Schatten im Paradies*. In this respect, *Der
Funke Leben* is a happy hunting ground. The Nazi camp
commandant, Neubauer, kept two Angora rabbits; and Ross refers
to the affection for these animals on the part of the "chief of all
concentration camps, Heinrich Himmler" (*Schatten*, p.81); and
when he later acts as adviser for an anti-Nazi film being made in
Hollywood, he proposes that the camp commandant should be
depicted as keeping white Angora rabbits, none of which he will
permit to be slaughtered. Descriptions of a concentration camp in
Schatten im Paradies closely resemble the camp in *Der Funke
Leben*. The striking image of the corpses in the crematorium
incinerator arching up as if the heat had brought them to life
occurs in both novels, as does a description of the interior of the
building with its hooks on the wall from which victims were
suspended.

Whilst it might be tempting to draw the unkind conclusion that
Remarque's flagging inventiveness had forced him to recycle old
material, it would be much nearer the truth to recognize that here,
as in the past, Remarque was deliberately and consciously forging
bonds with his other novels. Equally, *Schatten im Paradies* abounds
with references of an autobiographical nature, although here they
have become somewhat tongue-in-cheek. At one point, for
example, a visit is proposed to a Paulette Goddard film; and Ross's
cynical view of Hollywood — "Only God knows the ways of
Hollywood" (*Schatten*, p.85) — doubtless mirrors Remarque's
own, despite his success there.

Many of the comments which Remarque places in the mouth of
his first-person narrator have more than a touch of self-irony
about them; Ross emphatically declares that he is just a "lousy
journalist" and not a writer, (*Schatten*, p.96) and he more than
once describes himself as a kind of "con-man" with social pretensions:

"She just has the Rolls for this evening... Wouldn't you like to glide
through the world as someone with social pretensions for one night?"
I laughed. "I've been doing that for years. But not in a car. That would
be a novelty." (*Schatten*, p.91)[4]

Mention is made of Ross's penchant for "popular philosophy", (*Schatten*, p.19) a weakness — if it is a weakness — of which Remarque has frequently been accused by his critics; and at one point Ross's girlfriend, Natascha, feels constrained to defend the author's other principal failing, namely his sentimental lapses:

> Sometimes it is absolutely necessary to let oneself be flooded by a gigantic wave of sentimentality in which all caution and good taste gloriously perish. (*Schatten*, p.121)

In addition, Ross passes the occasional self-conscious remark about his own use of the cliché.

The setting for *Schatten im Paradies* is New York, Remarque's home for most of the time he spent in America, and a city which he always held in great affection. Ross also goes to Hollywood for a while, but — like Remarque — he soon tires of the articifiality of the place, and returns to New York. Several of Remarque's Hollywood friends receive a passing mention, Greta Garbo and Dolores del Rio among them, as do some of the German writers who shared Remarque's American exile. Indeed, Thomas Mann comes in for a degree of criticism at one point for his endorsement of the *furor teutonicus* in his *Gedanken zum Kriege* (Thoughts on the War) and *Friedrich und die Grosse Koalition* (Frederick and the Grand Coalition), written at the beginning of the First World War, although Remarque does qualify his observations by adding: "How deeply must the barbarism have been seated for it not to have been entirely eradicated in this humane and humanitarian author." (*Schatten*, p.263)

The novel also touches on the suicides of Stefan Zweig and his wife; Hasenclever's suicide — he is mildly disguised as Hastenecker — is also mentioned. A certain Betty Stern, whose Berlin salon was a popular meeting place in the 'twenties, is translated to New York under the name of Betty Stein, and there portrayed in some depth as a mother-figure and patroness of all German emigrés. Even Remarque's cook, Rosy, appears under her own name, as the Hungarian cook of the rich emigré Vrieslånder who — like Remarque himself — generously assists his less fortunate compatriots. The jobs which Ross takes, first in an antique shop assessing the value of Chinese bronzes, and then selling Impressionist paintings, give Remarque an opportunity to display his not inconsiderable knowledge of these subjects.

Another theme to which Remarque devotes much space in *Schatten im Paradies* is the issue of the responsibility of the Germans at large for the Nazis' rise to power, and his observations are scarcely calculated to endear him to his fellow-countrymen. As

147

in *Der Funke Leben,* he attributes much of the blame for the atrocities committed in the Second World War, not only to the consequences of the political beliefs of the National Socialist party, but also to certain basic characteristics which are to be found in the German nation as a whole, especially the strict sense of hierarchy, the willingness to take orders from above, whatever those orders may be:

> The man behind a desk doesn't have to wield the axe in his hand himself... And there are always people who carry out orders, especially in Germany. (*Schatten*, p.32)

Remarque claims that the Germans tend to regard all orders as sacrosanct, and hence seek to evade their own complicity in whatever their orders lead them to do:

> The Germans were no nation of revolutionaries. They were a nation of order-takers. Command replaced conscience. It was the favourite excuse. Someone acting on orders wasn't responsible. (*Schatten*, p. 399)

The bureaucratic chain of command, asserts Remarque, holds firm even when crimes and acts of inhumanity are to be committed, and this *Führerprinzip* is frequently adduced as a justification for the worst atrocities.

Although Ross is deeply offended when an American lawyer assumes that, as a non-Jewish German, he must be a Nazi, he goes a long way in the direction of making similar assertions himself about the German nation, when he puts forward the view that it is certain national characteristics which gave rise to Nazism, and that the Germans are a "schizophrenic nation. Skilled economists, scientists and mass-murderers". (*Schatten*, p. 377) He refuses to draw any clear distinction between the Nazis and the Germans as a whole; hearing a Nazi broadcast on the radio, Ross is made to remark: "That wasn't a party any longer. That was Germany." (*Schatten*, p.88) Remarque repeats the statement he made in *Der Funke Leben* through his depiction of the camp commandant Neubauer, namely, that the Nazis were quite ordinary Germans, and a phrase which occurs several times in *Schatten im Paradies,* with minor variations, is that "the Nazis didn't fall out of a clear blue sky and conquer Germany". Ross endeavours to make this point when he acts as adviser to the makers of anti-Nazi films, who find it difficult to believe either that the reality of the Nazi regime is far worse than their depiction of it on the screen or that the people who perpetrate the crimes and atrocities are quire ordinary people:

I explained to him time and again that the events in Germany were not instigated and carried out by people who had come down from the moon and conquered the country, but by good Germans, who without doubt still considered themselves to be good Germans. I explained to him that it was ridiculous to assume that all generals in Germany were so blind and had such bad memories that they knew nothing of the tortures and murders which were committed daily. (*Schatten*, p. 317)

Once again, the Church does not escape censure for the rôle it played in the rise of Nazism. Asked about his religious convictions, Ross replies that he is an atheist now, for, although he was born a Catholic, he left the Church when it signed the Concordat with Hitler.

Remarque also levels a different — but related — kind of criticism against his fellow Germans, namely, their lack of a sense of humour:

"The Germans have no sense of humour. That's right."
"What do they have instead?"
"*Schadenfreude*. An untranslatable German word." (*Schatten*, p.149)

The word *Schadenfreude* (implying a delight in the suffering of others) receives two mentions in the course of the narrative, and Remarque was clearly disturbed by the fact that this concept was a peculiarly German one. By contrast, he said of the Americans that one of the things he cherished most about them was their sense of humour.

Although humour plays nothing like so important a rôle in *Schatten im Paradies* as it did in *Der schwarze Obelisk,* the Wildean shafts of wit are still very much in evidence, and on occasion Remarque borrows from the earlier novel a device frequently employed there, that of using a joke to make a serious point. Ross's friend Kahn, for example, in seeking to indicate the kind of fate which most of the emigrés can expect in America, tells a story about a Paris nightclub run by Russian emigrés. The owner, trying to impress a visitor, points out a porter who was formerly a general, a waiter who had been a count, and so on. In the end, the owner notices the visitor's Dachshund and enquires of him what kind of dog it is. "In Berlin," the man replies, "that used to be a St Bernard." (*Schatten*, p.85)

The emigrés, then, are living unreal existences, are "shadows" of their former selves, compelled to live from hand to mouth, accepting whatever work they can get. Remarque highlights the ironic fate of a number of Jewish actors who find themselves playing — of all things — the rôles of Nazis in the Hollywood propaganda films. Such is their "Promised Land"; yet, in comparison with Germany, America does indeed appear to be a paradise for the emigrés, "an illusory paradise, if you like," says Ross, "a paradise to overwinter in". (*Schatten*, p.174)

References to the "shadowy" existence led by the emigrés abound, and convey both a sense of impermanence and even of criminality, since many of them do not possess legitimate papers and consequently become involved in the outer fringes of crime. The Russian Melikow, Ross's landlord, is one such individual: he is blackmailed into becoming caught up in drug-trafficking. Imagery relating to light and shade, always a common feature of Remarque's novels, is — as might be expected from the novel's title — very prominent, one frequently repeated image being that of insects flying round an electric lamp. The bright light of America attracts the emigrés, but many of them suffer the fate of the insect — although some prosper, several commit suicide, including Kahn, who has saved countless lives both by himself and in association with the French Resistance, but now he can find nothing to live for, no purpose in life. In words typical of a Remarque hero, his hopelessness is expressed in these terms:

> We are spoilt for normal life... We are ruined... Some have escaped with minor injuries, some have even profited, others have become crippled, and the wounded... will never find their feet again, and they will perish in the end. (*Schatten*, p.355)

So America turns out to be a false paradise for most of the refugees; few find anything of worth there, or in the post-war Germany to which a number of them, Ross included, return. Concluding — like so many of Remarque's other heroes — that "one cannot go back", (*Schatten*, p.400) Ross is left reflecting upon the transience of life and reminiscing about his love for Natascha, which — for a time, at least — seemed to hold out the hope of immortality: "Love with open fires, lamplight, the night wind, falling leaves, and confidence that nothing can be lost". (*Schatten*, p.260) The vibrant life of New York conspired to add a measure of credence to this illusion of immortality, but Ross's fear of death still lurked beneath the surface, a fear doubtless sharply etched in his author's mind. Nor can the vitality of the city overcome the realization of so many of Remarque's heroes that the individual is, in the last analysis, a solitary spark of life struggling against inevitable extinction.

CONCLUSION

Remarque's detractors have been many, varied and vociferous, from Marxists at one extreme outraged at his refusal or supposed inability to draw the "obvious" conclusions from the social ills he portrays with such compelling realism to academics at the other end of the scale convinced that success and literary quality are mutually exclusive propositions. Although half a century has gone by since *Im Westen nichts Neues* first appeared, the novel continues to stimulate acrimonious debate and stir critical passions: even the veteran journalist and *Times* columnist Bernard Levin, starved of a target for his barbed pen, was recently constrained to dismiss Remarque as not "even in the second rank", and his anti-war novel is pilloried as "little more than very superior pulp fiction" (or does he mean "slightly less than very inferior good fiction"?).[1]

Proponents and opponents of Remarque alike have consumed much of their energy in pursuit of different game than the actual works themselves. But the novels do reward serious investigation and fill an important niche in twentieth-century German literature, although it would be wrong to embrace a position opposite to that held by Levin and make exaggerated claims for Remarque's achievement. *Im Westen nichts Neues*, in particular, may be one of the most important books written in this century; but it is neither one of the very greatest, nor does it represent the best that Remarque himself achieved.

Remarque's real importance as a writer lies in the way in which he has charted the history of a generation of young men alienated not only from the past and the present but also from their own true selves: those who survive the devastation of the trenches return home filled with hope that there is a way back into normality for them, but they find that, having lived an animal existence constantly staring death in the face, everyday life seems lacklustre and meaningless by comparison. Their plight is compounded by the years of inflation and the rise of Nazism.

Any residual faith which Remarque may have had in humanity in general and the German nation in particular suffers an almost total collapse in the face of the Nazi phenomenon. At times, he even goes so far as to suggest that the horrors engendered by the Nazis are endemic, that Goethe's Faust with his titanism is not

151

Everyman, but specifically German man. In the words of Schwarz in *Die Nacht von Lissabon*:

> It was all part of the culture of Faustian man just like Goethe and Schiller, and I experienced it in a concentration camp in Germany. (*Nacht*, p.273)

Remarque's narrative technique is essentially dramatic, in that he allows his characters to reveal themselves primarily through the medium of dialogue and action without himself seeking to intrude; nevertheless, it is no difficult matter to distil from his works his major preoccupations as a writer. He sets out from what he regards as the inescapable facts of human existence; namely, that life is a relentless, irreversible process which inevitably culminates in the oblivion of death, that each individual is essentially alone, and that nothing endures. Such sentiments are expressed in the very last words of his to find their way into print, in the closing sentences of *Schatten im Paradies*:

> There is no way back, nothing stands still, neither oneself nor the other person. All that remains is the occasional evening filled with melancholy, that melancholy which we all feel because everything passes and man is the only member of the animal kingdom aware of that fact and also aware that it is a consolation, but one that he doesn't understand.
> (*Schatten*, p. 400)

Occasionally, a more optimistic note asserts itself, as in *Der schwarze Obelisk*, when Bodmer assures Isabelle that nothing is lost, despite the fact that time cannot be halted. Equally, in *Der Funke Leben*, the lovers survive the concentration camp; and *Zeit zu leben* holds out at least a measure of hope for the future.

But despite the insistent, if thin, vein of optimism that streaks his novels, Remarque is for the most part a seeker rather than a finder; for him, there are no clear positive answers, only questions. And the one question that dominates all the others is this insistent demand which first emerges in his early *Jugendstil* writings and which persists throughout his work (here put into the mouth of Schwarz):

> And what do we really possess? Why so much ado about things which at best are only loaned to us for a little while; and why so much talk about whether we possess them to a greater or lesser degree, when that deceptive word "possess" only means "clutching the empty air"?
> (*Nacht*, p.301)

So Remarque explores the paradoxes of human existence, and these find their most frequent expression in his novels in what might be termed — to twist a title from Thomas Hardy — "Life's big Ironies". Constantly he refers to the unfairness of life, and his work echoes with the complaint that the right things always happen to the wrong people. Equally, his characters' aspirations are shattered time and again, and the "miracle" which many of them hope for is either snatched from their grasp, or turns out to be no miracle at all. Schwarz has tickets for America and visas in his hands, when his wife dies; and although the man to whom he gives these priceless documents reaches America with his wife, their new life there soon turns sour, and she divorces him.

These paradoxes also find expression in the strong antithetical streak in Remarque's novels: in the contrast between home and the front line in *Im Westen nichts Neues*; the town and the sanatorium in *Drei Kameraden* and *Der Himmel kennt keine Günstlinge*; the town and the asylum in *Der schwarze Obelisk*; the hand-to-mouth existence of the refugee and the "paradise" of the USA; and, most compelling of all, the concentration camp and the white house on the hill in *Der Funke Leben*. It never appears possible to resolve the contrast between these opposites, just as Remarque finds it impossible to resolve the contradictions within some of his individual characters. Lohkamp expresses the fundamental reason for this profusion of paradox and antithesis in life in these words cited earlier: "The details are wonderful, but the whole has no meaning. As if it's made by someone who could think of nothing else to do with the wonderful variety of life but to destroy it again". (*Kameraden*, p. 273)

So it is somewhat aberrant of Remarque's detractors to accuse him of failing to measure up to the big issues of life simply because he refuses to conceive of them in terms of political ideology. Not that Remarque ignores social and political issues: politics is one of the central themes of *Der Funke Leben*. Time and again, he stresses both in this novel and elsewhere that all forms of political extremism are essentially the same in that they deny humanity and to seek to suppress any form of opposition with calculated brutality combined with a supreme confidence in the rightness of their actions. Remarque's concern for other major issues — unemployment, refugees, war, the plight of the underdog in a materialist society (the list could be extended, if not indefinitely, then at least considerably) — also assists in giving the lie to assertions that he turns his back on reality.

Of course, Remarque has his weaknesses: there is no denying that he tends on occasion to trivialize and sentimentalize, and he is given, when leaning heavily on plot, to cause compound fractures of the long arm of coincidence. Equally, there are moments when his gift for the apposite turn of phrase abruptly deserts him and he degenerates into cliché.

But such failings are more than compensated for by the im-

CONCLUSION

mense readability of his novels (an observation which is frequently taken as adverse criticism, but is not intended as such here), and the compelling authenticity of his narrative. Most important, his novels constitute a significant contribution to the fictional depiction of European man in this century and the social and political issues he confronts.

Perhaps Remarque's most impressive quality as a writer, and the one which has laid him open to so much adverse criticism, is his honesty, his overt admission that life may have moments of extreme beauty and happiness, but that does not compensate for the fact that the meaning of the totality — if it exists — eludes his grasp. He may indeed have regarded himself primarily as a writer who tried to crystallize meaning out of the stream of time which was rushing past him with increasing speed, a "Don Quixote who sought to tilt against the windmills of time". (*Nacht*, p. 155)

But, ironically, he has at least won a Pyrrhic victory, in the sense that his novels will live on for many long years after the events he has described so memorably have lapsed into history.

NOTES

R-S = *Remarque-Sammlung*, the collection of primary and secondary material housed in the Niedersächsisches Staatsarchiv in Osnabrück. The Roman numeral refers to the volume; this is followed by the item number.

INTRODUCTION

1 Erich Remark, "Die Frau mit den goldenen Augen", *Die Schönheit*, 1918, no. 4, pp.154-64.
2 "Kapitän Priemkes viertes Abenteuer", *Echo-Continental*, 1923, p.97.
3 The titles of Remarque's novels are given in German throughout the text. For the English version, and for the German edition to which the page number, when given, refers, see the Bibliography.
4 The work referred to is F. Baumer, *E.M. Remarque*, Berlin, 1976. The review is by A. Kerker, *"Im Westen nichts Neues und so weiter. Eine verfehlte Remarque-Biographie"*, *Die Zeit*, 11.11.1977, Literatur-Feuilleton, p.4. In fairness to Baumer it should be pointed out that Kerker's review is not without its blemishes; the date of publication given in the review, for example, is inaccurate.
5 The difficulties are compounded by the fact that his widow is in possession of a large number of papers, etc., which she has so far not released.

CHAPTER ONE

1 Mynona, *Hat Erich Maria Remarque wirklich gelebt?*, Berlin, 1929.
2 H.-G. Rabe, "Remarque und Osnabrück", *Osnabrücker Mitteilungen*, LXXVII (1970), pp. 201-2.
3 J. Witt, "Mit Remarque auf der Schulbank!". (R-S I, 28)
4 ibid.
5 *Der Spiegel*, 9.1.1952.
6 Konstantin, Prinz von Bayern, *Die grossen Namen. Begegnungen mit bedeutenden Deutschen unserer Zeit*, Munich, 1956, p.397. Burham Arpad falsely claims that Remarque made this statement about *Im Westen nichts Neues*. (See R-S III, 435a)

7 Erich Remark, "Aus der Heimat", Heimatfreund, IV, no.5, June, 1916. (Copy in R-S I, 29)
8 "Remarque und Osnabrück", p.211.
9 ibid. p.232.
10 Letter from Georg Middendorf to Hanns-Gerd [sic] Rabe 7.10.1969. (R-S I, 52)
11 "Remarque und Osnabrück", p.232.
12 Letter to Georg Middendorf, 25.8.1917. (R-S I, 40)
13 Letter to Georg Middendorf, undated. (R-S I, 40a)
14 The subject of his mother's death is discussed at some length between the semi-autobiographical narrator of Der schwarze Obelisk and the priest Bodendiek. (Obelisk, pp.87-88)
15 Erich Remark, Die Traumbude. Ein Künstlerroman, Dresden, 1920, p.202.
16 Letter 7.10.1969. (R-S I, 52)
17 Interview between Rabe and authors, 29.7.1975.
18 R-S I, 56, which is described as " 'Remarque über sich selbst. Gespräch mit Wilhelm Scherp', Kölner Zeitung, 26.11.1929". Arnim Kerker, however, maintains that there is no such article as "Remarque über sich selbst" by Scherp in the Kölner Zeitung, and that the interviews with Wilhelm Scharp (?) appeared in the Revue d'Allemagne in 1929, one of them then being published in a slightly shortened version under the title "Der Gefangene seines Ruhms" in the Kölnischer Zeitung. (See A. Kerker, "Im Westen nichts Neues und so weiter".)
19 Remarque und Osnabrück, p.222.
20 Letter from Dr. G. Wöste to Hanns-Gerd Rabe, 19.12.1967. (R-S I, 105)
21 Rabe, "Junglehrer Erich Paul Remark", Merian, no. 7, July 1971.
22 Letter to local authority in Osnabrück, 12.9.1920. (R-S I, 123)
23 Letter to Brand, undated. (R-S I, 117)
24 Letter to Brand, 8.11.1920. (R-S I, 133)
25 Letter 12.9.1920. (R-S I, 123)
26 See note 18.
27 Note by Rabe. (R-S I, 37)
28 "Abendlied" also appeared in Die Schönheit, as did several poems in similar vein by Remarque.
29 "Remarque und Osnabrück", p.225.
30 Der Spiegel, 9.1.1952, p.23.
31 Letter to local authority in Osnabrück, 20.11.1922. (R-S I, 144)
32 See Introduction.

33 R-S I, 158.
34 E.M. Remarque, "Uber das Mixen kostbarer Schnäpse", *Störtebeker*, no. 2, p.37.
35 Mynona, pp.91-92.
36 *Die literarische Welt*, 14.6.1929.
37 "Ein Leben wie ein Roman", *Stern*, 4.10.1970.
38 Conflicting views have even been expressed regarding Remarque's personal appearance: Mäti Robert describes him in *Merian* as having "thick black eyebrows", (R-S II, 258-59) while Harry Graf Kessler, in his *Tagebücher 1918-1937*, describes him as "blond, with blue eyes and blond eyebrows"! (R-S II, 265)
39 For example, Baumer, p.53, and M. Krell, *Die Welt*, 2.3.1961.
40 A. Antkowiak, *Ludwig Renn. Erich Maria Remarque. Leben und Werk*, E. Berlin, 1965, p.102.
41 H.W. Baum, "Remarque und seine Zeit", *Bibliothekar* VI (1957), quoted by Antkowiak, pp. 102-3.
42 A. Eggebrecht, "Gespräch mit Remarque", *Die literarische Welt*, 14.6.1929, p.1.
43 ibid.
44 Letter to Frau Hoberg, 5.8.1930. (R-S II, 227a)
45 I. Brandt, "Bei Remarque am Lago Maggiore", *Welt am Sonntag*, 16.4.1967.
46 K. Henkelmann (née Hoberg), "Erinnerungen an Remarque", written down by Rabe, November 1969. (R-S II, 260)
47 Letter to H.G. Hoberg, 31.10.1970. (R-S III, 440a)
48 Interview between Rabe and authors, 29.7.1975.
49 E. and K. Mann, *Escape to Life*, Boston, Mass., 1939, p.44.
50 H. Liepman, "Erich Maria Remarque: So denk' ich über Deutschland", *Die Welt*, 1.12.1962.
51 E. and K. Mann, pp. 44-45.
52 R. Lehrhardt, unnamed newspaper article. (R-S II, 364b)
53 "Gespräch mit Remarque", p.1.
54 E. and K. Mann, p.45.
55 "Begegnung mit einem Mann von Welt", *Stern*, 23.6.1968; also in "Ein Leben wie ein Roman", *Stern*, 4.10.1970.
56 C. Zuckmayer, *Gesammelte Werke. Die deutschen Dramen*, Frankfurt a.M. and Berlin, 1951, pp.290-91.
57 Rabe: "The legend that the house in which Remarque lives used to be the Böcklin villa is pure invention." (R-S II, 314)
58 *Osnabrücker Zeitung*, 6.4.1932, p.2.
59 "Gespräch mit Remarque", p.1.
60 R. Lehrhardt, unnamed newspaper article. (R-S II, 364c)
61 "Begegnung mit einem Mann von Welt"; also in "Remarque

und die Frauen", *Lesen* 7/8, 1971.
62 A. Whitman, "Erich Maria Remarque, Novelist, dies", *New York Times*, 26.9.1970.
63 *Frankfurter Neue Presse*, 18.6.1948.
64 H. Wagener, "Erich Maria Remarque", in J.M. Spalek and J. Strelka, *Deutsche Exilliteratur seit 1933. I–Kalifornien*, Part I, Berne and Munich, 1976, p.593.
65 F. von Reznicek, "So war Erich Maria Remarque", *Schweizer Rundschau*, LXIX (1970), p.399.
66 Letter to *Der Spiegel*, 19.7.1971.
67 Baumer, pp.53-54.
68 Konstantin, Prinz von Bayern, p.398.
69 Wagener, p.593.
70 Baumer, p.75.
71 ibid, p.76.
72 Wagener, p.593.
73 Rabe, *Freie Presse*, 1966. (R-S II, 329)
74 Letter from F. von Opel to *Frankfurter Allgemeine Zeitung*, 6.10.1970, p.12.
75 Letter from Peter Remark to G. Kruezmann, *Neue Osnabrücker Zeitung*, 23.11.1968.
76 "Begegnung mit einem Mann von Welt".
77 Letter to Hanns-Gerd Rabe, 20.6.1967. (R-S II, 341)
78 See R-S II, 267 and also a postcard from Remarque to Rabe, 31.12.1968, in which he writes: "I am deeply moved by the council's gesture of naming a street after my sister." (R-S II, 381)
79 D. Niven, *Bring on the empty Horses*, London, 1975, p.100.
80 "Remarque und die Frauen".
81 V. Wolff, "Erinnerungen an Remarque. Sehnsucht nach der Unruhe des Lebens", *Madame*, July 1971.
82 "Remarque und die Frauen".
83 Baumer, p.55.
84 Letter to Hanns-Gerd Rabe, 8.8.1966. (II, 325)
85 "Bei Remarque am Lago Maggiore".
86 H. Habe, *Die Welt*, 24.6.1971.
87 *Neue Osnabrücker Zeitung*, 31.1.1970. (Reprinting of an interview with a Prague journalist, R-S II, 389)
88 "Begegnung mit einem Mann von Welt".
89 Rabe, "Alkohol als Leitmotif in Remarques Romanen", *Osnabrücker Nachrichten*, 15.10.1971.
90 Wagener, p.601.
91 ibid.
92 "Remarque und die Frauen".
93 *Los Angeles Times*, 12.6.1948.

94 See Baumer, p.88.
95 See R-S III, 469.
96 "Bei Remarque am Lago Maggiore".
97 *Neue Osnabrücker Zeitung*, 29.9.1970.
98 For example, Rabe, *Osnabrücker Nachrichten*, 28.5.1971.
99 M. Lütgenhorst, "Emigrant zweier Welten". (R-S II, 362-63)
100 Letter from Peter Remark to Georg Kruezmann, published in the *Neue Osnabrücker Zeitung*, 23.11.1968, states:"... my daughter was unjustly executed. My wife fell into a depressed state and came to an unhappy end".
101 "Emigrant zweier Welten".
102 Letter to Hanns-Gerd Rabe, 9.5.1957. (R-S II, 281)
103 Letter to Hanns-Gerd Rabe, 2.1.1967. (R-S II, 332)
104 Letter to Hanns-Gerd Rabe, 21.8.1967. (R-S II, 342)
105 Letter to H.G. Hoberg, 31.10.1970. (R-S III, 440a)
106 H. Koar, "Remarque kommt im Frühling", *Freie Presse*, 26.11.1966. (R-S II, 343a)
107 ibid.
108 *Neue Osnabrücker Zeitung*, 31.1.1970.
109 "Emigrant zweier Welten".
110 *Rheinischer Merkur*, 2.10.1970. (R-S III, 450a)
111 H. Habe, *Welt am Sonntag*, no.41, 11.10.1970, p.25.
112 Quoted H. Habe, "Sein ganzes Werk drehte sich ums Sterben", *Kölnischer Rundschau*, 26.9.1970.

CHAPTER TWO

1 Quoted by A. Kerker, "*Im Westen nichts Neues*. Die Geschichte eines Bestsellers", broadcast by the Third Programme of the Norddeutscher Rundfunk, 3.4.1973. (Copy in R-S 228a-257)
2 ibid.
3 J. Wulf, *Literatur und Dichtung im Dritten Reich. Eine Dokumentation*, Gütersloh, 1963, p.46.
4 B.A. Rowley, "Journalism into Fiction. Erich Maria Remarque, *Im Westen nichts Neues*", in H. Klein (ed.), *The First World War in Fiction*, London, 1976, p.103.
5 "Gespräch mit Remarque", p.1.
6 C. Riess, *Bestseller. Bücher, die Millionen lesen.* Hamburg, 1960, p.60.
7 P. de Mendelssohn, *S. Fischer und sein Verlag*, Frankfurt a.M., 1970, p.1115.
8 ibid, p.1116.

9   *Frankfurter Allgemeine Zeitung*, 9.7.1962 and 26.7.1962.
10 "*All Quiet on the Western Front*", *Times Literary Supplement*, 8.4.1929, p.314.
11 E. Childers, *The Riddle of the Sands*, London, 1955, p.77.
12 "*All Quiet on the Western Front*", *New Statesman*, 25.5.1929, p.218.
13 K. Kroner, "Ein Arzt über *Im Westen nichts Neues*", *Neue Preussische Kreuz-Zeitung*, 27.6.1929 (Beiblatt).
14 For example, W. Müller Scheld, *Im Westen nichts Neues. Eine Täuschung*, Idstein, 1929, p.10.
15 P. Kropp, *Endlich Klarheit über Remarque und sein Buch "Im Westen nichts Neues"*, privately printed in Hamm, Westphalia, 1930, p.10.
16 E. Toller, "*Im Westen nichts Neues*", *Die literarische Welt*, V (1929), no. 8, p.5.
17 *Der Kampf um Remarque*, Berlin, 1929, unpaginated.
18 See B. Kempf, *Suffragette for Peace. The Life of Bertha von Suttner* (transl. R.W. Last), London, 1972, pp. 23-29 (*Die Waffen nieder!*); pp.53-63 (Nobel and his Will); pp. 134-63 (Extracts from English version of *Die Waffen nieder!* transl. T. Holmes).
19 G.N. Shuster in the Foreword to W.K. Pfeiler, *War and the German Mind. The Testimony of the Men of Fiction who fought at the Front*, New York, 1941, p.1.
20 H. Heisler, *Kreig oder Frieden. Randbemerkung zu Remarques Buch "Im Westen nichts Neues"*, Stuttgart, 1930, p.33.
21 G. Lutz, *Die Front-Gemeinschaft. Das Gemeinschaftserlebnis in der Kriegsliteratur*, Greifswald, 1936, p.71.
22 G. Nickl, "*Im Westen nichts Neues* und sein wahrer Sinn. Ein Betrachtung über den Pazifismus und Antwort an Remarque*", *Heimgarten. Monatsschrift für Unterhaltung und Aufklärung*, Sonderheft, 1930, p.12.
23 ibid, p.14.
24 Müller Scheld, p.28.
25 E.M. Requark (pseud.), *Vor Troja nichts Neues*, Berlin, 1930, p.22.
26 ibid, p.7.
27 ibid, p.24.
28 ibid, p.43.
29 Berlin, 1929.
30 ibid, p.11.
31 ibid, p.19.
32 See M.S. Jones, *Der Sturm. A Study of an Expressionist Periodical*, German Department, Hull University, 1979: chapter on Friedlaender.

33 A. Soergel and C. Hohoff, *Dichtung und Dichter der Zeit*, vol. 1, Düsseldorf, 1963, p.349.

34 W. Rothe (ed.), *Die deutsche Literatur in der Weimarer Republik*, Stuttgart, 1974, pp.204, 206, 208.

35 V. Lange, *Modern German Literature 1870-1940*, New York, 1945, p.104.

36 J. Rühle, *Literature and Revolution. A critical Study of the Writer and Communism in the twentieth Century*, London, 1969, p.153.

37 Letter in *Frankfurter Allgemeine Zeitung*, 4.9.1971.

38 H. Liedloff, "Two War Novels: a critical Comparison", *Revue de Littérature Comparée*, XLII (1968), pp. 390-406.

39 H. Swados, "Remarque's Relevance", *Book Week*, 23.10.1966, p.12.

40 H.M. Klein, "Dazwischen Niemandsland: *Im Westen nichts Neues* and *Her Privates We*", in O. Kuhn (ed.), *Grossbritannien und Deutschland. Festschrift für John W.P. Bourke*, Munich, 1974, pp.487-512.

41 "Journalism into Fiction", p.109.

42 Antkowiak, *Ludwig Renn. Erich Maria Remarque*, p.116.

43 I. Wegner, "Die Problematik der 'verlorenen Generation' und ihre epische Gestaltung im Romanwerk Erich Maria Remarques", Diss., Jena, 1965, p.32.

44 Liedloff, pp. 391-92.

45 Preface to *The Old Wives' Tale*, London, 1948, p.x.

46 "Remarque und Osnabrück", p.232.

47 ibid, pp. 199-200.

48 "Gespräch mit Remarque", p.1.

49 Nickl, p.38.

50 See Lutz, p.73.

51 P. Hagbolt, "Ethical and social Problems in the German War Novel", *Journal of English and German Philology*, XXXII, pp.21-32.

52 Liedloff, p.391.

53 Letter quoted by C. Day Lewis, "Paul Nash. A private View", in M. Eates, *Paul Nash. The Master of the Image*, London, 1973, p.xii.

54 ibid.

55 "Gespräch mit Remarque", p.1.

56 A.F. Bance, "*Im Westen nichts Neues*: A Bestseller in Context", *Modern Language Review*, LXXII (1977), p.372.

57 C. Cockburn, *Bestseller. The Books that Everyone Read 1900-1939*, London, 1972, p.11.

58 For example, Wegner, p.65.

59 "Gespräch mit Remarque", p.1.

60 W.K. Pfeiler, *War and the German Mind. The Testimony of the Men of Fiction who fought at the Front*, New York, 1941, p.142.

61 H. Meyer, "Bestseller Research Problems", in D.D. Richards, *The German Bestseller in the Twentieth Century. A Complete Bibliography and Analysis 1915-1940*, unpaginated.

62 Cockburn, p.3.

63 Obituary in *Daily Telegraph*, 26.9.1970.

64 Letter to Hanns-Gerd Rabe, 12.2.1929. (R-S I, 209)

CHAPTER THREE

1 I. Hamilton and E.M. Remarque, "The End of War?" (A correspondence between the author of *All Quiet on the Western Front* and General Sir Ian Hamilton), *Life and Letters*, III (1929), p.407.

2 "Gespräch mit Remarque", p.2.

3 Quoted by Antkowiak, *Ludwig Renn. Erich Maria Remarque*, p.135.

4 B. Reifenberg, "*Der Weg zurück*. Zu dem Nachkriegsbuch E.M. Remarques", *Frankfurter Zeitung*, 27.9.1931.

5 Antkowiak, *Ludwig Renn. Erich Maria Remarque*, p.137.

6 ibid. p.136.

7 ibid. p.140.

8 Wegner, p.72.

9 E. Löhrke, *Armageddon. The World War in Literature*, New York, 1930, p.4.

10 ibid, p.9.

11 L. Marcuse, "Der neue Remarque", (review of *Der Weg zurück*), *Frankfurter General-Anzeiger*, 1931.

12 Remarque's own Alsatian dog is also said to have accompanied him to war.

13 Modelled on Remarque's friend Rabe.

14 Weiskopf, for one, complains that the time and place of the action remain unclear, but he settles for "a German city around the year 1932". (F.C. Weiskopf, *Über Literatur und Sprache*, E. Berlin, 1960, p.126.)

15 Letter from Rabe to Herbert Gérold. (R-S III, 534)

16 K. Henkelmann (née Hoberg), "Erinnerungen an Remarque", written down by Rabe, November 1969. (R-S II, 260)

17 Antkowiak, *Ludwig Renn. Erich Maria Remarque*, p.147.

18 ibid, p.148.

19 A. Antkowiak, "Erich Maria Remarque: *Drei Kameraden*", *Sonntag*, 18.10.1953.

20 Antkowiak, *Ludwig Renn. Erich Maria Remarque*, p.148.
21 ibid. p.146.
22 ibid. p.144.
23 See notes 6 and 7.
24 Antkowiak, *Sonntag*, 18.10.1953.
25 Antkowiak, *Ludwig Renn. Erich Maria Remarque*, p.145.
26 Weiskopf, p.126.
27 See Chapter Two, p.50.
28 Antkowiak, *Ludwig Renn. Erich Maria Remarque*, p.144; Weiskopf, p.125.
29 Weiskopf, p.125.
30 ibid, pp. 125-26.
31 *Der Himmel kennt keine Günstlinge*, p.210, p.214; cf. T. Mann, *Der Tod in Venedig*, London, 1969, p.24.
32 W. Gresinger, in *Erich Maria Remarque zum 70. Geburtstag am 22. Juni 1968*, Cologne and Munich, 1968, p.29.
33 Antkowiak, *Ludwig Renn. Erich Maria Remarque*, p.207.
34 F. Sieburg, "Ein Gefühl von grosser Süsse", *Frankfurter Allgemeine Zeitung*, 16.6.1961.
35 See Chapter One, note 98.
36 See "Remarque und Osnabrück", pp. 234-36.
37 Modelled on Father Biedendieck, see Chapter One, pp.12-13.
38 See an article by Rabe of 4.10.1966, (R-S II, 326a) in which he refers to the interest of a certain Dr. W. in *Der schwarze Obelisk* and Remarque's "accurate description" of schizophrenia.
39 Based on Eduard Petersilie, owner of the Osnabrück hotel, the Germania (destroyed during the Second World War) and an aspirant poet. See "Remarque and Osnabrück", p.235.

CHAPTER FOUR

1 J.G. Stressinger, *Encyclopaedia Britannica*, Vol.XIX, 1972, p.71.
2 Antkowiak, *Ludwig Renn. Erich Maria Remarque*, p.165.
3 *Neue Osnabrücker Zeitung*, 31.1.1970. (Reprinting· of an interview with a Prague journalist, R-S II, 389)
4 Victoria Wolff, a neighbour of Remarque's in Ascona, records that she had a friend by the name of Kern, whom Remarque also knew. See "Erinnerungen an Remarque".
5 Antkowiak, *Ludwig Renn. Erich Maria Remarque*, p.155.
6 "Emigrant zweier Welten".

CHAPTER FIVE

1   F. Hrastnik, "Remarques Weise von Liebe und Tod", (review of *Zeit zu leben*) *Frankfurter Allgemeine Zeitung*, 24.9.1954.
2   R. Krämer-Badoni, "Der alte patriotische Eifer", (review of *Der Funke Leben*), *Neue Zeitung*, 27.9.1952.
3   Antkowiak, *Ludwig Renn. Erich Maria Remarque*, pp.173-74.
4   Weiskopf, p.230.
5   In the Krämer-Badoni review, for example (see note 2).
6   Antkowiak, *Ludwig Renn. Erich Maria Remarque*, p.188.
7   Letter to the authors from K. Witsch (25.7.1977). For a complete account of the controversy surrounding the various versions of *Zeit zu leben*, see R.W. Last, "The 'Castration' of Erich Maria Remarque", *Quinquereme*, II (1979), pp.10-22.
8   Weiskopf, p.336.
9   Witsch letter 25.7.1977.
10 ibid.

CHAPTER SIX

1   *Welt am Sonntag*, 27.9.1970. (R-S III, 463)
2   H.G. Schwark, *Rundschau am Sonntag*, no.42, (17.10.1971) p.7.
3   See *Die Welt der Literatur*, Beilage zur *Welt*, 22.7.1971. (R-S, III, 488)
4   Cf also *Schatten im Paradies*, p.100, p.102, p.172.

CONCLUSION

1   B. Levin, "... And some have Greatness thrust upon them", *The Times*, 22.3.1978, p.18.

BIBLIOGRAPHY

A. PRIMARY WORKS

Although Remarque always wrote his novels in German, a number were first published in America, occasionally under titles different from the German version. In the alphabetical list of the German titles given below, the title of the equivalent English published version follows in brackets. This is followed by a chronological list of Remarque's major publications in German and English and a list of the German editions cited in the text.

Arc de Triomphe (Arch of Triumph)
Der Funke Leben (Spark of Life)
Der Himmel kennt keine Günstlinge (Heaven has no Favourites)
Der schwarze Obelisk (The black Obelisk)
Der Weg zurück (The Road Back)
Die Nacht von Lissabon (The Night in Lisbon)
Die Traumbude (= The Dream-Den; not published in English, although it did appear in Dutch in 1931)
Drei Kameraden (Three Comrades)
Im Westen nichts Neues (All Quiet on the Western Front)
Liebe deinen Nächsten (Flotsam; literally: "Love thy Neighbour")
Schatten im Paradies (Shadows in Paradise)
Zeit zu leben und Zeit zu sterben (A Time to Love and a Time to Die; literally: "A Time to Live and a Time to Die")

Chronological list of Remarque's published novels in German and English

1920 *Die Traumbude. Ein Künstlerroman,* Verlag der Schönheit, Dresden.
1929 *Im Westen nichts Neues,* Propyläen, Berlin.
1929 *All Quiet on the Western Front,* transl. A.W. Wheen, Little, Brown and Company, Boston, Mass., and G.P. Putnam's Sons, London.
1931 *Der Weg zurück,* Propyläen, Berlin.
1931 *The Road Back,* transl. A.W. Wheen, Little, Brown and Company, Boston, Mass., and G.P. Putnam's Sons, London.
1937 *Drei Kameraden,* Querido, Amsterdam.
1937 *Three Comrades,* transl. A.W. Wheen, Little, Brown and Company, Boston, Mass.
1941 *Flotsam,* transl. Denver Lindley, Little, Brown and Company, Boston, Mass.
1945 *Arch of Triumph,* transl. Walter Sorell and Denver Lindley, D. Appleton-Century Company, New York and London.
1946 *Arc de Triomphe,* F.G. Micha, Zurich.
1952 *Der Funke Leben,* Kiepenheuer & Witsch, Cologne.
1952 *Spark of Life,* transl. James Stern, Appleton-Century-Crofts, New York.
1953 *Liebe deinen Nächsten,* Kurt Desch, Munich.
1954 *A Time to Love and a Time to Die,* transl. Denver Lindley, Harcourt, Brace, New York.

1954 *Zeit zu leben und Zeit zu sterben*, Kiepenheuer & Witsch, Cologne.
1956 *Der schwarze Obelisk. Geschichte einer verspäteten Jugend*, Kiepenheuer & Witsch, Cologne.
1957 *The black Obelisk*, transl. Denver Lindley, Harcourt, Brace, New York.
1961 *Der Himmel kennt keine Günstlinge*, Kiepenheuer & Witsch, Cologne.
1961 *Heaven has no Favorites*, transl. Richard and Clara Winston, Harcourt, Brace and World, New York.
1963 *Die Nacht von Lissabon*, Kiepenheuer & Witsch, Cologne.
1964 *The Night in Lisbon*, transl. Ralph Manheim, Harcourt, Brace, New York, and Hutchinson, London.
1971 *Schatten im Paradies*, Droemer Knaur, Munich.
1972 *Shadows in Paradise*, transl. Ralph Manheim, Harcourt, Brace, Jovanovich, New York.

German editions cited in the text

Im Westen nichts Neues, Kiepenheuer & Witsch, Cologne, 1971.
Der Weg zurück, Kiepenheuer & Witsch, Cologne, 1971.
Drei Kameraden, Arc de Triomphe, Liebe deinen Nächsten (in one volume), Kurt Desch, Munich, Vienna and Basle, 1973.
Der Funke Leben. Kiepenheuer & Witsch, Cologne, 1972.
Zeit zu leben und Zeit zu sterben, Kiepenheuer & Witsch, Cologne and Berlin, 1961.
Der schwarze Obelisk, Kiepenheuer & Witsch, Cologne and Berlin, 1971.
Der Himmel kennt keine Günstlinge, Kiepenheuer & Witsch, Cologne, 1972.
Die Nacht von Lissabon, Kiepenheuer & Witsch, Cologne, 1972.
Schatten im Paradies, Droemer Knaur, Munich, 1971.

B. SELECT BIBLIOGRAPHY OF SECONDARY WORKS CONSULTED

R.M. Albérès, *L'aventure intellectuelle du XXe siècle 1900-1950*, Paris, 1950.
P. Aley, *Jugendliteratur im Dritten Reich. Dokumente und Kommentare*, Gütersloh, 1967.
"*All Quiet on the Western Front*", *Life and Letters*, III (1929), pp.60-61.
"*All Quiet on the Western Front*", *New Statesman*, 25.5.1928, p.218.
"*All Quiet on the Western Front*", *Times Literary Supplement*, 8.4.1929, p.314.
A. Antkowiak, "Erich Maria Remarque: *Drei Kameraden*", *Sonntag*, 18.10.1953.
A. Antkowiak, *Ludwig Renn. Erich Maria Remarque. Leben und Werk*, E. Berlin, 1965.
"*Arch of Triumph*", *Times Literary Supplement*, 23.11.1946, p.575.
H. Arnold (ed.), *Deutsche Bestseller — Deutsche Ideologie. Ansätze zu einer Verbrauchspoetik*, Stuttgart, 1975.
A.F. Bance, "*Im Westen nichts Neues*. A Bestseller in Context", *Modern Language Review*, LXXII (1977), pp.359-73.
F. Baumer, *E.M. Remarque*, Berlin, 1976.
J. Baxton, *Hollywood in the 'Thirties*, London and New York, 1968.
"Begegnung mit einem Mann von Welt", *Stern*, 23.6.1968.
"Begegnung mit Remarque", *Neue Zeitung*, 23.7.1952.

166

N. Bentwich, *The Refugees from Germany. April 1933 to December 1935*, London, 1936.

W.A. Berendsohn, "Entstehung und Nachwirkung der neuen realistischen Dichtung", in E.J. Gumbel (ed.), *Freie Wissenschaft. Ein Sammelbuch aus der deutschen Emigration*, Strasbourg, 1938.

H.J. Bernhard, "Der Weltkrieg 1914-18 im Werk Ernst Jüngers, Erich Maria Remarques und Arnold Zweigs. Ein Beitrag zum Problem des Realismus in der Literatur des 20. Jahrhunderts", Diss., Rostock, 1958.

I. Brandt, "Bei Remarque am Lago Maggiore", *Welt am Sonntag*, 16.4.1967.

J. Brautzsch, "Untersuchungen über die Publikumswirksamkeit der Romane *Im Westen nichts Neues* und *Der Weg zurück* von Erich Maria Remarque vor 1933", Diss., Potsdam, 1969.

K. Brownlow, *The Parade's gone by . . .*, London, 1968.

U. Bruchmann, "Remarque und Plievier", *Umschau*, Mainz, 1948, pp.435-40.

A. Calder, *The People's War. Britain 1939-45*, London, 1969.

A. Casty, *Development of the Film*, New York, 1973.

A. Cesana, *Das Gesicht des Weltkrieges in der Literatur*, Basle, 1932.

C. Cockburn, *Bestseller. The Books that Everyone Read 1900-1939*, London, 1972.

C. Connolly (ed.), *The modern Movement. One Hundred key Books from England, France and America*, London, 1965.

"Das 'grösste Buch des Jahrhunderts' von einem Osnabrücker? Gerhart Hauptmann, Thomas Mann verstecken sich vor — Remark(que)!!", *Der Stadt-Wächter*, Osnabrück, 25.5.1929.

I. Deak, *Weimar Germany's left-wing Intellectuals*, Berkeley and Los Angeles, 1968.

"*Der Himmel kennt keine Günstlinge*", *Neue Zürcher Zeitung*, 3.10.1961.

"Der unbequeme Autor Erich Maria Remarque wird 60 Jahre", *Frankfurter Allgemeine Zeitung*, 21.6.1958.

M. Eates, *Paul Nash. The Master of the Image*, London, 1973.

A. Eggebrecht, "Gespräch mit Remarque", *Die literarische Welt*, V, no.24, 14.6.1929, pp.1-2.

"Ein Autor, der alle Leserschichten erreichte", *Frankfurter Neue Presse*, 18.6.1948.

"Ein Leben wie ein Roman", *Stern*, 4.10.1970.

"Erich Maria Remarque", *Frankfurter Allgemeine Zeitung*, 31.10.1964.

"Erich Maria Remarque in Berlin", *Giessener Anzeiger*, 12.9.1956.

Erich Maria Remarque zum 70. Geburtstag am 22. Juni 1968, Cologne and Munich, 1968.

E. Eyck, *A History of the Weimar Republic*, vol.II, Cambridge, Mass., 1964.

E. von Frauenholz, *Einführung in die Weltkriegsliteratur*, Berlin, 1932.

L. Furnhammer and F. Isaksson, *Politics and Film*, London, 1971.

M. Geismer, "Terror Marched with a Goose Step", (review of *The Night in Lisbon*) *New York Times Book Review*, LXIX, 22.3.1964, p.1.

R. Grimm and J. Hermann (eds.), *Die sogenannten zwanziger Jahre*, Bad Homburg, 1970.

H. Grimrath, *Der Weltkrieg im französischen Roman*, Berlin, 1935.

W. Grözinger, "Der Roman der Gegenwart: der anpassungsfähige Leser", *Hochland*, LIII (1960-1961), pp.567-75.

H. Habe, "Sein ganzes Werk drehte sich ums Sterben", *Kölnischer Rundschau*, 26.9.1970.

I. Hamilton and E.M. Remarque, "The End of War?" (A correspondence between the author of *All Quiet on the Western Front* and General Sir Ian Hamilton), *Life and Letters*, III (1929), pp.399-411.

M. Hardie and A.K. Sabin, *War Posters issued by the belligerent and neutral Nations 1914-1919*, London, 1920.

T. Harrisson, "War Books", *Horizon*, IV (1941), pp.416-37.

H. Heisler, *Krieg oder Frieden. Randbemerkung zu Remarques Buch "Im Westen nichts Neues"*, Stuttgart, 1930.

F. Hrastnik, "Remarques Weise von Liebe und Tod", (review of *Zeit zu leben und Zeit zu sterben*) *Frankfurter Allgemeine Zeitung*, 24.9.1954.

L. Jacobs, *The Rise of the American Film. A critical History*, New York, 1960.

E. Jirgal, *Die Wiederkehr des Weltkrieges in der Literatur*, Vienna and Leipzig, 1931.

C. Jödicke, "*Im Westen nichts Neues*", (Letter) *Frankfurter Allgemeine Zeitung*, 26.7.1962.

E. Jünger (ed.), *Das Antlitz des Weltkrieges. Fronterlebnisse deutscher Soldaten*, Berlin, 1930.

T. Kalkschmidt, *Der deutsche Frontsoldat. Mythos und Gestalt*, Berlin, 1938.

A. Kantorwicz, *Vom moralischen Gewinn der Niederlage*, Berlin, 1949.

B. Kempf, *Suffragette for Peace. The Life of Bertha von Suttner* (transl. R.W. Last), London, 1972.

A. Kerker, "Der Fall Remarque", (Letter to editor) *Frankfurter Allgemeine Zeitung*, 4.9.1971.

A. Kerker, "*Im Westen nichts Neues*. Die Geschichte eines Bestsellers", broadcast by the Third Programme of the Norddeutscher Rundfunk, 3.4.1973. (Copy in R-S II, 228a-257)

A. Kerker, "*Im Westen nichts Neues* und so weiter. Eine verfehlte Remarque-Biographie", (review of F. Baumer, *E.M. Remarque*) *Die Zeit*, 11.11.1977.

H. Kindermann, *Die Weltkriegsdichtung der Deutschen im Ausland*, Berlin, 1940.

H.M. Klein, "Dazwischen Niemandsland: *Im Westen nichts Neues* und *Her Privates We*", in O. Kuhn (ed.), *Grossbritannien und Deutschland. Festschrift für John W.P. Bourke*, Munich, 1974.

Konstantin, Prinz von Bayern, *Die grossen Namen. Begegnungen mit bedeutenden Deutschen unserer Zeit*, Munich, 1956.

R. Krämer-Badoni, "Der alte patriotische Eifer. Erich Maria Remarque: *Der Funke Leben*", *Neue Zeitung*, 27.9.1952.

K. Kroner, "Ein Arzt über *Im Westen nichts Neues*", *Neue Preussische Kreuz-Zeitung*, 27.6.1929 (Beiblatt).

P. Kropp, *Endlich Klarheit über Remarque und sein Buch Im Westen nichts Neues*, privately printed in Hamm, Westphalia, 1930.

F. Lafitte, *The Internment of Aliens*, London, 1940.

E.J. Landau, "Kehrseite der Humanität. Zu Erich Maria Remarques *Arc de Triomphe*", *Neue Zeitung*, 2.9.1950.

V. Lange, *Modern German Literature 1870-1940*, New York, 1945.

N. Laski, *Jewish Rights and Jewish Wrongs*, London, 1939.

H. Liedloff, "Two War Novels: a critical Comparison", *Revue de Littérature Comparée*, XLII (1968), pp.390-406.

H. Liepman, "Erich Maria Remarque: So denk' ich über Deutschland. Ein Interview", *Die Welt*, 1.12.1962.

S. Lietzmann, "Mickey Spillane mit Hakenkreuz. Remarque und Barrault bei den Berliner Festspielen", (review of *Die letzte Station*) *Frankfurter Allgemeine Zeitung*, 24.9.1950.

E. Löhrke, *Armageddon. The World War in Literature*, New York, 1930.

G. Lutz, *Die Front-Gemeinschaft. Das Gemeinschaftserlebnis in der Kriegsliteratur*, Greifswald, 1936.

E. and K. Mann, *Escape to Life*, Boston, Mass., 1939.

G. Meier, "Remarques Stellung zu Faschimus und antifaschistischem Wider-
standskampf, untersucht an seinem Roman *Der Funke Leben*", *Wissen-
schaftliche Zeitschrift der Pädagogischen Hochschule Potsdam*, (Sektion
Germanistik/Geschichte) XV (1971), pp.225-42.

P. de Mendelssohn, S. *Fischer und sein Verlag*, Frankfurt a.M., 1970.

A. Mendelssohn-Bartholdy, *The War and German Society*, New Haven, 1937.

H. Meyer, "Bestseller research Problems", unpaginated introduction to
D.D. Richards, *The German Bestseller in the Twentieth Century. A complete Bibliography and Analysis 1915-1940*, Berne, 1968.

W. Müller Scheld, *Im Westen nichts Neues. Eine Täuschung*, Idstein, 1929.

Mynona, *Hat Erich Maria Remarque wirklich gelebt?*, Berlin, 1929.

G. Nickl, "*Im Westen nichts Neues* und sein wahrer Sinn. Eine Betrachtung
über den Pazifismus und Antwort an Remarque", *Heimgarten. Monatsschrift für Unterhaltung und Aufklärung*, Sonderheft 1930.

Obituary, *Daily Telegraph*, 26.9.1970.

Obituary, "Mr. Erich Remarque. Author of controversial best-seller", *The
Times*, 26.9.1970.

P. Petr, "Bemerkungen zu einigen deutschen Prosawerken über den ersten
Weltkrieg", *Germanica Wratislaviensa*, VII (1962), pp.19-34.

W.K. Pfeiler, *War and the German Mind. The Testimony of the Men of
Fiction who fought at the Front*, New York, 1941.

H. Pörzgen, "Moskaus Lieblingsschriftsteller finden auch Kritik. Uber Remarque und Heinrich Böll: westliche Literatur in Russland (IV)", *Frankfurter Allgemeine Zeitung*, 2.9.1964.

H.-G. Rabe, "Remarque und Osnabrück", *Osnabrücker Mitteilungen*, LXXVII
(1970), pp.196-246.

H.-G. Rabe, "Alkohol als Leitmotif in Remarques Romanen", *Osnabrücker
Nachrichten*, 15.10.1971.

H.-G. Rabe, "Soldat Remarque. Ein verdunkeltes Kapitel seines bunten
Lebens", *Osnabrücker Nachrichten*, 9.6.1972.

H.-G. Rabe, "Remarque als Junglehrer in einem Hümmlingdorf", *Osnabrücker Nachrichten*, 27.7.1973.

H.-G. Rabe, "Osnabrücker Kunst und Künstler 1900-1970", *Osnabrücker
Mitteilungen*, LXXXI (1974), pp.1-127.

H.-G. Rabe, "Remarque war 1916 bei der 'Jugendwehr' ", *Osnabrücker
Nachrichten*, 1.3.1974.

M. Reich-Ranicki, "Knalleffekte in Todesnähe. Erich Maria Remarque von
Im Westen nichts Neues zu *Der Himmel kennt keine Günstlinge*", (review
of *Der Himmel kennt keine Günstlinge*) *Die Zeit*, 6.10.1961.

M. Reich-Ranicki, *Deutsche Literatur in West and Ost: Prosa seit 1945*,
Munich, 1963.

M. Reich-Ranicki, "Sein Geschmack war der von Millionen. Zum Tod Erich
Maria Remarques", *Die Zeit*, 2.10.1970.

B. Reifenberg, "*Der Weg zurück*. Zu dem Nachkriegsbuch Erich Maria Remarques", *Frankfurter Zeitung*, 27.9.1931.

"Remarques Bankdepot beschlagnahmt", *Osnabrücker Zeitung*, 6.4.1932.

W. Rey, "Die Bewältigung des Weltkrieges im nationalen Kriegsroman",
Diss., Neu-Isenburg bei Frankfurt a.M., 1937.

F. von Reznicek, "So war Erich Maria Remarque", *Schweizer Rundschau*,
LXIX (1970), pp.398-400.

D.D. Richards, *The German Bestseller in the twentieth Century. A complete
Bibliography and Analysis 1915-1940*, Berne, 1968.

J. Richards, *Visions of Yesterday*, London, 1973.

M. Rickards, *Posters of the First World War*, London, 1968.

C. Riess, *Bestseller. Bücher, die Millionen lesen*, Hamburg, 1960.

W. Ross, "Aus Ascona nichts Neues. Erich Maria Remarques nachgelassener Roman", (review of *Schatten im Paradies*) *Die Zeit*, 20.8.1971.

W. Rothe (ed.), *Die deutsche Literatur in der Weimarer Republik*, Stuttgart, 1974.

B.A. Rowley, "Journey into Fiction. Erich Maria Remarque, *Im Westen nichts Neues*", in H. Klein (ed.), *The First World War in Fiction*, London, 1976.

H. Rudolf, "Helden der Krise. Zu Erich Maria Remarques Emigrationsromanen", *Arbeiten zur deutschen Philologie*, II (1966), pp.83-93.

J. Rühle, *Literature and Revolution. A critical Study of the Writer and Communism in the twentieth Century*, (transl. and ed. J. Steinberg), London, 1969.

M. Ruppert, "Geschäfte mit dem Tod. Erich Maria Remarques neuer Roman", (review of *Der schwarze Obelisk*) *Frankfurter Allgemeine Zeitung*, 3.11.1956.

H. Schlötermann, *Das deutsche Weltkriegsdrama 1919-1937. Eine wertkritische Analyse*, Würzburg-Anmühle, 1939.

J. Schmidt, "Emigration, Trauma und Masche. Erich Maria Remarques nachgelassener Roman *Schatten im Paradies*", *Frankfurter Allgemeine Zeitung*, 14.8.1971.

F. Sieburg, "Ein Gefühl von grosser Süsse", (review of *Der Himmel kennt keine Günstlinge*) *Frankfurter Allgemeine Zeitung*, 16.6.1961.

J.L. Spivak, *Europe under the Terror*, London, 1936.

J. G. Stressinger, "Refugees", *Encyclopaedia Britannica*, vol. XIX, 1972, pp.71-72a.

D. Strothmann, *Nationalsozialistische Literaturpolitik. Ein Beitrag zur Publizistik im Dritten Reich*, Bonn, 1963.

A. Subiotto, "Hans Carossa's *Rümanisches Tagebuch*", in A.D. Best and R.W. Last (eds.), *Essays Presented to Dr. Baier*, Hull, 1975, pp.31-39.

H. Swados, "Remarque's Relevance", *Book Week*, 23.10.1966.

E. Toller, "*Im Westen nichts Neues*", *Die literarische Welt*, V (1929), no. 8, p.5.

H. Ullstein, "Im Westen nichts Neues", (Letter to the editor) *Frankfurter Allgemeine Zeitung*, 9.7.1967.

F. Vordemberge, *Arbeiten der Jahre 1966-1974. Gemälde, Aquarelle, Zeichnungen, Graphik*, Osnabrück, 1974.

H. Wagener, "Erich Maria Remarque", in J.M. Spalek and J. Strelka, *Deutsche Exilliteratur seit 1933. I Kalifornien*, Part I, Berne and Munich, 1976.

I. Wegner, "Die Problematik der 'verlorenen Generation' und ihre epische Gestaltung im Romanwerk Erich Maria Remarques", Diss. Jena, 1965.

F.C. Weiskopf, *Über Literatur und Sprache*, E. Berlin, 1960.

"Wer ist Erich Maria Remarque?", *Wetterauer Zeitung*, 31.12.1955.

A. Whitman, "Erich Maria Remarque, Novelist, dies", *New York Times*, 26.9.1970.

J.C. Witsch, "Erich Maria Remarque. *Die Nacht von Lissabon*", *Die Kiepe*, XI (1963), no.1, p.1.

V. Wolff, "Erinnerungen an Remarque. Sehnsucht nach der Unruhe des Lebens", *Madame*, July 1971.

J. Wulf, *Literatur und Dichtung im Dritten Reich. Eine Dokumentation*, Gütersloh, 1963.

C. Zuckmayer, *Als wär's eine Stück von mir*, Vienna, 1966.

W. Zukerman, *The Jew in Revolt. The modern Jew in the world Crisis*, London, 1937.

A. Zweig, *Über Schriftsteller*, Berlin and Weimar, 1967.

Index of Names

171